COASTLINE

BRITAIN'S THREATENED HERITAGE

COASTLINE
BRITAIN'S THREATENED HERITAGE

INTRODUCED BY LORD PETER MELCHETT
CHAIR, GREENPEACE UK
DESCRIBED BY KATE BAILLIE
PHOTOGRAPHED BY DENNIS GILBERT

WITH CONTRIBUTIONS BY
DOUGLAS ADAMS, BERYL BAINBRIDGE,
MELVYN BRAGG, DAVID DAICHES, HUNTER DAVIES,
MARGARET DRABBLE, JOHN FOWLES,
CLARE FRANCIS, ALASDAIR GRAY, TED HUGHES,
HAMMOND INNES, GEORGE MACKAY BROWN,
DENNIS POTTER, ALICE THOMAS ELLIS

KINGFISHER BOOKS

Abbreviations used in this book

AONB: Area of Outstanding Natural Beauty
DoE: Department of the Environment
MNR: Marine Nature Reserve
MoD: Ministry of Defence
NCB: National Coal Board
NCC: Nature Conservancy Council
NR: Nature Reserve
NT: National Trust
RSPB: Royal Society for the Protection of Birds
SSSI: Site of Special Scientific Interest
WHO: World Health Organization

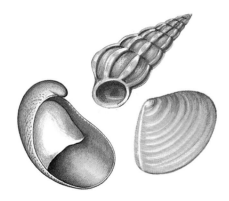

First published in 1987 by Kingfisher Books Limited
Elsley House, 24–30 Great Titchfield Street, London W1P 7AD
A Grisewood & Dempsey Company

BRITISH LIBRARY CATALOGUING IN PUBLICATION DATA
Greenpeace
Coastline: Britain's threatened heritage.
1. Coasts—Great Britain
2. Great Britain—Description and travel—1971–
I. Title
914.1'04858   DA632
ISBN 0-86272-213-6

Half-title: Unloading buoys for lobster pots at Whitby, North Yorkshire.

Title page: The Fleet lagoon and Chesil Beach, Dorset.

Chapter openers:
Page 14: The Thames at dusk, looking downriver towards Blackfriars Bridge.
Page 22: Looking north along the Suffolk coast from Minsmere towards Dunwich.
Page 36: Dockside scene at Hull.
Page 46: Tyneside shipyard at dusk.
Page 58: The fishing village of Crail, Fife.
Page 74: Sea loch in the Cuillins, Skye.
Page 88: Wigtown Bay, Dumfries and Galloway.
Page 100: The harbour at Whitehaven, Cumbria.
Page 108: Morecambe Bay, looking towards the Lake District.
Page 118: Threecliff Bay, on the Gower peninsula.
Page 134: The Severn Bridge, from the English side of the estuary.
Page 142: Godrevy lighthouse, on the north Cornwall coast.
Page 152: Salcombe, on the south Devon coast.
Page 168: Broadstairs, on the east coast of Kent.

PROJECT EDITORIAL DIRECTOR: CHARLOTTE PARRY-CROOKE
CONCEPT/DESIGN: REG BOORER, DOWN TO EARTH COMMUNICATIONS
EDITOR: JONATHAN ELPHICK
EDITORIAL: HAYLEY FRANCIS, ERIC SMITH
CARTOGRAPHY: PAUL OLDMAN, HOWARD DYKE
DESIGN ARTWORK: ANTONY DOMINY
INDEX: P.E. BARBER

Phototypeset by Southern Positives and Negatives (SPAN), Lingfield, Surrey
Colour photograph separations by Newsele Litho, Milan
Map separations by Scantrans PTE, Singapore
Printed in Italy by Vallardi Industrie Grafiche, Milan

CONTENTS

Interest in this project has been forthcoming from numerous sources. The publishers and the Greenpeace Environmental Trust would particularly like to thank the contributors, the consultants, the guest authors and all the following for their generous and valuable assistance during the preparation of the book.

CONSULTANTS AND CONTRIBUTORS

Scientific consultant: Dr Paul Johnston, Greenpeace Scientist, Queen Mary College, London
Campaign consultants/'Causes for Concern': Andrew Booth and Beverley Thorpe, Greenpeace Toxics Division
Ecology consultant/Wildlife features: Dr Tony Hare
Geographical consultant/'Regional Summaries': Keith Lye FRGS

OTHER ADVISERS

John A. Burton; CoEnCo (Council for Environmental Conservation): Edwina Milesi; CORE (Cumbrians Opposed to a Radioactive Environment): Jean Emery; Cumbria Trust for Nature Conservation; Bob Edwards; campaigners and staff at the London office of Greenpeace; IUCN (International Union for Conservation of Nature and Natural Resources): Sue Wells; Bryn Jones; Marine Conservation Society: Dr Susan Gubbay; Marine Research Assessment Group (Centre for Environmental Technology); Nature Conservancy Council: Andrew Currie (Skye), Pat Doody, Chris Lumb, Ian Mitchell (Golspie), John Shackles (Bury St Edmunds); Royal Society for the Protection of Birds.

PHOTOGRAPHER'S ACKNOWLEDGEMENTS

Ken Anderson Fishmonger, London SE23; B.J. Atkins, Pie & Mash, London SW6; Charles Barker Scotland: Alastair Sutcliffe; Frank Burstow, Kyle of Lochalsh; Daily Fresh Fish Supplies, London SW6; Topher Dawson, Scoraig; John Dixon, Beadnell; Eastern Photocolour, Edinburgh; Forsyth Hamilton Smoked Salmon, Ardrishaig; the Galloway Smokehouse, Carlsluith; Toon Ghose, Southern Aero Club, Shoreham; Colin and Anne Gibson, Shetland; Govan Shipbuilders, Glasgow; Hanimex (UK), Swindon (for Fuji film); Ian Jackson, Isle of Man; La Marée, London SW3: Henry White; Leeds Film & Hire, London WC1; Kathleen Macaskill, Skye; John Macleod, Skye; Manze's Pie & Mash, London SE8; Chris and Charles McLean, Redcar; Edwin and Elizabeth Mickleburgh, Aberdeen; Gunnie Moberg, Orkney; Photo-Technical Services, Aberdeen; James and Jane-Ann Robertson, Findochty; Messrs Smith & Burke, Dyble, New Billingsgate; Donald Stewart, Skye; Swan Hunter Shipbuilders, Wallsend; Bernard Thomas, coracle-maker, Dyfed; Andrew Walker, Footdee; Stu Walters, Padstow; Dennis Watt. Lerwick. Very special thanks to Triumph Processing, London SW15 and to Diane Mikula-Gilbert.

GENERAL ACKNOWLEDGEMENTS

Gaynor Cavell; the Chlachain, Mallaig; Dundee Chamber of Commerce; Mark Ellingham; European Year of the Environment; Steve Evans; Christopher Fagg; Theresa Farino; Geological Museum, London; J.R.E. and L.M. Hamilton-Baillie; Colin Haycraft; Andrew Hewson; Mrs Laura Huxley and Chatto & Windus (for permission to use the quotation on page 182 from Aldous Huxley's *The Doors of Perception*); Institute of Cornish Studies: Oliver Padel; Institute of Petroleum; Eileen Johnson; Lincolnshire Archives Office: Nigel Colley; Lindisfarne Priory; Manchester Ship Canal Company: David Thornley; John May, Greenpeace Books; Paint Research Association; Pan Books (for permission to use the extract selected by Douglas Adams from *So long, and thanks for all the fish*); Peter Polish; Port of London Authority: Martin and Sarah Pumphrey; Royal National Lifeboat Institution: Amble Station; Scottish Arts Council: Shonagh Irvine; Scottish Fisheries Museum; Scottish Maritime Museum: Campbell McMurray; Scott Lithgow Shipbuilders; Severn-Trent Water Authority: Robert Bishop; St Catherine's Point Lighthouse, Isle of Wight: Graham Ibbertson; Trinity House, London; The Welsh Office. The following kindly supplied or took the guest author photographs: BBC Television/Faber & Faber (Dennis Potter); Christopher Barker/*Portraits of Poets* (George MacKay Brown, Ted Hughes); Jonathan Cape/Fay Godwin (John Fowles); Duckworth & Co (Beryl Bainbridge); Duckworth & Co/Jerry Bauer (Alice Thomas Ellis); William Heinemann (Douglas Adams); John Johnson (Clare Francis); London Weekend Television/Hodder & Stoughton (Melvyn Bragg); Penguin Books/Mark Gerson (Margaret Drabble); Scotsman Publications Ltd (David Daiches, Alasdair Gray).

FOREWORD

If you go for a day out in Britain, you are far more likely to go to the seaside than anywhere else; the British make 300 million trips to the coast each year. So it is not surprising that almost all of us who live in Britain remember childhood trips to the seaside, and feel a particular love for somewhere we think of as our own bit of coast. I will always remember the excitement and joy of my first few strokes of unaided swimming off Brighton beach. More recently, on Skye, I marvelled at the stunning beauty of the view across the Sound of Sleat to Knoydart, as a family of Golden Eagles soared, calling to each other, high out over the sea.

These stretches of coast, and many other favourites – from North Yorkshire to Pembrokeshire, from Dorset to the Western Isles – I enjoy as a change. But, for me, the real coastline is north Norfolk. Here is a coast of sweeping saltmarshes, long golden beaches and biting east winds. Here, though admittedly not often, the sea can be hotter than the Mediterranean when a high tide has just come in over sand heated all day by the sun. But in January blizzards, roaring in off the North Sea, and blown sand can combine to blank out the beach in seconds, with a wind so strong and cold it is difficult to face into it.

This coast is always full of birds – great wheeling flocks of Brent Geese in winter; startlingly black and white Shelduck and Oystercatchers in spring; delicate snow-white, diving terns in summer. In the autumn, as the sun sets over the sea, great streams of waders fly in along the coast, when the high tide floods their feeding grounds out in the Wash. And always above, the huge expanse of ever-changing sky.

Much of the coast of Britain, particularly the areas between high and low water, has not been altered by people. Along with the tops of some of our highest mountains, the coastline is our wilderness. I feel this sense of untouched nature most strongly out in the Wash. At low tide, huge expanses of sandbanks are exposed. The sand is shifted by every tide, so it is possible to walk in a great, magnificent emptiness, where no one has been before. I imagine the sand is clean and untouched, free from human interference, with only the prints of gulls and seals ahead of me. Common Seals breed out on the sandbanks – mercifully, the butchery of previous years is ended here. But the next time I stand on the fresh, wet sand, I will inevitably think of the human sewage that Greenpeace discovered on the beaches to the east, of the industrial effluent and toxic wastes pouring into the sea to the north, swept down into the Wash on every tide. I will despair at what we do to the water the seals live in, and mourn the dolphins and porpoises already gone.

Compared to most developed countries, much of our coastline has been protected from bricks and concrete, from ribbon development. But industry, particularly the nuclear industry, still heads for the coast with more enthusiasm and grim determination than any day trip-per. This book shows the terrifying range of pollution and other hazards that threaten to engulf and destroy our coastline. Alongside the incredible beauty of the coast, it details the horrors that are being unleashed around every headland, on to every beach, beneath every cliff. The silent, often unseen poisons are the target of Greenpeace's campaign for clean seas.

Britain has one of the most beautiful and varied coastlines in the world. This magnificent book, and Dennis Gilbert's spectacular photographs, will convince everyone of that. On behalf of Greenpeace, and every-one who loves our coastline, I thank the contributors, consultants and advisers, everyone at Kingfisher Books, Dennis Gilbert, and particularly Ted Hughes and the other guest authors, who have written something especially for us, or chosen a favourite piece.

Greenpeace will go on campaigning peacefully, using scientific research and the courage and determination of our campaigners to confront those who would destroy the coastline, until our seas are clean again. Please read this book. Then join us.

Peter Melchett.

Lord Peter Melchett, Chair, Greenpeace UK

INTRODUCTION

Opposite: Major coastal and estuarine features of Britain and its offshore islands are shown on this map. Also shown are the towns and other places visited by the Greenpeace vessel *Beluga* on the 1986 Greenpeace coastal survey. (See also page 183.)

'THE SEA WASHES ALL MAN'S ILLS AWAY.'

Euripides, *Iphigeneia in Tauris* (414–412 BC)

In 1986, the Greenpeace research vessel *Beluga* and her international team of scientists made the first independent survey of the state of Britain's coasts and estuaries. The subsequent report of the survey's findings makes informative – but often depressing – reading. On the positive side, however, the report has thrown the problems of coastal and marine pollution into sharp relief, galvanized support for action, and brought new hope for the future. Indeed, it was the historic voyage of the *Beluga* that provided a major inspiration for this book, which attempts both to celebrate Britain's outstanding coastal heritage and to sound a warning about the threats it faces.

Britain has a coastline of immense variety and beauty. Its mainland and island shores include dramatic cliffs, long sweeping sandy bays, narrow rocky coves and great flat estuaries fringed with saltmarshes. An island itself, Britain is also a country of islands – over a thousand of them, as varied as the coastline itself, ranging from cliff-girt, wave-lashed Scottish outcrops to the genteel charm of the Isle of Wight.

As well as magnificent scenery, Britain's coastline has a remarkably rich geology – from the hard granite headlands of Cornwall to the chalk of the South Coast and parts of Yorkshire. Britain's complex geological history ensures that there is great variety in the rocks within relatively small stretches of coast; this variety is largely responsible for the many types of coastline found in Britain.

For most of its long history, much of Britain has been alternately exposed and submerged by shallow seas, gradually acquiring its modern shape over the last 25 million years or so. During the Ice Age, so much water was locked up in ice sheets and glaciers that the sea level fell and Britain was linked to Ireland and mainland Europe. As the climate grew warmer, and the ice melted, these bridges were drowned. Britain's isolation from the European mainland began around 7500 years ago, when the last remaining shallow link across the North Sea was submerged.

The rise in sea level also submerged many river valleys. Some, such as the Severn, formed great estuaries, while others, especially in south-western England, formed rias (drowned river valleys). On the West Coast of Scotland, the flooding of the steep-sided glaciated valleys produced the fiords characteristic of the region. The coast is still slowly sinking in some places – at the rate of more than twenty feet over the past 6,500 years in East Anglia – and slowly rising in others, such as in parts of Scotland.

Today's coastal scenery has been shaped not only by changes in sea level, but also by continuous erosion and deposition. Along much of the West Coast of Britain, old, hard rocks dominate. Although they are pounded relentlessly by great Atlantic breakers, they are more resistant to the immense erosive power of the waves, and the constant weathering by frost and sun, than are the generally softer rocks of much of south-eastern England. There, coastlines composed of unconsolidated glacial clays and sands can be eroded at a dramatic – and sometimes disastrous – rate.

Rock and shell fragments from the shore are ground down by the sea to form sand grains. Some of this material is washed out to sea. Some forms beaches, some is deposited by tides and currents to form spits and bars; and some is blown by the wind to form sand dunes, which may eventually become colonized – and stabilized – by tough, salt-resistant vegetation and grasses, such as Marram Grass.

Larger rock fragments are deposited as banks of shingle, of which Britain has impressive examples at Chesil Beach, Dungeness, Orford Ness and the Spurn peninsula. The largest rocks of all form the jumbled rocky shores, clothed in seaweeds and studded with rock pools, each a living world in miniature.

All the varied types of British coastline provide habitats for a rich heritage of wildlife. The more remote rocky western and northern coasts and islands are home to great seabird colonies of international importance. Twenty-four species of seabirds breed in Britain, some of them with a total population numbered in hundreds of thousands. On the same plummeting cliffs, tough, well-adapted plants cling to precarious crevices and crannies. The mainly deserted rocky coasts of the far north and west provide one of the last havens for the Otter. Grey Seals also favour the wilder rocky northern and western coasts.

Estuaries, although rather uniform environments, are also bursting with life. Although relatively few species of animals and plants have managed to adapt to the harsh uniform conditions of shifting mud and sand, with their dramatic extremes of temperature and changing salinity, those that do may occur in immense numbers. Beneath the mud and sand is a teeming world of molluscs, crustaceans and worms – with as many as 60,000 of the little shrimp-like *Corophium* or 90,000 ragworms in a single square yard. These creatures form a vital source of food for the huge numbers of wading birds that throng Britain's shores, especially in winter. Of the thirty or so estuaries in Europe and North America that are visited annually by more than 20,000 waders, half are to be found in Britain. In winter, British estuaries and other wetlands are thronged with more than half the total number of waders found in the whole of Europe.

Dissected by mysterious mazes of channels, saltmarshes are rich in plant life – from the salt-tolerant species of the intertidal mud to the grasses and bright flowers of the upper marsh. Saltmarshes also provide breeding and feeding sites for a variety of waders, as well as winter feeding grounds for huge numbers of wildfowl and other birds, such as the Skylark and the Short-eared Owl.

Sand dunes, although almost lifeless in their formative stages, soon become consolidated by robust, sand-gathering plants. Gradually, the dunes become larger and larger, providing homes for nesting Shelduck, spider-hunting sand wasps and many moths and butterflies. In the older dunes there are moist hollows, or 'slacks', where a rich flora, including rare orchids and other very localized plants, occurs. Sand dunes are also colonized by such scarce animals as the Natterjack Toad.

ORKNEY
ISLANDS

Westray

Mainland

Hoy

Pentland Firth

SHETLAND
ISLANDS

Unst

Yell

Fetlar

Mainland

CAPE WRATH

PENTLAND
FIRTH

OUTER HEBRIDES

LEWIS

HARRIS

SKYE

North West Highlands

MORAY FIRTH

KINNAIRDS
HEAD

Spey

Grampian Highlands

Dee

Aberdeen

MULL

JURA

ISLAY

KINTYRE

FIRTH OF CLYDE

NORTH CHANNEL

Clyde

FIRTH OF TAY

FIRTH OF FORTH

ST ABB'S HEAD

Berwick

HOLY I.

Tweed

Southern Uplands

Cheviot
Hills

Tyne

Gretna

Cumbrian Mts.

SOLWAY FIRTH

ST BEES HEAD

ISLE OF MAN

Grange-over-Sands

Pennines

MORECAMBE BAY

FYLDE

IRISH SEA

NORTH SEA

Tees

Middlesbrough

N. York
Moors

HOLDERNESS

FLAMBOROUGH HEAD

Humber

SPURN HEAD

Trent

LIVERPOOL
BAY

ANGLESEY

HOLY I.

Mersey

Queensferry

Dee

Skegness

THE WASH

LLŶN PEN.

CARDIGAN BAY

Cambrian Mts.

The Fens

Norfolk
Broads

THE SANDLINGS

Midland Plain

ST DAVID'S HEAD

Severn

Brecon
Beacons

Wye

Avon

Cotswolds

Nene

Great Ouse

Chilterns

Stour

The Mumbles

GOWER

BRISTOL CHANNEL

Mendips

FOULNESS

Thames

Southend

Margate

North Downs

Ilfracombe

Exmoor

Salisbury
Plain

South Downs

HARTLAND PT.

Dorset
Downs

DUNGENESS

BEACHY
HEAD

STRAIT OF DOVER

Dartmoor

Poole

I. OF WIGHT

Camel

LYME
BAY

I. OF
PORTLAND

LAND'S
END

FALMOUTH BAY

BOLT HEAD

ENGLISH CHANNEL

LIZARD POINT

BRITAIN'S COASTAL FEATURES

St
Martin's

Bryher

Tresco

St Mary's

St Agnes

ISLES OF
SCILLY

Even the extreme environment of a shingle beach has its own individual wildlife. In more stable areas, where the pebbles are no longer pounded and flung about by the waves, lichens can thrive, along with a number of specialized flowering plants and a few small animals. Given freedom from disturbance, such birds as terns and Ringed Plovers will nest on shingle beaches.

Britain's coastline – and the seas that wash it – has always been of supreme importance to its island people. From the earliest days of Britain's settlement, trade was carried on from its shores and food harvested from its waters. A navy developed to defend the country from periodic invasions; Britain's importance as a seafaring and naval power grew apace, leading eventually to its control over the world's oceans and to the long period of empire-building.

Great fishing and whaling ports grew up along its shores; during the 19th century, the Industrial Revolution left its grimy mark on many coastal areas. New coastal towns became established and doubled their populations in decades, while the increasing popularity of the coast with the holidaymaker led to further development, as seaside resorts, both large and small, appeared and expanded.

Most of Britain's coastline has been affected at one time or another by human activity. Along parts of it, such as the South Coast, continuous ribbons of towns and suburbs now cover long stretches with very little of the natural landscape remaining; in other areas, large expanses of saltmarsh have been 'reclaimed' for agriculture – at the expense of shellfish breeding beds, wading birds and wildfowl. Ironically, the planners' use of the word 'reclaimed' often describes the claiming of a natural saltmarsh for human use for the first time. A variety of ambitious schemes has been put forward for 'reclaiming' major estuaries and bays – including Morecambe Bay and the Severn estuary – for reservoirs and tidal barrages. Less dramatic, but far more insidious, is the continual small-scale loss of areas of saltmarsh to a variety of developments, from agriculture, power stations, chemical complexes, oil refineries, ports and marinas to rubbish dumps. Taken together on a national scale, these individual assaults are diminishing Britain's remaining saltmarshes at a disturbing rate.

Dune systems, too, are vulnerable to human interference. Their inherent mobility means that the encroachment of agriculture, golf courses or building sites can destabilize them; even regular use of footpaths can loosen the sand enough to start a blow-out. Although dune erosion can be hard to spot, it can happen remarkably quickly – a 30-foot-high dune can vanish within a month. Replacing it might take two years, and it may not be fully stabilized for a further four. Large areas of dunes have been completely altered by plantations of conifers. Shingle beaches, although they appear tough and resistant, have been damaged by such things as gravel extraction and over-exploitation by tourism to the extent that their breeding birds, particularly terns, have declined markedly.

By the early 1960s, the private car had begun to replace the railway as the major means of transport; while many railway stations in small seaside resorts were closed, new trunk roads and a network of motorways were built. The increased personal mobility brought about by the motor car changed the stay-put seaside holidaymaker into a tourist, able to reach some of the least developed, most unspoiled stretches of the coast. Today, narrow fishing-village streets are clogged by traffic jams and beautiful bays despoiled by car and caravan parks; the greatly increased pressure on the coast in the most popular spots is, not surprisingly, having a serious effect on the landscape and its wildlife.

While tourism and leisure activities have become increasingly important to the economies of numerous seaside towns and villages, many traditional coastal industries and skills have declined. Britain was once the world's greatest shipbuilding nation, but the slump in the industry's fortunes during the 20th century has led to massive unemployment among its highly skilled workforce. The same story is generally true of many of Britain's once-busy docks, which now handle only a fraction of their former shipping – although a few, such as Felixstowe in Suffolk, have grown in stature.

Traditional fishing still continues, but on a greatly reduced scale. Today,

To the north of the British mainland lie the remote and rugged Scottish islands. In the Shetland Isles no point is more than three miles from salt water. Today, even here, many of the traditional coastal livelihoods have given way to developments of the modern age, especially the oil industry.

While some areas of Britain's coastline are being added to by natural forces, others are being eroded – often at an alarming rate. Along Britain's East Coast, erosion has proved a major problem for centuries. Here, at Mundesley in Norfolk, large landslips have occurred, taking great circular bites out of the cliff face and putting paid to turn-of-the-century plans for developing the town as a holiday resort.

fishing is an increasingly competitive and technological business that has led to the decline of local small-scale fisheries. These are often unable to compete with the modern purse-seiner, equipped with the latest echo-sounding and radar fish-finding equipment, whose purse-shaped nets may be larger than St Paul's Cathedral and can catch in a single day more fish than an old steam drifter could in a month. The taking of larger and larger catches has led to the serious overfishing of many fish stocks in Britain's offshore waters, notably of herring, skate and mackerel. Other fish, such as sand-eels, formerly ignored because they are not considered edible, are now taken in increasing numbers for processing into oil, fishmeal and fertilizer. Their depletion could have disastrous effects on many sea creatures, such as Puffins and other seabirds, that form part of the sea's intricate food chains. Modern fishing causes other problems, from the scouring of the seabed by fish trawls or shellfish suction dredgers, which can devastate whole communities of seabed creatures, to the drowning or injury of seals caught in nets, and the strangling of seabirds which use pieces of non-rottable plastic netting for nest material.

Completely new coastal industries have also left their mark on many of Britain's shores and seas over the last few decades. Oil-drilling rigs, oil-production platforms and oil terminals, nuclear power stations, and huge complexes of petrochemical and other industries now line many shores and estuaries. These bring with them huge problems of pollution. While it was once in a sense true that the sea could 'wash all man's ills away', by diluting his wastes, today's continuous outpouring of an alarming variety of pollutants – from oil, coal waste and sewage sludge to toxic heavy metals and radioactive emissions – is creating the most serious threat Britain's coastal waters have ever faced.

Despite the massive problems that face the coastline and its communities of both people and wildlife, there are success stories in the fight to preserve its magnificent heritage. Nature reserves have been created to protect habitats and species, while many particularly beautiful stretches of the seashore have been kept from development through purchase by the National Trust, the National Trust for Scotland and other bodies. In addition to the creation of new land-based reserves, 1986 saw the formation of the first Statutory Marine Nature Reserve, around the island of Lundy in the Bristol Channel, through the efforts of a relatively new conservation group, the Marine Conservation Society.

This Society was among the many organizations that advised on certain specific marine pollution problems before the Greenpeace vessel *Beluga* left on her 1986 survey of Britain's coastline. The route taken by the *Beluga*, and the regions on which her scientists reported, form the basis for the division of the following chapters in this book. The voyage of the *Beluga* played a vital role in a major campaign to save and preserve Britain's coastal heritage – a continuing campaign whose aims unite numerous other environmental pressure groups and conservation organizations with Greenpeace. As part of Greenpeace's ongoing coastal programme, this book provides a timely reminder of both the beauty and importance of Britain's coastline and the forces that threaten it; hopefully it will inspire participation in the fight to save it – before it is too late.

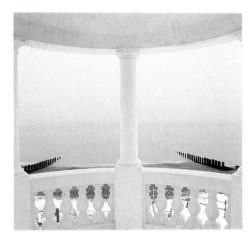

Along Britain's South Coast stretch the results of the Regency and Victorian boom in seaside resorts. One such is Bexhill, in Sussex, developed by the de la Warr family, along an area of coast that was then almost empty, and retaining today – especially in winter – some of its original charm.

Some of the loveliest bays in Britain lie along its West Coast. Here, waves break on the great sweep of Rhossili Bay, one of the many beauty spots on the Gower peninsula in Wales. The headland is protected from commercial development by the National Trust, which owns this coastal stretch.

THE THAMES ESTUARY

DOUGLAS ADAMS

The deep roar of the ocean.

The break of waves on further shores than thought can find.

The silent thunders of the deep.

And from among it, voices calling, and yet not voices, humming trillings, wordlings, the half-articulated songs of thought.

Greetings, waves of greetings, sliding back down into the inarticulate, words breaking together.

A crash of sorrow on the shores of Earth.

Waves of joy on – where? A world indescribably found, indescribably arrived at, indescribably wet, a song of water.

A fugue of voices now, clamouring explanations, of a disaster unavertable, a world to be destroyed, a surge of helplessness, a spasm of despair, a dying fall, again the break of words.

And then the fling of hope, the finding of a shadow Earth in the implications of enfolded time, submerged dimensions, the pull of parallels, the deep pull, the spin of will, the hurl and split of it, the flight. A new Earth pulled into replacement, the dolphins gone.

Then stunningly a single voice, quite clear.

'This bowl was brought to you by the Campaign to Save the Humans. We bid you farewell.'

And then the sound of long, heavy, perfectly grey bodies rolling away into an unknown fathomless deep, quietly giggling.

THE THAMES ESTUARY
MARGATE TO SOUTHEND

'THE SHADOWY SHIPS IN THE RIVER
SLOWLY CHANGED TO BLACK SUBSTANCES: AND THE SUN, BLOOD-RED ON
THE EASTERN MARSHES BEHIND DARK MASTS AND YARDS, SEEMED FILLED
WITH THE RUINS OF A FOREST IT HAD SET ON FIRE.'

Charles Dickens, *Our Mutual Friend* (1865)

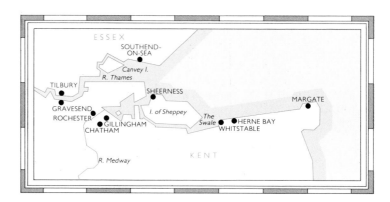

Although found mainly on fresh waters, the Tufted Duck winters on a few estuaries, including the Thames. Its rapid increase since it first bred in Britain in the 1840s is due to the greater availability of suitable habitats and the spread of the Zebra Mussel, a major food, from the London docks.

When Dickens wrote the novel from which the quotation above is taken, the Thames was alive with activity yet dark, diseased and depressing. But its long and proud history encompasses far more than the gloom and doom of its Victorian past. For centuries, this great river was the very lifeblood of the nation, providing the gateway to a steadily expanding world. From Roman times, when the first quays were built, London was the most important trading centre for northern Europe, and the Thames Britain's main waterway. Trade was based on the historic heart of the capital, the 'square mile' of the City of London, established on the north bank of the river, around which over the centuries the vast metropolis has grown.

Remnants of the once thriving Royal Victoria Dock, these cranes were known to the dockers as 'moonshots'; they are preserved at present, but may soon end up on the scrapheap.

The Great Trading Centre
Already a thriving business and administrative centre in Roman times, the City of London grew in importance as merchants from Britain and the Continent established their trading bases there. London's prestige and power lay in its control of trade carried via the Thames to and from the Baltic, the Rhine and, later, every port in the world. The great river, and the destinations to which it led, formed the vast network of markets for which the City of London became the management. Almost all the famous financial institutions in existence today have their basis in the trade conducted by the sailing ships that at one time had to queue for weeks to berth in the busy Pool of London between the Tower of London and London Bridge.

The Life and Death of the Docks
It was not until the early 1800s that the first modern enclosed docks spread eastwards from the City, both north and south of the river, thanks to the Crown's fear that their construction would encourage shippers to evade customs duties. Despite this late start, the vast dock system – which eventually extended east from the Tower of London to Newham, with an outpost at Tilbury 23 miles downriver from London Bridge – soon became one of the wonders of the world, confirming London as the leading international port. In 1908, the Port of London Authority was established to control this vast enterprise, formerly owned by a number of private companies. Under the Authority's jurisdiction, the Port of London comprises the tidal portion of the Thames, extending from Teddington lock to the seaward limit, at the Tongue light vessel, a distance of 95 miles.

The huge area of the docks, including by the 1930s some forty-four miles of quays, was served by an army of dockers, stevedores and lightermen. Ships from every corner of the globe filled the great basins, disgorging a bewildering variety of cargoes into giant warehouses and vaults, redolent with aromas of a multitude of different commodities, from exotic spices and hops to tallow and rubber. Each dock, or a quay within the dock, specialized in particular cargoes – flour, wine and fruit at Millwall, for instance, and meat and tobacco at the Royal Victoria. The cold stores for meat could accommodate half a million carcases.

As recently as the mid-1960s, the London docks were still thriving. Then they went into a rapidly accelerating decline, so that by 1981, when the last docks, the three 'Royals', closed, the incredible diversity of sounds and sights and smells was gone forever, together with thousands of jobs and entire communities. The chief cause

trade. Tilbury Docks, though not built until 1886, had room for expansion. With container and ro-ro berths, grain and timber terminals and tanker repair yards, they are thriving, too.

St Katherine's Dock, by Tower Bridge, is now well established as a marina and floating museum of famous ships. At other docks, over the last few years, deserted quayside buildings have been speedily converted into television studios and artists' workspaces, alongside new office centres making up one of the largest office developments in the world. The upwardly mobile, able to afford a quarter of a million pounds or more for flats in converted warehouses, are also attracted by the area's proximity to the City. Working and shopping elsewhere, the inhabitants of this surreal world of luxury homes are

Since 1984, the 45 square miles of Inner London that were so vulnerable to flooding have been protected by the gleaming Thames Barrier, whose design allows boats to pass through unhindered on normal tides.

Sea Wormwood grows on windswept saltmarshes. Its absinthe-scented foliage is eaten by the caterpillar of the Essex Emerald Moth. The moth, at the edge of its range here, survives in only a handful of sites in Essex.

of this sudden death was the alteration in the methods of handling dry cargo. With the advent of containerization and the development of 'roll-on roll-off' ('ro-ro') vessels, cargoes could be driven by road to and from ports in the same container, thus greatly reducing the handling required. The existing facilities at the huge London docks became obsolete, there was no room for further expansion, traffic congestion made access to the quays increasingly difficult and the larger ships could not pass through the locks. The London docks lost out to the specialized container ports of Rotterdam, Felixstowe and Harwich – save for a single wharf on the south bank of the river by the Blackwall Tunnel entrance, the Victoria Deep Water Terminal, which is able to profit from the container

overwhelming the original community of East Enders, who receive little in return.

Another dramatic change has been caused by the Thames Barrier, completed in 1984, which straddles the river near Woolwich like the gleaming but discarded helmets of a party of giant knights. The biggest movable flood barrier in the world, its construction involved the destruction of areas of marsh and foreshore used by waders and wildfowl. And new embankments have had to be built, replacing or covering the old clay walls all the way down to the sea, causing the loss of much of the rich specialized flora. Earlier, too, wildfowl lost the valuable area of Woolwich Bay during its mid-1970s reclamation for the new town of Thamesmead, now the home of many exiled East Enders.

In the early morning light, two different worlds meld across the low tide creeks and flats of the Medway (right): an old beached dinghy, used perhaps for gathering shellfish, and the distant chimney of Kingsnorth power station on the Isle of Grain, where important research has been carried out into the effects of the warm-water effluent from the power station on the estuary's wildlife.

Grey Herons are found on many estuaries, as well as by inland waters, and breed in nearby woodlands. The largest British heronry is at one such site, in Northward Hill, overlooking the north Kent marshes.

Opposite: The lower Thames is still a waterway: for ferries and container ships at Sheerness (left); for the Port of London Authority's pilot boats and an oyster smack at Gravesend (above right); and for cockle boats from Leigh-on-Sea (below centre) that work the Maplin Sands. Even at Margate (below right), a few people still opt for the pleasures of sailing rather than the rides of the amusement park.

The Splendour of the Thames

Despite its recent problems, the riverside still contains much beauty. Lining its banks are some of the finest buildings in London – from Hampton Court and Kew Palace to the Houses of Parliament and the South Bank complex. Perhaps the finest of all the Thameside architecture is to be seen at Greenwich. This was the site of one of the Thames's seven royal palaces, built in the 15th century. Henry VIII was born here, and it was at Greenwich that he acquired the passion for ships that encouraged him to found two new naval dockyards and victualling yards on the river, at Woolwich and Deptford, and to build up the Royal Navy. At the end of the 17th century, Queen Mary had Sir Christopher Wren rebuild the palace, creating the Royal Naval Hospital, a masterpiece of Baroque splendour. In 1873, the hospital was converted into the Royal Naval College for training officers.

As well as its proud tradition of naval history, which it shares with the former naval dockyard at Chatham on the Medway in Kent, the Thames has a long tradition of regal pageantry which has lasted until the early 20th century, with great flotillas of royal barges often turning out for weddings, coronations and funerals. This pageantry was at its height in Tudor times, when the river was much wider than it is today, and lined with noblemen's houses. The progressive embankment of the Thames from the 1760s onwards has created one of the greatest changes in its appearance as its banks were extended.

The bridges, too, while linking north and south London, have transformed the Thames. Of the many bridges that span the river today, few existed before the Victorian era. Old London Bridge was the greatest. The roar and thunder of the tide as it raced through the narrow channels between the great piers must have been an impressive sound.

Most spectacular of all the public events the river has seen must have been the great Frost Fair in the severe winter of 1683–4, when the water froze over completely. Crowds of people skated or sledged to and fro, watched the horse and coach races or visited the tents that had been erected on the ice for puppet plays, drinking or other entertainment. There was bull-baiting, too, and oxen were roasted on great spits.

Marshes and Islands

The marshes fringing the lower reaches of the Thames, on the south bank of the estuary in Kent, have changed little since the days when Dickens knew them – although they are now much reduced in area, due to land reclamation and conversion to arable land or sites for urban expansion. Today, the slow flight of the Heron and the sweet song of the Nightingale redeem Dickens's grim descriptions of hangings of convicts. Both species are among the many protected at the RSPB nature reserve at Northward Hill, site of the largest heronry in Britain.

Nearby, Cooling Marshes have long been converted for sheep grazing, while to the east lies the Isle of Grain – its name comes from the Old English word *greon*, meaning 'sand' or 'gravel' – almost separated from the mainland by the narrow Yantlet Creek. A power station and an oil refinery loom above the steadily chewing sheep. Across the mouth of the Medway more industrial structures surround the high brick walls of Sheerness Dockyard, with its car ferry and container terminal.

Oysters, Resorts and Barges

Although the oysters harvested in Essex are more famous, Whitstable, on Kent's north coast, can boast one of the largest oyster hatcheries in Europe. After a decline in the industry in the 1950s, due to pollution and storm damage, oyster farming flourished again, only to face a new threat today from the anti-fouling paint, TBT.

Other parts of the north Kent coast were transformed when sea-bathing first became fashionable. By the late 1700s, as many as 20,000 trippers were being carried down the Thames every summer, in small passenger boats called 'hoys', to the expanding town of Margate. By the early 19th century, Southend, on the opposite shores of the estuary, had grown from a village to assume the status of an elite resort, although later it was to become the classic Cockney eel-and-pie seaside town, swallowing neighbouring villages, as did Margate.

Many of these resorts had impressive piers; Southend's, over $1\frac{1}{4}$ miles long, is the longest pleasure pier in the world. The original purpose of the piers – as landing stages for holiday-makers, who otherwise faced an unpleasant walk across tidal mudflats – has long since been superseded and forgotten. Some lifeboat crews still launch their vessels from pierheads, but modern day-trippers – and commuters – arrive by road or rail, packing the trains and filling the town and suburbs with the noise and fumes of traffic jams. A broad ribbon of offices, factories, oil storage tanks and housing estates now links London with Southend.

The one thoroughfare that is no longer busy is the Thames. A touch of glamour is introduced by the sleek yachts in the new City marinas, and the rust-red sails of restored Thames barges bring a splash of colour from time to time, while historic ships like the *Cutty Sark* and HMS *Belfast* testify to the greatness of the river's past. But the Thames is mostly quiet, its daily traffic almost non-existent save for the ships that enter its expansive mouth to dock at Tilbury or Sheerness.

Cleaning up the Thames

In 1766 on a single day, 130 Thames salmon were sold at Billingsgate fish market, while London apprentices are said to have complained about their monotonous diet of this now-prized fish. Before long, however, few creatures, let alone the noble salmon, could survive the toxic

In the last few decades, the authorities have taken on the mammoth task of cleaning up the Thames. By the end of the 1960s, it was once again a river where fish could swim. Even the salmon had returned, albeit in very small numbers. But the news is not all good. The sewage no longer pumped into the Thames is instead loaded onto ships and carried out to sea near Clacton, where it is dumped uncontained. Currents drift it back to the coast and the problem merely shifts location. Over a hundred pipelines still discharge wastes into the river, and mercury has found its way into the bodies of Thames eels. Every year since 1979, the Thames Water Authority has had to spend £65,000 on restocking the river with salmon. In 1985, eleven salmon were caught with rod and line in the Thames – compared with eighteen in 1812, when the river was far more polluted than it is today.

Since the docks closed, the river has lost part of its identity. But it is still much valued by Londoners, both as their great landmark and, recently, for its recreational potential. Hopefully, the interests of anglers, birdwatchers and others – and the new watersports clubs, marinas and prestige riverside flats for the privileged – will ensure further cleaning-up programmes. Those who worked in the docks mourn the lost vitality of the river. Their jobs have gone and a share of the riverside is denied to them, but Old Father Thames is still loved. He is old and not very well, but he can yet be rejuvenated.

Few of the bridges that now span the Thames, carrying millions of people daily between north and south London, existed before Victorian times. Battersea Bridge (above) replaced an earlier wooden structure in the 1880s. Framed within its arch is Albert Bridge, which is as delicate as it looks. It has needed reinforcement and traffic is restricted.

mix of the river at its most polluted. It became the opaque and evil-smelling channel that symbolized so well the squalor of the city's life. It was as a consequence of the great expansion of the population in 19th-century London that the river's role as dustbin and open sewer first became an acute problem.

To the surprise of many tourists, the glass dome behind the prow of the *Cutty Sark*, preserved as a reminder of London's great maritime tradition in a Greenwich dry dock, covers the lift shaft for a foot tunnel beneath the river. This emerges on the Isle of Dogs, an area where once-thriving docks have been redeveloped into huge office and workshop areas and residential accommodation.

REGIONAL SUMMARY

THE THAMES ESTUARY

The coast of the Thames estuary (Margate-Gravesend; Tilbury-Southend) is about 70 miles (113km) long. The Tideway (that part of the Thames affected by tides) extends 69 miles (111km) inland to Teddington.

PHYSICAL PROFILE

The mostly muddy estuarine coasts are made up mainly of London Clay, with chalk outcrops on the Isle of Thanet. (Thanet was an island in Roman times – the channels separating it from the mainland have silted up.) The coast is sinking and the sea-level rising by about 2 feet (0.6m) per 100 years. There is a danger of floods when storms coincide with spring tides. (On the night of January 31, 1953, 58 people were drowned on Canvey Island.) The Thames Barrier at Woolwich now safeguards central London from tidal surges that might have flooded the capital's underground railway tunnels.

Climate: One of Britain's driest coasts, with rainfall averaging 19–22 inches (490–560mm) a year. Summer temperatures often exceed 80°F (27°C), but sea breezes are cooling. Winters are chilly. Snow is common when winds are in the east.

HUMAN PROFILE

The region is now a resort and industrial (especially oil-refining) area. Resorts include Margate (pop 53,300) and Southend-on-Sea (156,700), whose 1¼ mile (2km) long pier is Britain's longest. Southend and Gillingham (93,700) are residential areas. Canvey Island (35,300) has many holiday homes. Sheerness, part of Queenborough-in-Sheppey (33,400), and Tilbury, part of Thurrock (127,000), are container ports with ferry services. Gravesend (58,000) is HQ of the Port of London's Navigation Service.

Sites of historic interest: Reculver was a Roman fort guarding the approach to the Isle of Thanet. The former Roman encampment of Rochester (52,000) is now noted for its Norman castle and cathedral. Hadleigh Castle, Essex, was built in the 1360s to guard against French attack. Tilbury Fort (1682) defended the Thames against the Dutch and French. Chatham (61,900) is the site of a former Royal Navy dockyard (founded 1547). Sheerness was the scene of the Nore Mutiny (1797).

Museums: Charles Dickens Centre, Rochester; Dolphin Yard Sailing Barge Museum, Sittingbourne; Prittlewell Priory Museum, Southend.

Famous personalities: Dickens spent his early childhood (1817–23) in Chatham and his honeymoon (1836) at Chalk. His final years (1860–70) were spent at Gadshill, near Rochester. The area features in several of his novels.

Marine industry: Fishing: Whitstable, Europe's biggest oyster hatchery. Boat- and shipbuilding: Rochester on Medway, Tilbury.

Commerce/industry: Oil refining: Coryton, Isle of Grain, Thurrock. Oil-fired power station: Isle of Grain. Paper: Gravesend. Flour, saw-milling and engineering industries: Chatham.

NATURAL PROFILE

Wildlife: Special habitats, with rare plants, include old sea (and river) walls. Grazing marshes behind the walls are rich in flowers, insects and birds. There are saltmarshes, estuarine muds and fast-vanishing docklands, including abandoned wharves, with their unique wasteland flora.

Attractions: In Kent, South Swale and The Swale (NCC); Elmley Marshes (RSPB); Chetney peninsula and Medway Marshes – breeding and wintering wildfowl; High Halstow Marshes; Northward Hill (RSPB) has Britain's largest heronry. In Essex, Fobbing and Vange Marshes – grazing marsh with old sea walls – Essex Emerald Moth, Emerald Damselfy and Britain's largest population of Willow-leaved Lettuce; Leigh Marsh – rich in plant species and large numbers of wintering Brent Geese. *Footpaths:* Margate-Reculver-Herne Bay, about 10 miles (16km); parts of the Gravesend-Rye Saxon Shore Way, including sections along the Swale estuary and the Graveney Marshes; Leigh-Shoeburyness, 7 miles (11km). *Beaches in Kent:* Margate, St Mildred's Bay, Minnis Bay, Herne Bay, Leysdown (noted for fossils). *Beaches in Essex:* Leigh-on-Sea, Westcliff, Southend.

CAUSES FOR CONCERN

Direct dumping: 4.9 million tons (5 million tonnes) per annum of contaminated sewage is dumped 10 miles (16km) off Clacton. This is Europe's largest dumpsite. Because sewage contamination affects cockles, fishermen at Brightlingsea boil their catch for four minutes before it is safe.

Pipeline discharges: Almost 150 pipelines discharge millions of gallons of waste into the Thames estuary every day. The emission of warm water from the cooling systems of conventional power stations has raised the temperature of some regions by 5.4°F (3°C). Warming, combined with sewage washed out of the antiquated sewerage system by heavy rainfall, causes deoxygenation of water. This can kill thousands of fish, as in July 1986.

Radioactive discharges: Three inland research centres discharge liquid radioactive wastes into the Thames: Harwell, Oxon (UK Atomic Energy Authority); Amersham International plc, Bucks; and Aldermaston, Berks (MoD).

Oil pollution: Risk of major spills from oil terminals at Thames Haven, Canvey Island. Most damaging has been the regular run-off from the huge concentration of industrial and private oil users surrounding the Thames and its estuary.

Beaches: Southend has sewage contamination above EEC guidelines.

Threatened wildlife: The 100,000 to 150,000 waders that winter in the Thames estuary, representing 5 to 7.5% of the total on British coasts, are threatened with habitat loss. Wildfowl numbers have declined sharply in some areas. Although the Thames, Medway and Swale estuaries are now protected under the international Ramsar Convention, 48% of grazing marshland has been drained since 1935.

The Salmon's much-heralded return to the Thames has been achieved by the determined clean-up of the river in recent years, although the fishes' numbers are maintained by annual reintroductions, and pollution problems still occur.

The ground-nesting Hen Harrier retreated as the agricultural revolution advanced. It was persecuted, too, by grousemoor gamekeepers. With protection, it has recovered, breeding in the uplands, and visiting south and east coasts – including the Thames estuary – in winter.

EAST ANGLIA
AND THE WASH

HAMMOND INNES

Here were the Belgae, the Romans, the Saxons, the Jutes, the Angles and the Danes. Here the Rhine ran north to an Arctic sea before the Channel was born or the great bulge of land between Wash and Thames was formed. Here in East Anglia a sainted king was slain, his body incorrupt and stolen away.

Here stands the greatest concentration of medieval churches in England, with the finest roofs, the finest screens, the finest wood carvings, and more angels, in flight or couchant, to the square foot of great oak hammer beams than anywhere else.

Here stood Hereward of the Fens on the Isle of Eels in defiance of the Norman Conqueror, and on that same island, over a period of two and a half centuries, a band of monks built what I think to be the most marvellous of all cathedrals, for it rides like a great galleon above the flat of the black peat, and when the nave collapsed Alan of Walsingham rafted eight great oaks up from Bedford and erected that incredibly beautiful lantern as the centrepiece of his reconstruction.

Here once was a world of oaks, all forest from Breckland heath to Thames marsh. Here now is rich farming, the landscape changing, birds and insects disappearing from sprayed habitats.

But the key to East Anglia's unique quality is not land, it is water – long sea estuaries thrusting deep, rivers and streams like veins, fens and washes, the Norfolk Broads, and, at the mouth of those rivers and estuaries, England's gateway to Europe.

And it is here, on the coast, that you find that wonderful lost world of sea marsh and sea bird.

23

EAST ANGLIA AND THE WASH
SOUTHEND TO SKEGNESS

'THE SUNBURNT TAR THAT BLISTERS ON THE PLANKS,
AND BANK-SIDE STAKES IN THEIR UNEVEN RANKS,
HEAPS OF ENTANGLED WEEDS THAT SLOWLY FLOAT
AS THE TIDE ROLLS BY THE IMPEDED BOAT.'

George Crabbe, 'Peter Grimes' from *The Borough* (1810)

The percussion of pebbles as the sea retreats and advances on the East Coast shingle and the seemingly infinite expanses of low-tide sand on the northern beaches bordering the Wash are the two chief characteristics of this watery, elusive coast. Often literally invisible from out to sea, because it scarcely rises above the waves, the shoreline is so ill-defined in the northern marshes and so close to inland waters in the Broads that it frequently loses its identity altogether. Lacking good communications with the rest of the country, its people found it easier to travel to the continent of Europe than to London or Liverpool, with the result that East Anglia has been peculiarly isolated for much of its history.

Marram Grass is
the dune builder.
Stopping wind-
blown sand with its tough,
stiff leaves, it raises the
young sandhill grain by
grain, building it up with
its roots. Buried by a
heavier drift of sand, it
will grow up and out
incredibly fast.

Floods and Farmland

Gales can build the waves in the southern part of the North Sea to a surge that rises above the highest tide. Accompanied by bucketing rains and flooded rivers, the relentless sea can bring a death warrant to the coastal communities of East Anglia. Records of floods and devastation go back more than seven hundred years. During the last great inundation, in 1953, almost three hundred people were killed. The low, soft cliffs crumbled, and the miles of sand dunes and shingle walls were powerless to hold back the angry seas as they burst through the coastal defences like a battering ram.

Yet, life on the East Anglian coast has a great serenity and beauty. Arctic birds find winter warmth and food on its marshes and estuaries. Men cut reeds in huge beds to keep traditional cottages thatched. Children gather cockles on the endless vistas of sand and mud, and summer warmth-seekers find a sheltered spot and sunny weather for all the bitter winds. Cottages of local flint or pastel-pink plaster glint in the sun and merge with the sky and sea on darker days, and the bold vertical lines of church towers and lighthouses punctuate the flat, watery landscape.

The Great Drainages

East Anglia is on the way to nowhere but the cold grey North Sea. As a destination in itself, before the days of railways, the journey overland from Lincoln, Bedford or London meant taking a

long, circuitous route that skirted forests, swamps and large expanses of water. Travelling by sea was more direct, though not without its hazards. But once through the Wash, or past the harbour piers of Lowestoft and Great Yarmouth, two great waterway systems – the Broads, linked together by the rivers Waveney, Bure and Yare, and the dykes and rivers of the Fens – opened up the interior. Cambridge, Norwich and Peterborough could all be reached by sail or punt. In fact, there was little choice but to go by boat across the watery fens that stretched around the Wash – from Lincoln almost to Cambridge and from Gibràltar Point to King's Lynn. While flooding and the tide keep most of the area awash, it also brought about the building-up of

great morasses of mud and silt into islands. The Lincolnshire names Gedney, Stickney and Haxey share the Old Norse suffix *ey*, meaning 'an island' – and islands in the fenlands these places certainly were for a very long time.

The nature of this watery landscape was changed forever with the major drainage programmes of the early 17th century during which vast areas of saltmarsh were reclaimed and then the fenland behind drained. As the drainage progressed, so islands became hummocks, and villages and towns – that once had overlooked the sea – became inland as opposed to coastal settlements, while roads, and eventually railways, transformed communications and travelling. Wisbech, Holbeach, Skeldyke, Fosdyke,

The vast sand- and mudflats of the Wash stretch for miles at low tide. Viewed here in the glow of the setting sun from Snetti-sham, Norfolk, they look serene and unspoiled, but land reclamation and pollution have taken their toll on this internationally important wildlife area.

These crabbing boats, hauled by tractors up Norfolk's Cromer beach, lay pots for the local speciality. The long-renowned Cromer crabs have a ready market from tourists, but pollution could easily harm the industry.

Once wool and herrings made East Anglia rich – now arable farming is the main money-spinner. Here, at Boston (right), grain is loaded in bulk onto ships for export to Europe. On a smaller scale, the granary on the waterfront at Wells must be carefully approached by vessels through the deep-water channel marked by this buoy at Holkham (centre right).

By filtering seawater to obtain its food, the Common Mussel also concentrates pollutants, which can lead to food poisoning. The mussel harvest in the Wash is affected, but the cause – untreated sewage in the sea – could easily be avoided.

Lade Bank and Wainfleet Bank are among the many places in the area that bear witness to the immense changes that transformed this corner of England out of all recognition.

Moulton Sea's End and Surfleet Sea's End, south of the Wash, settlements pushed out from their mother villages, have since been superseded many times over. Holbeach has spawned no less than five villages to seaward bearing its name, including Holbeach St Matthew and Holbeach St Marks. The current sea wall is a good six miles north from the original Holbeach, across fields of turnips and potatoes, sheep pastures, drainage ditches and single-track roads high above the farmland where once grew the saltmarsh plants Eelgrass, Sea Lavender and Sea Purslane.

The majority of the attempts at draining the fenlands and marshes over the centuries were successful, but some were doomed to spectacular failure. A Victorian venture to drain a vast area of the Wash near King's Lynn cost the speculators a third of a million pounds for a fraction of the land they had hoped to gain. They had not understood what their more cautious predeces-

sors knew – that reclaiming land from the sea is only done with the sea's co-operation. The build-up of the raw material can be speeded up by constructing walls and ditches, or by importing and encouraging stabilizing plants such as Marram Grass and Common Cord Grass, and salt removed with the use of leaching agents, but the process from the initial build-up of land to salt-free arable soil can take almost a decade.

Grand schemes destined to make the Victorian planners look small-minded surfaced in the 1970s with a feasibility study of a plan to turn the whole of the Wash into a reservoir. Whether a barrage was technically possible was not ascertained for sure, and with the realization that such a volume of water was way beyond present needs, the project was shelved until the year 2000. The fall-back scheme of building offshore storage tanks was deemed uneconomic and axed. Although the rich and abundant wildlife of the Wash has been saved from this development, other threats face this fragile and special environment – despite the establishment of designated Sites of Special Scientific Interest.

The timber skeleton of a boat at Brancaster Bay (left) and the cleaned and repainted buoys on the quayside at King's Lynn (above) are a reminder of the constant dangers of the low-lying, deceptive Norfolk coast.

Where Land and Sea Meet

All along the north Norfolk shoreline, between the dramatic bands of ochre and cream chalk and sandstone that make up the cliffs at Hunstanton and the soft but steep cliffs at Sheringham and Cromer, the nebulous coast switches from farmland to mudflats, from reed-beds and brackish lagoons to tidal marsh, and from sand dunes to shingle spits. The human contrivances of old wooden jetties and simple log bridges, each house with its own design of flint or pebble and worn red brick, the tall medieval churches and the slanting masts of mud-beached dinghies merge with the wide open skies, rumpled plains and shallow seas into the unique entity of the north Norfolk coast.

Where land and sea meet on the Norfolk saltmarshes – which are among the largest in Britain – the pattern resembles the convoluted shapes in the bottom of a fortune-teller's tea cup. Against a background of matt green and grey, sprinkled with the pale blue and yellow of Sea Aster and Sea Purslane, a thousand muddy creeks and channels wind their way back and forth between the sea and strand. Way out beyond the mudflats, across the patches of salty samphire and seablite, the low-tide line is audible from its silty gurglings, but as invisible as the horizon. Within hours, as if the fortune-teller required another showing, the cup is filled again and all the curling complexity disappears, the scene now resembling a pane of cloudy glass, reflecting the movements of a flock of Redshank or Dunlin or the light, buoyant flight of terns.

The shaping of Blakeney Point and Scolt Head Island by the eastern drift of the sea's load of shingle has been going on for centuries. The more the shingle was built up, the more the shore behind it was sheltered – deposited silt raised the sea-bed into mudflat, and then as plants took hold, marsh. While such natural changes have re-drawn this coastline, the land-hungry human touch has been at work as well. For those who gathered mussels or the Stiffkey cockles known as 'Stewkey blues', the land that the sea slithers over provided a livelihood. Men who knew the creeks and the tides as intimately as their village streets guided ships in the days of sail to the

Although Glasswort is known as 'poor man's asparagus', it fetches high prices in city shops. In East Anglia, it is called samphire and is eaten the way it tastes best – freshly picked from the saltmarshes where it grows, and pickled.

The grey hulk of the nuclear power station dominates the shoreline at Sizewell (right), less than two miles from the town of Leiston. Many local people welcome the employment prospects offered by the construction of a new reactor, Sizewell B – despite the fact that they are short-term only, and official pronouncements on the reactor's safety are not so reassuring since the Chernobyl accident.

Having bred regularly along the East Coast, the Avocet had become extinct in Britain by 1825, wiped out by drainage of wetlands and by persecution. It returned to the East Anglian coast in the 1940s and now breeds there annually at several RSPB reserves.

Opposite: Admiring the colour-washed houses with their Flemish gables at Aldeburgh (left), walking for miles at the little Norfolk resort of Wells (above right) or crewing lovingly preserved old Thames barges (below right) at Maldon, Essex, are among the pleasures afforded by the East Anglian coast.

Norfolk havens of Wells, Salthouse, Cley, Brancaster, Burnham and Thorham. And large landowners, families such as the Cokes of Holkham – famous for their innovations in the traumatic years of agrarian revolution – continued to reclaim marsh for arable land.

Habitats Preserved

Despite its continued profiting from shoreline land reclamation, the beauty of this coast is that some stretches of marsh still remain untouched. From Snettisham on the east coast of the Wash to Salthouse beyond Blakeney, over half the shore is under the protection of wildlife trusts. The tidal sandbanks in the Wash are where Common Seals breed, their new-born pups taking their first breath at low tide, and their first swim as the water rises and lifts them from the sand. The Wash colony is one of the largest in Britain – and would have been the first victim of any barrage construction. So, for the moment, the seals have at least until the 21st century to keep their home in the Wash and the waters all the way to Blakeney Point.

Nowhere else in England serves as a temporary stopover or permanent home for so many species of bird as Norfolk's north coast. Bitterns breed in the reed-beds of the RSPB reserve at Titchwell Marshes, alongside the ingeniously suspended nests of Reed Warblers. Seeds and snails in the tidal marshes feed Pintail and Shoveler while Marsh Harriers sail majestically low over the reeds, ready to pounce on any unwary Moorhen or Water Vole. Cley-next-the-Sea provides one of the best birdwatching areas in England, with an unrivalled record of rarities. The nature reserves at nearby Blakeney Point and at Scolt Head, about fifteen miles to the west, provide shingle shores for Little, Sandwich and Common Terns to make their simple nest scrapes, without the threat of disturbance from visitors or their trampling feet.

On the Suffolk coast, Minsmere, Walberswick and Havergate Island are other areas high on the birdwatchers' list of coastal 'hot-spots'. Minsmere is the RSPB's most famous reserve and among the most popular, with tens of thousands of visitors each year. Over 280 species of birds have been recorded there, and 110 species nest there – the greatest variety of breeding birds at any reserve in Britain. An artificial fen, originally flooded in 1940 as a defence against Hitler's tanks, it contains a wide variety of habitats, from lagoons, reed-beds, gravel 'scrapes', mudflats, dunes and shoreline to mixed woodlands and coastal heathland. At Minsmere and Havergate summer visitors can see breeding Avocets.

The Unstable Coast

While land has been reclaimed around the Wash and in north Norfolk, it is water that lays claim to the land of Suffolk as it curves south down to Aldeburgh and Orford Ness. The most striking and tragic illustration of the savage dismember-

ment of the precarious, soft-rocked cliffs and anything built near them, is the story of the doomed town of Dunwich.

By Norman times, Dunwich was the most populated town in the region. During the reign of King John it was rich enough to buy a charter, and by 1235 it could spare King Henry III thirty of its ships. Its port flourished, merchants set forth in boats built in local yards and the fish catch was good. Palaces, mansions, merchants' houses, monasteries and even a mint were enclosed by the high city walls. Ipswich was only half the size of Dunwich.

On March 23, 1286, a high spring tide advanced towards the shore with a wind behind blowing ever more fiercely as darkness fell. By midnight two whole parishes, their great stone churches, their fortified defences, their houses, hovels and barns had been swept away, smashed by the waves and buried on the sea-bed. Within a lifetime, another high tide, combined this time with a winter gale, snatched three more churches, made half the population homeless, destroyed the harbour and began to close the book on the history of this unfortunate town.

A map of Dunwich in 1587 shows an unindented shoreline without a hint of a harbour, and just a scattering of medieval buildings. By the 17th century, every high tide was flooding the market place. People started pulling down the buildings to save the stone. In 1919 the medieval church of All Saints – and its graveyard – finally tumbled down the cliffs. The war waged on Dunwich by the relentless sea has never abated.

Dunwich was not alone along the Suffolk coast in its defeat. To the north, Easton and Covehithe hardly exist any more, while to the south, just outside Aldeburgh, the last traces of Slaughden vanished this century. Aldeburgh itself seems so secure today with its half-timbered Moot Hall protected by a sea wall with a road and parking spaces in between. But this apparent security conceals the familiar story of destruction by the sea – until three hundred years ago, three streets lay between the Moot Hall and the beach.

Some stretches of the Suffolk coast, however, do not recede – or at least have a long enough history of stability for erosion not to be a major issue in the siting of nuclear power stations. The Magnox reactor at Sizewell, south of Dunwich, has been in operation since the 1960s. In January 1987, construction of a second nuclear power station, Sizewell B – this time an American-style PWR (pressurized water reactor) – was given the go-ahead, after the longest public enquiry in British history. Despite the list of accidents associated with PWRs around the world, including Three Mile Island, and the mention in the final Sizewell B report that more research was needed on the possible medical effects of reactors, economic interests appear to have outweighed any potential risks. The enquiry closed before one of the reactors caught fire at the Soviet Union's Chernobyl plant in April 1986.

Boats, Birds and Oyster Beds

On a cold, windswept day, the prospect of the North Sea as it churns up pebbles, eats up sandflats or slaps against shored-up cliffs, is hardly inviting. To be at the helm upon its waves requires a hardiness and nerve, and advanced navigating skills. There are no headlands or heights to signal the opening of an estuary or the nearness of the land along this eastern coast. Instead, the mariner must rely on lighthouses, and, more importantly, on the myriad buoys and lightships, which have to be moved with the shifting shoals, banks and bars that dog these shallow waters. Around Harwich the flickering lights are as complex as the runway beacons on an airfield, while the curve of the coast between Cromer and Hemsby is one of the most dangerous stretches in the country.

At the dawn of history, the problem of a safe landing may not have arisen. In prehistoric times, one could probably have walked from East Anglia to Holland. Then, the River Thames joined the Rhine, flowing out across the land that now lies beneath the shallow North Sea. Among the remnants of the now drowned river valleys are the great expanses of the Foulness and Maplin sands that appear on the south-eastern coast of Essex at low tide. 'Foulness' means 'Isle of Birds', and the promontory of Foulness Island provides a haven for thousands of Brent Geese, other wildfowl and waders. The birds can feed and rest undisturbed by visitors, who are prevented from visiting Foulness by the Ministry of Defence, which tests its weapons on the island. Fortunately for the birds, the proposal to site London's third airport on Maplin Sands was thwarted when the hazard they posed to aircraft was accepted as a major objection to the scheme.

From Foulness north up the Essex coast towards Harwich lies a maze of muddy creeks, uninhabited islands and reclaimed marshes, penetrated by the watery tendrils of the Essex rivers – the narrow Roach and Crouch and the wider expanses of the Blackwater and Colne. The most northerly last cluster of Essex creeks and islands is at Walton-on-the-Naze, just south of Harwich. The timeless atmosphere of this backwater is rudely interrupted by the looming

Tollesbury's 19th-century sail lofts (right) could so easily have disappeared with the livelihoods they served, but for their rescue by dedicated pleasure sailors who now preserve them. Similarly, at West Mersea (below right), also in Essex, old yachts and other vessels have been refitted to serve as houseboats.

Like so many medieval Suffolk churches built with the riches from the wool trade, Blythburgh (centre) now presides over a shrunken parish that earns its wealth elsewhere. Once a thriving port, its harbour, on the muddy River Blyth, fell into disuse when ships grew too large to reach it.

concrete hulk of Bradwell nuclear power station on the eastern edge of the Dengie peninsula.

Across the water of the River Blackwater at Tollesbury, stand old wooden slatted sail lofts, some of them now carefully restored. They date back to the turn of the century, when Tollesbury had a fleet of over a hundred fishing smacks – the local Essex sailing boats for catching shrimps and other shellfish. Today, many of the communities that built the craft and lived off the catch use their skills to service the yachts in the modern marinas on which the local economy now depends. Burnham-on-Crouch is no longer a centre for the cockle, whelk and oyster harvest, but for yachting folk and their vessels. Maldon, Brightlingsea, Wivenhoe and Mersea have a shipbuilding history that goes back for centuries – they still build boats or repair old ones like the Maldon 'stackies', which carried whole 'stacks' of corn up the creeks to the surrounding villages.

One traditional industry that still thrives on the coast of Essex is oyster cultivation. The oyster beds lie in the River Colne and along the creeks and channels of Mersea Island and Brightling-sea. The famous Oyster Feast, when the first oysters of the season are sampled by royalty and other dignitaries, is still held on the last Friday of October in the ancient city of Colchester.

Medieval Ports and Waterways
Of all the East Anglian ports that thrived from medieval days – on incoming shipments of wine, skins and spices, on the sprat and herring catch and exports of corn, of oak for the king's Thames-side shipbuilding yards, and on local ship-wrights' skills, but most of all on wool and cloth – few still make a living from their docks. In Suffolk, some, like Dunwich, have neither dock nor town today. Others have lost their harbours to the sea or to the sea's silt. Blythburgh's magnificent church, that at night, illuminated, seems to float on the water, presides over a port to which ships no longer come. At the mouth of the Blyth, Walberswick, once Dunwich's great rival, hosts only yachts and pleasure craft. The same is true for Woodbridge on the River Deben, where the restored tidal mill overlooks the trim masts and polished decks of luxury yachts, and for

The dramatic loss of unimproved pastures and meadows has restricted once common flowers like the Common Spotted Orchid to a few safe havens. In East Anglia, these include grassy cliffs – oases of grass in deserts of arable land.

Both Southwold and Woodbridge in Suffolk were once renowned for their fishing fleets. Today, the journey up the Deben estuary to the restored tidal mill at Woodbridge (above left) is the preserve of yachting folk and few moorings remain at Southwold (left), a graceful Victorian resort that is in danger of becoming more commercialized.

At Lowestoft harbour, plaice, turbot, sole, cod and haddock are still landed from deep-sea trawlers. The town's fortunes have fluctuated with the fishing for over five hundred years and today, tourism, food processing and service industries are more important than fishing.

Victorian Southwold, its last remaining fishing boat moorings threatened by a proposed marina. In Norfolk, the towns of Cley, Wells and other smaller fishing ports have been distanced from their harbours since the drainages and no longer deserve the description 'next-the-Sea'.

Of the larger East Anglian towns, Ipswich and Boston have survived as ports, though diminished and dependent on new channels, downstream docks and dredging. King's Lynn's record is unbroken, but its current cargoes of tractors, steel and timber cannot compare with the trade that financed its splendid 15th-century Guildhall. Great Yarmouth and Lowestoft, once great centres of the herring trade, are past their prime and now rely chiefly on the tourist trade. Harwich will never be a naval base again and the town wears a sad, decrepit gown, despite the ferries and container ships busying back and forth. Across the Stour and Orwell estuary, Felixstowe alone can boast expansion.

There are no great cities on the East Anglian coast. Minor roads form a chequerboard pattern around the dykes and fields, and no dune or clifftop coast road clings to the eastern shore. In the past, coast and country were linked together in the movement of boats on river, dyke, Broad and creek, that all reached inland and out to the sea. That essential link has now been forgotten. Today, the Broads are used for recreation, not for commerce, and the pressure of huge numbers of waterborne visitors is taking its toll on this once quiet landscape and its wildlife. If the Broads – and indeed, the whole of East Anglia's coast, with its strange and soulful atmosphere – are to be preserved for future generations, then more effort in cleaning up pollution is needed. East Anglia is no longer the isolated region it once was. The coast may look idyllic, and the Broads unchanged by time, but they, too, are suffering from the same effects of 20th-century neglect as other areas of Britain's coastline.

REGIONAL SUMMARY
EAST ANGLIA AND THE WASH

Excluding estuaries, the generally low-lying coasts between Southend-on-Sea and Skegness extend about 220 miles (354km). Foulness Island (MoD-owned) is closed to the public.

PHYSICAL PROFILE

London Clay occurs in the south, but most of East Anglia is underlain by chalk and masked by glacial deposits. Chalk cliffs appear in north-eastern Norfolk. The Wash is underlain by Jurassic clays. Coastal sinking has created the rias in the south, while erosion is taking place, especially between Aldeburgh and Weybourne. A shingle spit south of Aldeburgh has diverted the River Alde south by about 9 miles (14km).

Climate: The average annual rainfall is 19 inches (480mm) in the south and 26 inches (660mm) in the north. Temperatures average 37°F (3°C) in January and 62°F (17°C) in July. North Sea storms at high tide periodically cause floods.

HUMAN PROFILE

The largest settlements are the ports and industrial towns of Colchester (81,400) and Ipswich (120,400). Major resorts include Clacton (43,600); Felixstowe (20,900), also a container port with cross-Channel services; Lowestoft (55,200); and Great Yarmouth (48,300). Other ports include Harwich (15,100), King's Lynn (33,300) and Boston (26,400). King's Lynn and Aldeburgh (2,900) have annual music festivals; the Aldeburgh Festival was founded by Benjamin Britten and Peter Pears.

Sites of historic interest: Colchester has Roman remains and a Norman castle. St Peter's-on-the-Wall (AD 654), at Bradwell-on-Sea, is one of England's oldest places of worship. Other features include 19th-century Martello Towers in Essex and Suffolk, and Sandringham (1870), the Queen's Norfolk home.

Museums: Castle Museum, Colchester; Ipswich Museum; Dunwich Museum; Maritime Museums at Lowestoft and Great Yarmouth; Lifeboat Museum, Cromer; King's Lynn Museum; Borough Museum, Boston (in the medieval Guildhall).

Famous personalities: Cardinal Wolsey (born Ipswich), George Crabbe (born Aldeburgh), Benjamin Britten (born Lowestoft), Lord Nelson (born Burnham Thorpe), Fanny Burney (born King's Lynn).

Marine industry: Boat- and shipbuilding: West Mersea, Wivenhoe, Brightlingsea, Ipswich, Woodbridge, Lowestoft, King's Lynn. Main fishing port: Lowestoft. Cockles: Stiffkey. Crabs: Cromer, Sheringham. Oysters: Colchester, Mersea I.

Commerce/industry: Colchester: diesel engines, photographic equipment. Ipswich: fertilizers, engineering products, clothing, brewing. King's Lynn: food processing, refrigerators. Boston: brewing, canning; food processing.

NATURAL PROFILE

Wildlife: Habitats on this low coast include salt-marshes (those in northern Norfolk are among Britain's best); sand dunes, sand and shingle beaches and spits; grazing marshes and sand/silt flats in the Wash; chalk cliffs in north-eastern Norfolk; inter-tidal zones, especially in the north.

Attractions: In Essex, Foulness and Maplin Sands include large sand/silt flats, with Britain's largest shell beaches off Foulness Point; Colne estuary, which has a wide range of habitats. In Suffolk, the Sandlings, a narrow strip along most of the coast from Felixstowe to Kessingland, have rich flora and fauna — it includes Orford Ness (shingle spit and saltmarsh); Havergate Island (RSPB), Britain's largest Avocet breeding ground; and Minsmere (RSPB). In Norfolk, the Winterton Dunes and the North Norfolk Coast, which has a rare, threatened habitat, a brackish lagoon at Salthouse. The Wash has flats for wintering wildfowl, saltmarshes and Britain's largest Common Seal breeding ground. *Footpaths:* Nature trails at the Naze, near Walton, and on Scolt Head Island; Suffolk Coast Path (Lowestoft-Felixstowe) — about 50 miles (80km) long. *Areas of Outstanding Natural Beauty:* Suffolk Coast and Heaths; Norfolk Coast. *Beaches in Essex:* Seawick, Jaywick, Clacton, Holland, Frinton, Walton. *Beaches in Suffolk:* Felixstowe, Lowestoft. *Beaches in Norfolk:* Great Yarmouth, Mundesley, Cromer, Sheringham, Wells, Hunstanton.

CAUSES FOR CONCERN

Direct dumping: Sewage sludge is dumped off Harwich. There is an industrial waste dumpsite at South Falls, off the Essex coast.

Pipeline discharges: A pesticide plant is causing mercury pollution in Norfolk's River Yare. This is one of the UK's worst examples of heavy metal pollution. The River Orwell, Suffolk, is badly contaminated with sewage.

Radioactive discharges: Sizewell A nuclear power station, soon to be joined by Sizewell B, and Bradwell nuclear power station discharge slightly radioactive cooling water into the sea.

Agricultural run-off: Nitrates from fertilizers cause eutrophication (over-enrichment) of the Wash and Norfolk Broads, threatening marine life. Pesticide run-off is also a problem.

Oil pollution: Gasfield off Great Yarmouth: production water and drilling muds cause local contamination of the sea bed.

Beaches: Great Yarmouth contaminated by raw sewage outfall.

Threatened wildlife: This coast has experienced a five-fold increase in the import of hazardous chemical and heavy metal waste from Europe, for treatment and burial in land-fill operations. The Wash is threatened by extensive drainage. Pesticide damage and disturbance have also caused the most serious decline of Otters in Britain. Possible barrage schemes for freshwater storage will seriously affect waders and wintering wildfowl. Possible loss of Fagbury Flats, Orwell estuary; Felixstowe Docks expansion would encroach into an important SSSI. Herring and mackerel have been overfished since the 1960s.

The Common Seal breeds in sheltered coastal sites, hauling out on sandbanks. Its name is misleading, as it is less common than the larger Grey Seal. One of its strongholds is the Wash.

The best and sweetest Edible Crabs come from Cromer, on the north Norfolk coast. The crab fishing industry is a local lifeline, but it may well be under threat from increased pollution in the area.

Coastal livelihoods

Fishermen have made a living from British waters since time immemorial. The boats, the nets and the catches may have changed, but not the danger nor the hardship of the job. Onshore, fish markets, family smokeries and processing factories still follow the fortunes of the fleet, as do traditional wooden boat-builders whose work still graces some ports.

Once, whole communities were employed in the great variety of tasks that go to build a

great ship – from those who welded and riveted the hull to the craftsmen who fitted out and decorated the cabins. Today's launches, few and far between, are almost always of naval vessels.

Oil rigs, and the service industries they spawned, brought different opportunites for coastal work, and the increase in foreign travel has boosted the ferry trade – though the Channel Tunnel may have an effect on this. Many islanders still depend on ferries for food and fuel as well as for transport.

Today, though, most coastal livelihoods are based on leisure – tending ornamental flowerbeds in the resorts, building yachts, doing lifeguard duty or repairing piers, not to mention feeding, accommodating and entertaining holidaymakers.

LINCOLN, HUMBERSIDE AND NORTH YORKSHIRE

MARGARET DRABBLE

The coastlines of childhood imprint themselves forever on the memory, and I still dream, forty years on, that I am walking barefoot along Filey Brigg, picking my way across the limpets and barnacles. And when I wake, I cry to dream again. So shall we all cry, and cry perhaps in vain. I have never dared to return to the Brigg, for fear that it is already ruined, a paradise lost: for fear that the pink rock pools are polluted, and the rocks covered with cement. But I know that the little fishing boats still wait on the cobbles at Filey and Bridlington, that one can still walk along the dizzy grey grass paths at precipitous Flamborough Head or along the crumbling bleeding red clay earth towards Scarborough. Whole families of fishermen lie still in the churchyard, with their epitaph, 'Lost at Sea', and the children still build sand castles and make sand pies and crown them with little paper flags.

When I was a child, the North Sea was so full of fish that we could go out into the bay any day and catch our tea – codlings, whiting, haddock, mackerel. There was a primal brightness upon everything, a glittering light that fell on beach and cliff and Amusement Arcade and green canvas bathing huts. It is true that we swam amongst sewage, released nightly, I believe, from a great metal gate in the sea wall, but we cared nothing for that, as we bobbed about and swallowed it down and shivered, goose-pimpled, in the brisk Yorkshire air. Sometimes we went on excursions to faraway places, to Whitby or Robin Hood's Bay, but the journey usually made me sick, and I preferred the charm of the familiar. I have since visited some of the most spectacular coastlines in the world, but none of them can match the emotional power of that stretch of North Yorkshire.

In later years I've come to know other, more workmanlike parts of the region – Hull, Grimsby, Redcar, the strange inland port of Boston. A pause seems to hang over them, as though they were out of time, forgotten by time. Will time preserve them? The sea washes, the cliffs erode, the sands silt, and the fish have swum away from land. There was once plenty, abundance. Is it one's own childhood that one mourns, as one remembers? The land itself grows old.

LINCOLN, HUMBERSIDE AND NORTH YORKSHIRE
SKEGNESS TO MIDDLESBROUGH

'... THE SMOOTH, WIDE SANDS, AND THE LOW ROCKS OUT AT SEA –
LOOKING WITH THEIR CLOTHING OF WEEDS AND MOSS, LIKE LITTLE GRASS-GROWN
ISLANDS – AND ABOVE ALL . . . THE BRILLIANT, SPARKLING WAVES.'

Anne Brontë, *Agnes Grey* (1847)

Bird's Foot Trefoil
favours grassy places.
Where grassland has been
cultivated, the plant still
flowers on clifftops. It has
over seventy local names,
including 'Eggs and Bacon',
from the flowers,
and 'Tom Thumb',
from its finger-like
seed-pods.

From the level plains of Lincolnshire to the secret harbours between the North Yorkshire cliffs, this is, above all else, England's fishing coast. Hull and Grimsby are the prime ports and Grimsby's quayside market is the biggest in the country. The fishing itself has declined but fish processing and packaging is still a major business in the area. As the fishing fleets make their way down the Humber to the North Sea grounds, container ships, ferries, tankers and river barges head for the commercial docks at Immingham, Hull and Grimsby.

The complex currents at
the mouth of the Humber
slowly build up the inner
shore of the Spurn penin-
sula, while the outer face of
this narrow spit – in places
only 50 yards wide – is
subject to erosion.

Contrasting Cliffscapes

The banks of the Humber are heavily industrialized, the main activities being oil-refining
and the making of plastics, fertilizers, paint
pigments and tin products as well as breaded
fillets. The longest single-span suspension bridge
in the world, opened in 1981, has replaced the
Humber estuary ferry, forming a 4,600-foot-long
conveyor-belt extension to the great cluster of
production lines.

In contrast to the industrialized Humber, the
shores to the north and the south are almost as
lonely and deserted as in the days when Vikings
clambered from their longboats to raid and
pillage – or to settle, giving towns and villages

names that to this day show their Danish origin in the suffixes 'by' (settlement), 'thorpe' (farm), 'brough' (shelter) and 'ness' (promontory).

Summer still sees visitors to Lincolnshire resorts like Mablethorpe but the once regular crowds from the Midlands towns are largely gone. North of the Humber – from the shifting sand and shingle spit of Spurn Head, dangling like a bait in the Humber mouth, to the bay of Bridlington – the coast of Holderness mocks human attempts at permanence. The soft clay cliffs erode at rates that break all records in the British Isles. Six feet of solid ground can tumble to the beach overnight, leaving houses teetering on the edge. Save for Withernsea and Hornsea, where massive sea defences have been built and rebuilt, only caravans and chalets stand between the wheatfields and the edge.

Further on, at Flamborough Head, the cliffs change to tougher chalk that does not crumble. Instead, it cracks to form sharp indentations, stacks and arches. Britain's only mainland colony of Gannets breeds on Bempton Cliffs (now an RSPB reserve), along with crowded ranks of Fulmars, Razorbills, Guillemots, Puffins and Kittiwakes. Precarious nests dot the ledges on the 400-foot-high vertical walls of chalk, and the sea and air are filled with the birds' comings and goings and their raucous cries.

Other habitats to the south and north of the Humber that are rich in wildlife include the Lincolnshire marshes and sand dunes, the mile-long rocky finger of Filey Brigg, with its rock pools rich in plant and animal life, and the mudflats sheltered by Spurn Head. The cloudy blue and silver Sea Holly is perhaps the most beautiful of the scarce plants that grace these sandy shores.

Beyond Flamborough Head, Scarborough's 12th-century fortress heralds the change in countryside and coastline as the North Yorkshire moors begin. Some 650 years before the fortress was built, the Romans had constructed a signalling station here to give advance warning of raids from across the water. The current early-warning station, for ballistic missiles, lies five miles inland at Fylingdales, its giant, golf-ball radomes a chilling landmark. The rolling heathered ground drops suddenly from here through steep pastures as the coast approaches. The cliffs are overgrown and tumbled and cut by numerous creeks, and the shore is of rocks. Settlements are set back from the sea, save where a bay or river gorge gives shelter to a fishing fleet.

The Great Fishing Industry

By the mid-19th century, when trawling had become the established offshore fishing method, smacks from the Channel ports worked the Dogger Bank and used Scarborough for their market and their summer base. As the fleets got bigger, some of the smacks moved to the Humber, where the whaling port of Hull had ample space, and where the Grimsby Harbour Com-

Many sites near industrial areas of Britain's coastline can provide welcome havens for wildlife, as here on the south bank of the Humber, where a wilderness of reed-beds and marshes lies in the shadow of the world's longest single-span suspension bridge. However, pollution from the industries lining the south bank is always a possibility.

The Royal Navy frigate HMS *Argonaut* pays a visit to Grimsby's commercial docks (above). Although it is still a major centre for the fish trade, Grimsby has few local fishermen now, thanks to the Cod Wars and the decline of the herring fishery through overfishing. At Scarborough (left), ornate Victorian hotels await the annual invasion of holidaymakers on which the town depends.

The over-exploitation of the Herring in the past had serious effects – not only was an important food source nearly exhausted, but a whole culture and means of employment was almost lost as the herring industry declined.

The old Yorkshire fishing village of Staithes nestles in the hollow of the cliffs (right). The potash mine at nearby Boulby has replaced the fishing industry as Staithes's chief employer, resulting in the village's straggling expansion back from the coast.

Fishermen's huts at Redcar (centre) play a far less important part in the town's economy today than the steelworks half a mile up the coast.

Trawlers can still be seen at Bridlington's small, neat harbour (right), even though most of them, like the *Cassandra*, come from neighbouring ports and land their catches at Grimsby.

pany had completed a new fishing dock.

The real turning point for Hull and Grimsby came with the chance discovery by a Brixham boat, blown off course with her trawl still down, of the Silver Pits, a ground rich with the finest sole. By 1848 a railway linked Grimsby with London and in 1852 the Royal Dock was opened. Boats, fishermen, shipwrights and capital converged on Grimsby from Cornwall, East Anglia and London. Three railway companies from the Midlands formed the Deep Sea Fishing Company to profit from the fishing boom. One unschooled lad from Suffolk called Harrison Mudd founded a firm of fishing agents, still going strong today, an ice manufacturers, and the North Sea Trawling Company, which by the mid-19th century was the largest fishing concern in the world.

In the latter half of the 19th century, when cod was the prime catch, Hull lost out to Grimsby, lacking harbour space for the floating 'chests' that stored live fish. Using hand lines or long lines to catch the richest populations of cod in Icelandic waters, and keeping them alive in the ship's 'well', was a fine art. Handling and feeding the catch were critical, as was turbulence in the

well. The fish would die along with the profits if the ship were becalmed or if a storm were suddenly to blow up.

The herring, its vital place in history commemorated in its old name 'king of the fishes', has been hunted off the English, Welsh and Scottish coasts since the Dark Ages. Unlike the cod, it cannot be caught with hook and bait. Herring busses – wooden square-rigged ships of thirty tons or more, equipped with drift nets – sailed from Bridlington, Whitby, Hull and Scarborough from the 12th to the 18th century to hunt the silver shoals. But silting harbours necessitated lighter craft, so the Staithes 'yacker' was developed. Clinker-built in oak, it sported two lug sails and a triangular mizzen.

Then in 1850, a Whitby shipwright produced the Marshall Lugger, which could be handled by a crew of five instead of seven. It carried a small open boat from which the fish were caught once the grounds were reached. This was the coble, the most common inshore fishing boat of the East Coast, whose design is thought to have come from Viking longships. Cobles can still be seen in use at Bridlington, Whitby and the old fishing villages of Filey, Staithes and Robin Hood's Bay.

From sail through to steam and diesel, the herring fleets employed the same drift-net system, towing a curtain of nets across the path of the shoal. The nets had a mesh just big enough to trap the fishes' heads by their gills. Some twenty years ago, however, overkill began with the introduction of the purse-seine net. Towed in a circle round the shoals, its bottom rope acts as a drawstring to pull up a 'purse'-full. Belatedly, herring fishing was banned in the North Sea for six years, in the hope that stocks would recover. Fishing may have resumed, but the catch is half the tonnage of two decades ago – demand, too, has decreased.

Iceland's extension of territorial limits – the issue that led to the Cod Wars of the 1960s and 1970s – and the decline of the herring trade were major blows to the English fishing fleets. But overfishing, of cod and other fish as well as herring, has decimated stocks worldwide, and continues to do so. In the North Sea the constant stream of pollutants pouring out from the rivers of the Netherlands, Germany and Britain, is creating, with alarming acceleration, areas of sea in which the fish – and the complex food chains of which they are part – may not survive at all.

Trawling and Trading Today

First light at Grimsby, however, still sees the workforce known as 'lumpers' sorting gleaming fish by size and laying out hundreds of shallow boxes around the covered quays of the fishing dock. By 7.30am, porters and lorry-drivers are at the ready as auctioneers and merchants congregate at the south-east end of the market, where the fish from distant waters are stacked.

'Here-we-go-thirty-six-pounds-here-we-go-again - forty - seven - pounds - do - I - have - forty-seven? ...' booms out into the cold morning air, as apparently indistinguishable gestures cement the deal, and the party moves on to the next batch while the buyer's labels are scattered over the fish. Some of the men jump from box to box, occasionally lifting up a specimen for examination. Radio telephones keep them in touch with prices in Holland and in the wholesale markets of Northampton and New Billingsgate, in London's Isle of Dogs. The pace is brisk and business-like, for all that an occasional gum-booted foot slips onto the slithery merchandise.

As the final quayside boxes find their buyer, a rickety chute from the Victorian brick-built ice factory fills the hold of a small side trawler. The

Boxes of cod and codling marked with their buyers' names await collection at Grimsby (above), while mended fishing nets are winched back aboard one of the few trawlers still based at Hull (left).

The fury of the sea is often apparent on the dramatic bays along the north Yorkshire coast, site of a number of old fishing villages. Robin Hood's Bay (right) and Runswick Bay (below right) were once thriving fishing communities, but the fishing declined as long ago as the 1900s. The Ship Inn at Saltburn (centre) provides a welcome haven for the few remaining lobster fishermen forced to remain ashore in bad weather.

The caterpillars of the Common Blue eat Bird's Foot Trefoil, and the butterfly flies in summer wherever the food plant flourishes, as it does on coastal grasslands. Many inland colonies have disappeared due to intensive farming.

crew may be heading back to their home port at Bridlington, Scarborough or Whitby, or preparing for the next trip before stepping ashore for the few, short hours that are available for them to spend with their families.

Midnight had seen the arrival of the catch – cod, haddock, rock salmon (Spiny Dogfish), monkfish, whiting, coley, skate, rays, plaice, scallops, turbot, sole, dab and flounder. Harvested from the North Sea, the Atlantic and Arctic Oceans, and the Irish Sea, some will have travelled hundreds of miles by road to Grimsby, the consignments carrying the names of the ports where the fish were landed: Lochinver, Kinlochbervie, Mallaig, Fleetwood. Container ships from Iceland and the Faeroes will have brought in cod that fetches higher prices here than in their home markets.

Only a small proportion of the fish auctioned at Grimsby and at Hull is caught by local vessels. Since the Cod Wars of the 1960s and 1970s with Iceland, the English East-Coast fleets have dwindled to a few seiners working inshore waters. Though the Scottish East-Coast fishermen reign supreme, Grimsby's fishing dock still holds its key position in the first stage of distribution, as New Billingsgate does in the wholesale markets. Once the fish is bought, it may go no further than Humberside's processing factories before being sent to fill supermarket shelves.

Resorts and Retreats

Scarborough, on the North Yorkshire coast, was the first town in Britain to become a planned resort. The discovery there of natural springs, whose waters were believed to cure melancholy and hypochondria, turned the ancient borough into a fashionable seaside spa. While Georgian and, later, Victorian architects set to work designing the two seafront crescents – divided by the castle with such appealing symmetry – the traditional fishing trade continued. Today, the

ing resorts are well away from the slipstreams of the Humber's industries and the record on sewage disposal is above average. But local tourism has declined, providing serious problems for those whose livelihood depends on it, though peace and quiet for the birds, such as the Shelduck and Short-eared Owls, that nest in watery slacks behind the dunes at places like Gibraltar Point. A wealth of sand-dune plants is also able to flourish undisturbed while the rare Natterjack Toad runs across the sand without disturbance from night-time beach parties.

For those who seek the picturesque, a retreat for art or contemplation, or the ideal antidote to city life, the old fishing villages of the North Yorkshire coast offer the greatest temptation. At Robin Hood's Bay, the close-knit lanes and cottages dare to touch the shore, leaning down upon it as if the uppermost houses might at any minute somersault to the tiny dock far below. Two hundred homes have been lost in as many years, not through being sited half-way up the cliff but because they were built right by the waves. A few traditional boats still venture forth with lobster pots, but fishing as the mainstay of village life came to an end in the 1900s.

At Runswick, white painted houses overlook a sandy, sheltered bay. Disaster struck the original village in 1664, when a landslip sent every single house save one crashing into the sea. The new village, built on the south side of Lingrow Beck, ceased to be a self-contained community forty years ago. Again, the fishing declined, local on-shore jobs disappeared, and those who dreamed of a life beside the sea replaced those for whom life had never been anything else.

The Ancient Port of Whitby
You might arrive at Whitby on the North Yorkshire coast in a car, a coach or train, but the classic entrance is by boat – and not any old boat, at that. It must be a Russian schooner scorning a summer night's storm and all-enshrouding sea-fog, hurtling full-sailed through the narrow entrance of the harbour to crash on the sandy bank below East Cliff. The corpse of the captain still stands at the helm, his hands and a crucifix lashed to the wheel. A great black dog jumps from the ship and disappears into the darkness. On board the cargo is nothing but silver sand and large wooden boxes filled with mould. Thus the scene is set for the arrival in England, in canine form, of Count Dracula of Transylvania.

The ethos of Whitby has changed little since Bram Stoker researched his seminal version of the Dracula legend in the 1890s. Streets whose names figure in Domesday records form a tight knot along the east side of the harbour, with a handful of fish-smoking houses emitting their distinctive aroma into the air. Steps of medieval origin rise above pink pantiled roofs to the churchyard where gravestone inscriptions have been whorled away by the wind. The church, still without electric light, illuminates its nautical

nets around the harbour, the whelk and cockle stalls, the bingo halls and elegant hotels combine to give Scarborough a peculiarly mixed appeal.

Skegness, on the Lincolnshire coast, is just the opposite, a 20th-century resort in every respect, although its transformation from a tiny fishing village had started in the 1880s. Billy Butlin opened his original holiday camp here in 1936. New amusement fads are speedily catered for, and continuous rebuilding, revamping and demolition has been the guiding principle. The one constant is a piece of marketing dating back to 1908: the railway poster of a jolly fisherman announcing three shilling return fares from King's Cross with the slogan 'Skegness is *SO* bracing'. John Hassall's tubby fisherman skipping across the golden sands has been used to promote the town ever since.

The virtues of the bracing East Coast air are still trumpeted as a tonic for the jaded and a curative for the sick. Skegness and its neighbour-

Whitby's natural harbour, sheltered by the steep banks of the Esk estuary, forms the central focus of this ancient fishing and whaling port. Today, its narrow winding streets are packed with tourists, who provide the town's main income, with the whaling days long gone and the fishing seriously declined.

The Shore Lark breeds in the dry Arctic tundra, but small flocks can sometimes be seen in winter drifting along the lonely shores of the East Coast.

The assortment of boats that can be seen at Whitby harbour includes sleek yachts and small fishing boats, which are also built in the town, and a few larger fishing boats like this one, complete with a canary in a cage.

interior by skylights. Beyond the churchyard on the summit of East Cliff, visible from miles out to sea and from every part of the town, stand the arched, gaunt ruins of Whitby Abbey. It was here, within the walls of its Saxon predecessor, that the unstructured, grass-roots Celtic church lost out to the rich and hierarchical Roman church at the AD 664 Synod of Whitby.

Across the gorge of the Esk another arch, of whale jawbones rather than Norman stone, frames the sea on West Cliff. In the days of Arctic whaling expeditions the town's street-lighting ran on blubber oil. The town's most famous whaling captain, and inventor of the crow's nest, William Scoresby, reached the open water in the vicinity of the North Pole in 1806, and still holds the world record for the most northerly point reached in a sailing ship.

Captain Cook learnt to sail in Whitby and chose local colliers for his South Pacific voyages. Ships that had known no other cargo than Newcastle coal brought back chestloads of exotic commodities and mementoes. A corner of the local museum has a selection – Maori flax bags and dried human heads, breadfruit from Tahiti and Solomon Islands sharks'-teeth knives.

Along with herring and cod fishing, post-Synod missions to Rome, smuggling, imports of coal and exports of locally quarried alum, Whitby's seafaring ventures kept shipyards in business over centuries. They still build fishing keels and cobles here as well as yachts, and trade with Scandinavia keeps the port alive. Though the fishing fleet is much depleted, the ghostly night-time scene of trawlers setting out for the Dogger Bank continues every season.

The supernatural may not manifest itself today, but the reality of Whitby is startling enough – on the moors behind, the white golf balls of Fylingdales' early warning system; from West Cliff, a midsummer view of sunrise and sunset, both over water; and the town itself, a perfect microcosm of English coastal history.

REGIONAL SUMMARY

LINCOLN, HUMBERSIDE AND NORTH YORKSHIRE

The coast between Skegness and Middlesbrough, excluding estuaries, is about 140 miles (225km) long. There is an RAF firing range between Mablethorpe and Theddlethorpe St Helen.

PHYSICAL PROFILE

The coasts of Lincolnshire (north of Skegness) and Humberside are composed mostly of glacial boulder clays. The underlying chalk surfaces in spectacular cliffs at Flamborough Head. The cliffs of North Yorkshire and Cleveland are made up of Jurassic shales, clays, sandstones and limestones. Outcrops of softer clays have been eroded into such inlets as Robin Hood's Bay. Erosion is most severe on the Holderness coast, which is receding at a faster rate than any other in Europe. Since Roman times, it has been cut back by 2 miles (3.2km). Some eroded material is deposited at the Spurn peninsula. New land is forming from alluvium on the banks of the Humber estuary.

Climate: The average annual rainfall is low – 22–23 inches (560–580mm). Average July temperatures are around 60°F (16°C). Periodic North Sea storms generate waves that can lower beaches by 10 feet (3m) in a few hours.

HUMAN PROFILE

The largest settlements are the ports and industrial centres of Kingston upon Hull (268,000) and Grimsby (92,100). Resorts include Skegness (14,400), Mablethorpe and Sutton (7,500), Cleethorpes (35,500), Withernsea (6,000), Hornsea (7,200), Bridlington (16,400), Filey (5,700), Scarborough (44,400), Whitby (13,800), Saltburn and Marske-by-the-Sea (20,000) and Redcar (84,900), which is also an industrial centre.

Sites of historic interest: Dane's Dyke, dug across Flamborough Head to protect the headland, is at least 2,000 years old. Roman sites include the foundations of a signal station at Scarborough, which also has a 12th-century Norman castle. Whitby's first abbey was founded in AD 657. The present abbey is 13th-century. The Pilgrim Fathers left Immingham on Humberside in 1608 for Holland – the first leg of a journey which ended in North America in 1620. The Humber Bridge, opened in 1981, has the world's longest main span – 4,626 feet (1,410m).

Museums: Town Docks Museum, Kingston upon Hull; North Holderness Museum of Village Life, Hornsea; Bayle Museum, Bridlington; Scarborough Museum; Lifeboat Museum, Whitby; Whitby Museum; Zetland Museum, Redcar (this museum contains the world's oldest surviving lifeboat); Captain Cook Birthplace Museum, Marton, 2 miles (3km) south of Middlesbrough.

Famous personalities: Stevie Smith, William Wilberforce (born Kingston upon Hull), Edith Sitwell (born Scarborough). As a young man, Captain Cook lived in Whitby: his ships were built there.

Marine industry: Grimsby and Kingston upon Hull are major fishing ports, with many industries associated with fishing. Bridlington and Scarborough are smaller fishing ports. Whitby and Goole are boat-building centres.

Commerce/industry: Humberside is a major industrial region, with oil refineries, chemical plants and engineering and steel works.

NATURAL PROFILE

Wildlife: Habitats include particularly good sand dunes, with saltmarsh, mud- and sand-flats, sand and shingle beaches, a sand and shingle spit with tidal mudflats (Spurn peninsula), and the Humber estuary. The coasts are low in the south, with cliffs towards the north.

Attractions: In Lincolnshire, Saltfleetby-Theddlethorpe National Nature Reserve, home of the rare Natterjack Toad, has a wide range of habitats between the seashore and freshwater marsh. In Humberside, the Humber estuary (including Blacktoft Sands) has important flats and marshes – birds include Pink-footed Geese and Bearded Tits (in reedbeds); Spurn Peninsula (Yorkshire Naturalists' Trust); and Bempton Cliffs (RSPB) with Britain's only mainland Gannet colony (has viewing platforms). In North Yorkshire, undercliffs with rich flora at Speeton; Robin Hood's Bay-Ness Point, with its wave-cut platform below steep, boulder clay cliffs – has important littoral communities of algae and invertebrates. *Footpaths:* Flamborough Head; Bempton Cliffs; Cleveland Way – part of which is between Filey and Saltburn-by-the-Sea.

Beauty spots: Coasts bordering the North York Moors National Park. *Beaches in Lincolnshire:* Skegness, Ingoldmells, Chapel St Leonard's, Anderby Creek, Sutton-on-Sea, Mablethorpe. *Beaches in Humberside:* Cleethorpes, Bridlington. *Beaches in North Yorkshire:* Filey, Cayton Bay, Scarborough, Whitby, Runswick Bay. *Beaches in Cleveland:* Saltburn-by-the-Sea, Marske-by-the-Sea, Redcar.

CAUSES FOR CONCERN

Direct dumping: The Humber estuary is the third most polluted estuary in the UK. The outer estuary receives the heaviest dumping of contaminated dredgings – 6.9 million tons (7 million tonnes) per annum.

Pipeline discharges: Local industries create the UK's largest single discharge of arsenic into the North Sea and one of the two of the UK's greatest discharges of cadmium is into the Humber estuary. The effects of the highly acidic wastes from the titanium dioxide industry in the Humber estuary are apparent over 6.6 sq miles (17km²).

Oil pollution: Run-off from industrial plants and also other land users.

Beaches: Raw sewage contamination at Skegness and Cleethorpes (potential public health risk).

Threatened wildlife: Britain's only mainland gannetry at Bempton Cliffs (about 650 pairs) suffers from marine litter in its nests. Many Gannets have been killed by entanglement in plastic fishing nets. Industrial pollution probably caused the collapse of the pink shrimp industry in the Humber estuary, which occurred in the 1950s.

Over two-thirds of the entire world population of Gannets breeds around Britain's coasts, nesting in noisy colonies on precipitous cliffs. But Bempton Cliffs, Yorkshire, is Britain's only mainland gannetry.

TEESSIDE, TYNESIDE AND NORTHUMBERLAND

MELVYN BRAGG

Although the coastline holds magnificent pleasures – from the magical castle at Bamburgh to fishing villages as serenely self-absorbed as any you might once have seen around the Mediterranean – it is the islands which furnish this stretch of Britain with its unique character.

Holy Island, still today approached over the causeway which gave the Celtic monks the isolation they desired, maintains its power to mesmerize the visitor. Here was a place where religion and learning carried a torch for almost a hundred years while most of Europe yielded to barbarism. The smallness of the place; the knowledge that here the wonderful Lindisfarne Gospels were created; the awareness of the quiet devotion of heroism of those men of God illuminates the island for anyone inclined to dream.

The Farne Islands are one of our greatest national treasures. When St Cuthbert withdrew there in 676, he was adopted by the Eider Duck (which became known as 'cuddy's duck') and he laid down the first rules for cultivating the wildlife there. He banished the crows! A boy stoning Kittiwakes had his hand withered and gnarled! Standards which have been maintained.

Grace Darling's grandfather, her father and then she herself became the first diarists of the islands. Their tradition continues. Now the crowds follow the diaries. The birds have become used to it. You can go to the islands and walk by them even in the nesting season. It is a rare instance of long habit breeding out so-called 'natural' fears. 247 different species have been recorded on these islands whose principal occupants are Puffins (21,000 pairs the last time I was there), Guillemots (12,000), Kittiwakes (unstoned), Razorbills, Shags, terns . . . and browsing offshore, magisterial Grey Seals. To take children there, as I do, is to take them to another Eden.

Down the coast the industrial towns of Newcastle and Middlesbrough are in the throes of decay and one hopes revival, fallen giants, their thin coils of smoke too much like a funeral pyre. But for the people in those towns, as for all of us, the long barren sweep of ancient coastline is both a place of restoration and a stern, perhaps even bracing, reminder of the power as well as the transience of man the maker. It is a coastline of history and mysticism as well as one of great beauty and lonely charms.

TEESSIDE, TYNESIDE AND NORTHUMBERLAND
MIDDLESBROUGH TO BERWICK

'... AND I HAVE THIS DAY DINED UPON FISH, WHICH PROBABLY
DINED UPON THE CREWS OF SEVERAL COLLIERS LOST IN THE LATE GALES.'

Lord Byron, letter to Thomas Moore from Seaham (1815)

Lilac drifts of Sea Aster colour and soften saltmarshes and estuary banks all around Britain's coast. This tough plant can survive in the least promising spots, even those washed by the tainted waters of great industrial rivers.

Part of the coast of Cleveland, Durham, Tyne and Wear and Northumberland is a junkyard of 19th-century industries heaving out their dying throes to a world that can buy cheaper elsewhere. Polluted estuaries, lifeless beaches and old communities torn apart are the legacy of the once-great wealth that flowed from the capital of coal. The other part, from the northern limit of the Northumbrian coal mines to the Scottish border, is a world of undisturbed sand dunes and rocky cliffs, silent but for the cries of seabirds and the singing of the wind. Grey Seals play off the islands and cattle graze above the sand dunes. Fishing and farming provide a living, as they have for some twelve centuries – from the time when Celtic Christianity was cradled in the kingdom of Northumbria.

The main bridge across the Tees at Middlesbrough (right) can be raised to allow ships to pass beneath it, but few do so these days, now that the region's major industrial sites are all downstream, near the mouth of the river.

The Legacy of the Past

At Swan Hunter's two remaining Tyneside yards yet more men leave with compulsory redundancy notices in their pockets. Conditions of work are tightened as the company goes down on its knees for contracts from the Ministry of Defence. On the Tees, the last cargo vessel from the last shipyard is waved on its way by a crowd of thousands – families surviving on the dole. Without orders for more ships, the steel and engineering works have no more business. The coal that powered all this industry is no longer wanted. Even the chemical plants are cutting

back on labour. It is no surprise that the highest rates of long-term unemployment in Britain are found between the Tyne and Tees.

Recession has not diminished the assault on the environment. Rather it has given every manager the excuse that cleanliness costs dear. The workforce in the mines, chemical plants, aluminium smelters and the rest often back their bosses, for their jobs are always in the balance.

The coastline is black with coal slurry from which most birds, plants and sealife have been banished; lethal cocktails of effluents reduce levels of oxygen to zero in the estuaries; the sea itself is condemned to die. The landscape of slagheaps, contorted pipes and chimneys, empty warehouses and silent docks with immobile cranes above them, speaks plainly of a double disaster. There is no work – and the work of the past bequeaths an environment in which nature often finds it hard to survive, let alone function.

Coal, Ships and Iron

In the Middle Ages, surface coal around Newcastle, eventually destined for the domestic hearths of London, was scraped up into baskets and carried to the wooden wharfs, or 'staithes', along the Tyne to be loaded into sturdy colliers.

During Elizabethan times, new industries requiring coal – brewing, soap- and salt-making – and the development of water-driven pumps led to the first deep mines. Bigger ships were needed to carry the 'black gold' – the coal that became synonymous with Newcastle. By the mid-19th century, the North-east was catapulted into the dramatic, and often dark and dangerous, transformations of the great industrial age, heralded by the coming of the railways.

The first permanent public steam railway in the world opened between Darlington and Stockton-on-Tees in 1825. Driving the locomotive – which he named *Locomotion* – was its inventor, George Stephenson, son of a Tyneside colliery engine man. The jubilant Stockton crowds did not yet foresee themselves as passengers – the chief success of the railway was the ease with which it could move coal from Durham's largest mines to the waiting Teesside ships.

In addition to the railways, four other industrial activities underpinned the path the 19th-century world was to take. Shipbuilding, coal mining, iron- and steel-making, engineering and railway construction had the combined effect of turning Britain into 'the workshop of the world' and its economic and military master.

The great city of Newcastle-upon-Tyne was once the centre of a major shipbuilding industry. Today, most of the ship-yards are closed. This view looks upriver towards the most recent of the five bridges that span the river – the New Tyne Bridge, built in 1928.

At one of Swan Hunter's two remaining Tyneside shipyards (right), workers add the final fittings to RFA *Sir Galahad*, the replacement for the smaller landing ship lost in the Falklands conflict. Now that *Sir Galahad* is in service, the future of the shipyard workers is uncertain. Blyth (below right) was one of Europe's biggest coal ports in the 1960s. Today, the ships carry bauxite instead, destined for a nearby aluminium works.

The cranes that form a background to this Jarrow street (above) have little work to do today, as shipyards continue to hand out redundancy notices. The economic deprivation of this Tyneside area echoes the grim days of the 1930s, when shipyard closures threw thousands out of work.

Their effect in this north-east corner of England was overwhelming. Middlesbrough, a tiny hamlet near the River Tees, was transformed into a sprawling, slum-filled and smog-laden city with a population in the hundred thousands by the First World War. Waste from the coal mines of Durham and Northumberland gave a pitted, bumpy outline to the gentle landscape and a black dusty coat to the shoreline. Coastal villages from Seaham in Durham to Amble in Northumberland had harbours built where fishing cobles once beached upon the sand, to export coal in quantities that multiplied tenfold between 1800 and 1865.

The fog in cities such as Newcastle and Middlesbrough was no natural meteorological phenomenon, but the result of the clinging vapours from coal fires, smelting works, glassworks and the nascent chemical industry. Across the waters of the Tyne, the Tees and the Wear a constant storm of sound echoed from the banks:

familiar noises, but now so much louder, of cargoes being unloaded; new noises of hammering and riveting steel from the shipyards, and the whining and thumping of machine tools in the quayside factories. The surface of the thick and grimy waters of the estuaries was hardly visible for the mass of barges bringing coal from the mines upriver, ore carriers from Sweden coming into port, vessels going out with rails, coal and machinery, tugs and boats servicing the ships or working on the ever-expanding harbours, all belching steam and smoke.

By the end of the 19th century, the miners, the iron, steel and chemical workers, the shipbuilders and the dockers were employed by a handful of dominant companies suffering fierce foreign competition. The economy rode on massively profitable loans to the Empire and to South America – manufacturing played second fiddle. After the First World War the bottom fell out of Britain's industrial base. Communities that had

This fiery sunset over Middlesbrough (left) is no natural phenomenon: it results from the light being refracted through the haze from the huge concentration of steel and chemical plants along the Tees estuary.

As night falls over Sunderland (above), a foreign ship enters a shipyard for repairs. As at the Tyneside yards, many workers have been laid off in recent years.

grown up around a single business collapsed, bringing immense human misery. When Palmer's shipyard on the Tyne closed in 1933, eight out of ten of Jarrow's working population were without a job and without any hope of finding one. In 1936, two hundred of the unemployed men – those still with strength enough to do it – marched almost 300 miles to London to bring attention to their plight. The production of coal and ships has never returned to the heights of 1913. In 1986 the Jarrow march was repeated to protest again at the denial of human needs in the name of economic rationality.

The Tyne-Tees Coast Today

The open space around Tynemouth's ruined priory gives views across the deserted rivermouth. Though once in a while a bulk carrier churns its way out to sea, most of the boats are trawlers, dwarfed by the harbour piers, bringing their catch back to the North Shields market. In South Shields a municipal fountain adorned with painted stone shells, an amusement park, and lawns reaching down to the sand dunes mark this as a resort, despite the presence of Westhoe colliery a stone's throw away from the beach. At Blyth and Newbiggin seaside piers were built alongside the coal ports for skilled Tyneside workers whose wages could cover weekend fun. Huge expanses of green front the long line of bay-windowed guest-houses that overlook the sea at Whitley Bay, where Glaswegians now outnumber Geordies every summer. In contrast to this urban sprawl the open sea is a joy.

On Teesside, from the transporter bridge of Middlesbrough to the golf course among the dunes of Seaton Carew, reed-beds and sheep or cattle pastures are juxtaposed with oil-storage tanks and the huge complex of chemical plants belonging to ICI and Tioxide UK. The reclaimed coal-tip flats of Seal Sands, at the mouth of the Tees, have the largest concentration of

In the days of sail, when voyages were long and food was poor, sailors often suffered from scurvy. Scurvy Grass grows by the sea and was taken aboard to treat the disease. It contains vitamin C – unnamed then, but no less effective.

The most abundant British gull, the Kittiwake was once shot for sport and for the hat trade, which used its wing-feathers. It has recovered well under legal protection, and now nests on seaside warehouses as well as rocky cliffs.

chemical industry in western Europe. Beyond Seaton Carew's 1930s-style promenade, gleaming yellow clock-tower and cracked hotels, three wooden masts tower above the walls of Hartlepool docks. They belong to HMS *Warrior*, the first iron-hulled battleship, built in 1860 and now a floating museum. At Sunderland they still build ships beneath Wearmouth Bridge's bower of steel, but the workforce has been drastically cut. Today, when a foreign vessel comes in for repair, laid-off craftsmen watch from the bridge to pinpoint design faults with expert eyes.

A number of the mines that still operate on the coast between the Tees and Tyne dump their slurry on the shore nowadays. Parts of the cliff are nothing but slagheaps, and along the great sweep of dark and lifeless beach below Peterlee, a corrugated iron chute borne aloft on stilts disgorges the black slurry onto what was once golden sand. Laid-off miners come to pick the beach for coal to eke out winter fuel bills. 'Seacoalers' gather sackfuls, to make a living from others for whom the price of proper-grade coal is unaffordable. The working miners rightly fear for their jobs for the management say they cannot pay for better waste disposal and keep the mines open. No one wins.

But seabirds still gather just south of the Tyne on a natural arch of limestone, more reminiscent of a Roman structure than the iron and steel cat's cradles of the Tyne and Wear bridges. Kittiwakes are the main residents of Marsden Rock, their bulky nests dotting the wind-cut ledges. Cormorants can be seen spreading their wings to dry on the top of the rock, and a few Fulmars may be fulminating against the lack of fishing boats to follow.

Between the coal towns north of the Tyne, the autumnal backdrop to the coast is of stubblefields and cylindrical bales of hay. Hints of the wide and wild north Northumbrian shores appear in flashes of white sand between the pitheads, power lines and aluminium works. At Cresswell, pale yellow stone takes over from the industrial brick and the long, lonely crescent of Druridge Bay begins. Less than twenty miles north of the River Tyne, and with a hinterland scarred by open-cast mines, this stretch of dunes might belong to the shoreline of a deserted island. Clear waves ripple onto sand as fine as castor sugar. Above the strandline the wind erases every print and track, blowing the tiny sandgrains into shapes as smooth as marble and as transient as thistledown. Piebald horses graze behind the dunes and foxes may make moonlit visits to explore the seaweed-covered shores. Sea fog can roll onshore, wrapping the bay into yet more seclusion and unworldliness. This magic place is scheduled as a site for the next pressurized water reactor after Suffolk's Sizewell B.

For Those in Peril on the Sea

For all Tyneside's historic importance as a shipbuilding centre, entering the rivermouth in the days of oar and sail was a nightmare in rough weather. On the north side lurked the Black Middens rocks and on the south the preferable but still treacherous Herd Sands. In 1789, people on the shore watched in horror and helplessness as the *Adventure*, from Newcastle, went aground with the loss of every life on board. One of a long line of disasters, it prompted a fund-raising effort by the concerned and well-to-do citizens of South Shields to fund a prize for the best design of life-saving vessel. The end result was a 30-foot boat with extra buoyancy from cork in the seats and the hull lining. It was crewed by twelve oarsmen and could carry eight others. Launched in 1799, the *Original* remained in service for thirty-odd years until claimed by the Black Middens. Before this first purpose-built lifeboat was wrecked, the Royal National Lifeboat Institution had been founded.

Today, between the Tees and Seahouses on the Northumberland coast, there are eleven lifeboat stations, a concentration matched only on England's South Coast. All are manned by volunteers and one full-time mechanic. North of Druridge Bay at Amble, where the harbour was originally built for the coal mines, the profile of the lifeboatmen is typical. About half are fishermen, and rarely out to sea when needed, since their small cobles do not handle well in rough weather. Three of the men – a pitman, a construction worker and a prison officer – may be on call between shifts.

Bobby used to work for the mines as a trimmer, levelling off the cargoes in the colliers to ensure that the ships were seaworthy. The Honorary Secretary, Ken – who contacts the crew – is a retired teacher with a Master's Certificate from fifteen years at sea. When asked why they volunteer to risk their lives, the men confess, after jokes about arm-twisting and being damned stupid, that it is hard to say. There may be a tradition in the family, but some of them have no previous connection with the sea. Rodney, the youngest of the crew, comes to the point: 'You can offer a service, you've got the experience and you can put it to good use'. One of the fishermen, Jock, adds that in his business you do all you can to rescue even your worst enemy when boats are in trouble out at sea. Whenever lives of lifeboatmen have been lost, there is never any shortage of replacements.

The Amble crew have lifted men off burning tankers and towed a capsized RAF boat into port to extract a lad alive after he had been trapped for nine hours. But the commonest calls are for amateur sailors, surf-boarders and 'people trying to reach Norway on air-beds'. Around a thousand lives are saved by the RNLI each year. The equipment – at Amble a 44-foot, twin-engined steel boat with a range of 97 miles, and a speedy inflatable – is all of first-class quality. The cost of the RNLI service – some £23 million a year – is met entirely by voluntary contributions, much of it from legacies. Were the RNLI to become a

public service, it is unimaginable that government funding could match the present income. But there are other reasons why the lifeboatmen prefer things as they are. When new gear or parts are needed, they arrive within a day. Amble's mechanic, Gordon, would have no such faith in an organization bound by red tape. The men feel, too, that as a full-time job, the urgency and commitment, and the easy way they work together, might disappear.

Wild Northumbria

Amble marks the end of the Northumbrian coalfields. The density of human habitation of the Tyne-Tees industrial belt suddenly fades, giving way to one of the most sparsely populated coastal regions of England. Here are fine sand-dune systems, born on the beach where the Sand Couch and Prickly Saltwort collect the sand, which is then built up by Marram Grass. Away from the sea it matures into bush, scrub and wet 'slacks', which lie low among the dunes. The sands are rich in lime – from sea shells – and lime-loving flowers like the startlingly purplish-red Bloody Cranesbill thrive. In the slacks grow the beautiful Grass of Parnassus and the Northern Marsh Orchid, and with them the rare, pale Coral-root Orchid, which draws nourishment from decayed organic matter in the ground. The wind-combed Marram Grass and acres of sand, its colours ranging from amber to milky white, suffuse every scene with softness, interrupted only by outcrops of hard rock, on which grows a carpet of grass, together with Primroses, Harebells and Lesser Knapweed.

At Alnmouth and Amble tiny open boats – the traditional cobles – catch salmon heading for the Aln and Coquet every summer. Lobsters and crabs are the commoner catch, though a few Amble trawlers make trips to Scotland to net the more commercial fish. A regular supply of herring arrives at Craster, coming overland from western Scotland in recent years, due to the ban on North Sea stocks. Pale pink kippers smoked over oak-sawdust fires for fourteen hours are the speciality of this fishing village. Some of the curing houses date back well over a century, as do the methods used. At Berwick-upon-Tweed on the border, boats lay out salmon nets that are drawn in from the shore. Upstream, at Norham, the nets are blessed at midnight at the start of the salmon season. Berwick celebrates mid-season with a feast and carnival and the crowning of a Salmon Queen. The small fishing fleets of Beadnell, Seahouses and Lindisfarne harvest scallops, winkles and mussels.

The villages along the Northumbrian coast are few and far between, playing the smallest part in the coastal drama of rocks and sand, with its cast of birds, seals and early saints. The long ridge of once molten rock, on which much of Hadrian's Wall is built, meets the coast just south of Craster. Reddish sandstones and grits abruptly change to dark dolerites with rocks like giant, rounded paving stones spreading across the beach. The outcrops, which include the Farne Islands, are topped by castles whose unassailable splendour has for centuries inspired fear, awe and artistry alike.

The Tudor ruins of the castle on Holy Island (Lindisfarne), remodelled in this century by Lutyens, sit like a ship atop a precipitous wedge of rock. St Aidan's statue and the ruins of the Priory bear witness to Holy Island's 7th-century role as the cradle of Celtic Christianity – from here Columba's disciple Aidan tackled the conversion of Saxon England. On the mainland the colossal Bamburgh Castle looks out towards the Farnes. But Bamburgh, for all its glory, cannot match the imposing scene and setting of the ruined castle at Dunstanburgh further south.

Birds and Beasts

On the Farne Islands St Cuthbert's Eider Ducks are still present, though since his time they have been threatened by hungry medieval monks, and much more recently by the number of visitors to this lovely archipelago. With impressive colonies

Virtually wiped out in Britain by the beginning of the 20th century, the Grey Seal has recovered under increasing degrees of protection – although it can still be culled under government licence, as at the Farne Islands off the Northumberland coast.

The adult male Dragonet seems too exotic to swim in British waters, but it is a fairly common fish of sandy seabeds. The courtship display is spectacular, the male puffing himself out and showing his striking colours to full effect.

Ross Back Sands, and Ross Back Links behind them (right), surrounded by water on three sides, are typical of the unspoiled coastline north of the industrial Tyneside area.

of breeding seabirds, it is hard to imagine how St Cuthbert could have found peace and quiet in his retreat here 13 centuries ago. The harsh guttural calls of Guillemots, Razorbills and Cormorants, the incessant nasal repetition of their name by the Kittiwakes, the 'aahing' and 'oohing' of the Eider Ducks and the shrill, grating cries of the terns fill this sanctuary with a cacophony of sound.

Apart from its birdlife, the other star attraction of the Farnes is its colony of Grey Seals. About half the world's population breeds around the coast of Britain and the Farnes have the largest English colony. The seals have been culled periodically by conservationists because the increase in the population was considered by some to be a threat to other wildlife. That the seals themselves had become unhealthy and aggressive was added to the argument. On the other hand, large numbers of pups were dying, which might have been nature's own way of regulating the colony's size.

Pale-bellied Brent Geese from Greenland and Spitsbergen and Whooper Swans from Iceland

Rural depopulation has affected the children of the small community on Holy Island (also called Lindisfarne), who have to cross this causeway twice daily to travel to and from their school on the mainland, now that the island's school has closed.

The little town of Alnmouth (below) has hardly grown since 1806, when the River Aln changed course, making this once busy Northumbrian port redundant. Further north, Bamburgh Castle (bottom) retains little of its original medieval structure, having been extensively rebuilt by its owner in the late 1800s.

The statue of the Celtic bishop St Aidan stands silhouetted in the grounds of the 11th-century Lindisfarne Priory on Holy Island, with Lindisfarne Castle in the distance. Holy Island has rich plant and bird life, and is Britain's only regular wintering site for Pale-bellied Brent Geese.

An abundant coastal breeder from Northumberland and Lancashire northwards, the Eider has benefited considerably from protection after past persecution. It is one of the world's most numerous sea ducks.

Inner Farne is the main, innermost island of the 28 islands and islets of the Farne group. Purchased by the National Trust as long ago as 1925, the Farnes are probably the oldest seabird sanctuary in Europe; the 7th-century hermit St Cuthbert protected their birds, giving Eiders (known locally as St Cuthbert's or Cuddy's Ducks) his special blessing.

feed on the algae and Eelgrass that grow on the tidal flats between Holy Island and the mainland. They know the tide timetable as well as the people living on the island, who are cut off for ten hours in every twenty-four.

Life has been hard on England's most northerly coast. The long dune-backed beaches and the islands close to the Scottish border have seen minimal change over the last few hundred years compared with the convulsions between the Tyne and Tees. On Lindisfarne no one locks their doors and no policeman or woman has the island as their beat. But the children have to go to a mainland school, their numbers no longer justifying education on the island. A world away, in the great industrial conurbations, people also have to leave – in search of work. The black Durham beaches, the closed shipyards and the boarded-up estates, the poisoned and empty estuaries are the tragic truth for which the haunting loneliness and loveliness of the coast towards the border sings the sad lament. Yet still there is immense beauty along this coastline of contrasts and the fighting spirit of its people gives hope for the future.

REGIONAL SUMMARY
TEESSIDE, TYNESIDE AND NORTHUMBERLAND

The distance between Teesside and Berwick-upon-Tweed, excluding estuaries and islands, is about 95 miles (153km).

PHYSICAL PROFILE
Apart from the Triassic rocks south of Hartlepool, the north-eastern coasts of England are mostly composed of Paleozoic coal measures, limestones and sandstones, often masked by glacial deposits and silt. The Durham coast has yellow cliffs of magnesian limestone, but the coasts in the south are largely disfigured by industrialization. Northern Northumberland's unspoiled coast is composed of Carboniferous rocks, crossed in places by the igneous Whin Sill, which extends to the Farne Islands. Lindisfarne Castle stands on a dolerite outcrop on Holy Island, which is cut off by tides for over ten hours a day.

Climate: Average temperatures are 37°F to 39°F (3°–4°C) in January and 60°F (16°C) in July. The rainfall averages 25 inches (635mm) a year.

HUMAN PROFILE
The coast between Teesside and southern Northumberland is densely populated. Major settlements include Middlesbrough (149,800), Hartlepool (90,300), Seaham (21,100), Sunderland (196,200), South Shields (87,200), Jarrow (27,100), Newcastle upon Tyne (192,500), Tynemouth (60,000), Blyth (36,500) and Berwick (36,500). Resorts include Whitley Bay (37,100), Newbiggin-by-the-Sea (12,100) and Amble (5,400).

Sites of historic interest: The Roman Hadrian's Wall starts at Wallsend, near Newcastle. A monastery was founded on Holy Island in AD 634, but the present priory dates from 1093. The Venerable Bede wrote his history of the English church at St Paul's, Jarrow (founded 685).

Museums: Maritime Museum, Hartlepool; Central Museum and Art Gallery, Sunderland; Bede Monastery Museum, Jarrow; Museum of Antiquities, Newcastle; Grace Darling Museum, Bamburgh.

Famous personalities: Sir Compton Mackenzie (born Hartlepool), Grace Darling (born Bamburgh), whose father was the keeper of the Longstone Lighthouse on the Farne Islands.

Marine industry: Shipbuilding and marine engineering: Hartlepool, Sunderland, Newcastle. Coble boat building: Amble. Fishing ports: Hartlepool, North Shields, Boulmer, Craster, Berwick. Kipper smoking: Craster. Salmon fisheries: Berwick.

Commerce/industry: Coal shafts in the Northumberland and Durham coalfield extend up to 4½ miles (7km) under the sea. The main industrial regions are Teesside and Tyneside, which produce oil and oil products, iron and steel, machinery, chemicals, cars, and electrical and electronic goods.

NATURAL PROFILE
Wildlife: Habitats include mudflats at the mouth of the Tees. Farther north are denes (gorges). North of Sunderland are high cliffs, while the Farne Islands and Holy Island, with their mudflats, are in northern Northumberland.

Attractions: In Cleveland, mudflats and marshes, with waders and wildfowl, at the mouth of the Tees. In Tyne and Wear, Marsden Cliffs (magnesian limestone). In Northumberland, Newton Pool Nature Reserve (NT); Farne Islands (NT) – breeding ground of Grey Seals; Lindisfarne National Nature Reserve. *Footpaths:* Marsden Bay; Boulmer to Dunstanburgh; nature trail on the largest of the Farne Islands; Spittal to Seahouses. *Beauty spots:* The Northumberland Coast AONB extends 43 miles (69km) from Amble to just south of Berwick. It includes the Farne Islands and Holy Island. *Beaches in Cleveland:* Seaton Carew. *Beaches in Tyne and Wear:* Whitburn, Marsden Bay, South Shields, Whitley Bay. *Beaches in Northumberland:* Seaton Sluice, Newbiggin-by-the-Sea, Druridge Bay (NT-owned shoreline), Low Newton, Beadnell Bay, Seahouses, Bamburgh, Holy Island, Spittal.

CAUSES FOR CONCERN
Direct dumping: Two million tons of colliery waste are dumped every year on Durham's beaches, smothering sea-bed creatures and devastating the offshore shellfish industry – the NCB has no plans to use infill or other alternative disposal methods. Acidic sulphate waste from chemical industries is dumped just off Teesmouth.

Pipeline discharges: Complex of chemical industries on Teesside contributes to the DoE's classification of the estuary as a Class D river (the most polluted category). The Tees estuary is the UK's second most polluted estuary.

Incineration at sea: The port of North Shields, Tyne and Wear, is used for loading highly toxic pharmaceuticals, pesticides and other wastes for incineration in the North Sea, in such ships as the Dutch *Vulcanus*, beyond the reach of national air pollution controls. Hazards also include transport of wastes to the port and risks of spillage on shore or at sea.

Radioactive discharges: Hartlepool nuclear power station discharges slightly radioactive cooling water into coastal waters. Druridge Bay is the proposed site of a nuclear power station.

Oil pollution: Run-off from industrial plants and also other land users.

Beaches: Coal slurry tipped on to once sandy beaches has led to their partial abandonment for recreation on a stretch of the Durham coast, notably at Seaham.

Threatened wildlife: Pesticide pollution is causing thinning of seabird eggshells, a cause of breeding failure. In the last 100 years, intertidal mudflats have been reduced at Teesmouth from 59,000 acres (24,000ha) to 432 acres (175ha). The last remaining area is earmarked for a port expansion programme. The Tees will thus become the first British estuary to lose virtually all its intertidal zone, and Grey Seals, waders and wildfowl are being deprived of their resting and feeding grounds.

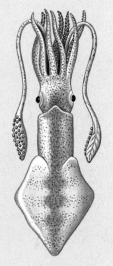

Mediterranean holidays, and Greek restaurants in our towns, have helped make the Common Squid an increasingly popular dish. It is landed from our fishing ports and is now a familiar sight on many fishmongers' slabs.

EASTERN SCOTLAND

DAVID DAICHES

When I was a child I fell in love with the eastern coastline of Scotland from Eyemouth, Cockburnspath, Dunbar and Port Seton to the fishing villages of Fife. We always spent our summers somewhere there, most often at Crail on the East Neuk of Fife, and the combination of beach and cliff, of rock pools – my brother and I spent many enchanted hours watching the life in rock pools – and sandy beaches, of picturesque fishing harbours and threatening barriers of rock and sandbank, still seems to me absolutely magical. The shift in atmosphere and feeling, from a sunny evening with little waves plashing gently on the shore to the stern grey coast with curled breakers shattering and the hissing of retreating pebbles as they were sucked back afterwards – this shift could take place in a few minutes – was dramatic and exciting. The names of the Fife fishing villages – Dysart, Largo, Pittenweem, St Monance, Anstruther, Crail – were romantic in themselves, and the coast between them, where as a youngster I scrambled and explored so often, was an enchanted land. To walk along the shore from Crail to the historic old grey town of St Andrews – right round the very East Neuk itself – was a journey in history as well as geography.

Later, I got to know the East Coast of Scotland further north, the splendid rocky shore between Montrose and Aberdeen, its deep coves visible from the train as it hugs the coastline, and again between Aberdeen and Fraserburgh, with its unexpected perfect beaches as well as its rocks and cliffs and stretches of unspoiled sand. I think, too, of the south shore of the Moray Firth from Banff to Buckie, with its little bays, its beautiful sand, its fishing harbours, its dramatic outcrops of rock. Beautiful, dramatic, comforting, threatening, surprising, moving in its reminder of human activity and human danger, the East Coast of Scotland is a perpetual source of wonder and a challenge to the imagination.

EASTERN SCOTLAND
BERWICK TO ABERDEEN

'STORMS THERE THE STACKS THRASHED, THERE ANSWERED THEM THE TERN
WITH ICY FEATHERS; FULL OFT THE ERNE WAILED ROUND SPRAY-FEATHERED . . .'

The Bass Rock passage from *The Sea Farer* (7th century)

Named after the holy mountain of Apollo, Grass of Parnassus is an uncommon flower of fens and dune slacks, mainly in Scotland and northern England. It has declined as its habitats have been drained.

Scotland's three capitals – present-day Edinburgh, medieval Perth and Celtic Dunfermline – all lie in the eastern Lowlands, sited on the banks and estuary shores of the Tay and Forth. From the days of the earliest human settlements, these firths, or estuaries, embraced sea routes to northern Europe and also formed the chief arena for trade, and conflict, with England. With some of Britain's richest agricultural land, with great ports, such as Dundee, sheltered by the funnelling firths, and with a wealth of mineral deposits, the East Lowlands, together with Glasgow on the West Coast, have been the economic driving force of Scotland, and alone form its unrivalled historic heart.

The sea is not always so placid off the neat little village of St Abbs as in this serene summer view. In rough weather, the village's harbour is a welcome refuge for boats, since it is one of the few sheltered havens along a stretch of coastline edged with sheer cliffs for miles. Although fishing has declined, turbot, haddock and cod are still caught offshore.

North from the Border

The River Tweed is Scotland's ancient border and remains so today, save for the loop to England's advantage around Berwick-upon-Tweed. Low cliffs south of the river mouth announce the frontier and beyond it rise to a sheer line of high limestone rock that carries the coastal scenery into the dramatic chaos of St Abb's Head and a different world altogether from the gentler Northumbrian shore. The once horizontal strata of the rocks have been pushed and twisted into sculpted surfaces painted by lichens in every shade, from lizard green to mustard yellow. Glossy fronds from a forest of kelp gleam through the clearest water off eastern

Scotland's coast, with flashes of reds and pinks from sea urchins and sea anemones. High above, smooth turf dotted with Thyme, Thrift and Wood Sage slopes beguilingly to sudden drops. Inlets, caves, half-submerged rocks and the excitement of the unknown around the next jagged corner entice exploration northwards to Fast Castle and beyond – until the grim shape of Torness Point nuclear power station serves as a rude reminder of present-day realities.

Further north, by the firths of Forth and Tay, industry and intensive agriculture dominate the gently rolling hills and flat reclaimed farmlands. But out beyond the estuaries, fishing villages have grown up around tiny coves set in the headlands of contorted red sandstone rock. Some perch on cliffs with rough-hewn steps leading down to unprotected beaches. The most exposed and unrelenting coast of Angus and The Mearns has long harboured fishing fleets. All along the rocky shores there are caves that have served as Celtic shrines, smugglers' caches and storage for fishing gear. Sharp, high basalt cliffs are interrupted by soft white dunes from Lunan Bay north to Milton Ness, and by the shingle of Inverbervie beach, where wave-polished fragments of agate, jasper, cornelian, cairngorm and amethyst gleam and sparkle among the pebbles. These lowland shores of eastern Scotland are well fringed with sweeps of sand dunes. The vibrant white of Grass of Parnassus and the blue of Clustered Bellflower, the pink of Centaury and Maiden Pink, and the early gold of Cowslip are all here. Late autumn brings the shiny orange berries of the Buckthorn shrub, which has been introduced here, as it has on the West Coast, and has spread all along the sandy soil of the East Lowlands coast.

The dunes at Montrose were transformed long ago into a golf course, or 'links' as it is called in

Fringed with almost continuous red sandstone cliffs, the coastline to the north of Arbroath is one of the finest in eastern Britain. This view from Boddin Point looks across the six-mile curve of Lunan Bay.

Scotland, the word originally meaning 'an undulating sandy sea-shore'. From Eyemouth just north of the border, to Stonehaven just south of Aberdeen, there are 50 seaside links, with the halfway-point of St Andrews famous as the international capital of the sport. Thought to be of Flemish origin, the game as played in Scotland is old enough to have had medieval statutes banning it. The authorities feared its popularity was at the expense of archery practice. The advent of gunpowder removed objections to the game, which the Scottish monarchs took up with relish. Today, local youngsters from the fishing villages, Americans on golfing tours, and businessmen from Aberdeen or London follow in the footsteps of the game's early players against a backdrop of the island-studded firths of Forth and Tay and the cold North Sea.

The Fringe of Gold
The peninsula of Fife between the firths of Forth and Tay was the 'fringe of gold' around the 'beggar's mantle' as James VI of Scotland described his kingdom at the end of the 16th century. It was this coast that traded with the Baltic and the Netherlands, nurtured the first Scottish university and led the Scottish church in pre-Reformation days. Line fishing for cod and haddock sustained the local population, while the Dutch ruled the seas as far as the herring fishery was concerned. By the time Scottish fishermen had joined the hunt for the silver shoals, the newly discovered coal beneath the 'fringe of gold' was being mined and poured into the furnaces of iron foundries. Not just the Fife coast between Largo and Kincardine, but also the Lothian coast on either side of Edinburgh threw up a squalor of dust, debris and darkening clouds from a hundred chimneys and pitheads. Today the herrings have gone and coal-fired and nuclear power stations squat upon the Forth shores, flanked by paper mills, cement and linoleum works, oil refineries and rig construction works. Not much purer are the valuable but heavily fertilized farming lands in the remaining open spaces along the Forth or in the less industrialized and more fertile Carse of Gowrie, the Tay's northern bank.

Far from railways and motorways and untouched by the oil industry, St Andrews, famous for its ancient university and renowned as the world's golfing capital, attracts huge numbers of tourists who contribute to its prosperous image.

The past dependence of the Scottish East-Coast communities on the fishing trade is commemorated in the church completed in 1905 at Port Seton (right) on the Firth of Forth. Today most Port Seton trawlers are based at Eyemouth (centre right), one of the largest and most sheltered harbours of eastern Scotland.

The fishing folk of St Monance on the Fife peninsula used to wash their nets at the shrine of their Celtic saint not for magic, but because the iron in the spring water extended the life of the hemp. But they would 'touch cauld iron' to avert ill luck and dreaded certain words and sights with a dogged superstition. Carrons Ironworks, which opened in the mid-18th century at Falkirk, south of the Forth, would have appeared to them as a creation of the devil. Within a hundred years, the people of Inverkeithing, Burntisland, Kirkcaldy and Buckhaven on the opposite shores were to see their enlarged harbours blacken with dust and grime, their cottages rattle from the passing railway trucks and their moorings reduced to make way for the ships exporting coal, iron and the new manufactured goods.

In the fishing villages of this coast, the dangerous business of setting out to sea, the cold and messy business of salting and drying, and the hard graft of selling went on with only occasional respite. The women of these communities, who prepared the fish and packed it on their backs in wicker 'creels' to take to neighbouring towns,

were famous for their strength, quick wits and sharp repartee. One annual event was the football match between the fishwives and the unmarried women of Musselburgh and next-door Fisherrow, east of Edinburgh, which the married team invariably won. Musselburgh golf course had its local fisherwomen players long before any landowner's wife or daughter took up the game. The big occasions for the fishing villages were the processions at the end of the herring season. At Cockenzie and Port Seton near by, the event was marked by the burning of an old boat and with it all the bad luck of the preceding year. The Musselburgh procession, known as the 'Fishermen's Walk', still takes place, with all the fishing families dressed in their traditional costumes, the shawls, striped petticoats and aprons of the women handed down from generation to generation. Along with other games and sports, there is a race in which the contestants thread bone net-making needles as they run.

The oyster bars of Edinburgh once provided an inexhaustible market for the winter trade of such Lothian fishing villages. The beds of the

In recent years, the Grayling butterfly has become increasingly restricted to the coast, where its caterpillars feed on grasses, including Marram. Sand dunes, such as those at Tentsmuir, Fife, still hold large populations.

Siccar Point's dramatic cliffs, backed by rolling farmland of the Borders, are typical of those along much of the unspoiled East Coast of Scotland.

Firth of Forth yielded some thirty million oysters a year in the days of Edinburgh's 18th-century renaissance. Mussels, too, were abundant – hence Musselburgh's name. Ferries across the Firth of Forth provided another living – some of it of an unscrupulous nature, judging by travellers' accounts of mid-passage threats. Leith to Burntisland and Kinghorn was a standard crossing, until the commercial shipping trade pushed out both fishermen and ferrymen. The Queensferry route had its origins in the Middle Ages, carrying pilgrims visiting the shrine at Dunfermline. In the Victorian era, paddle steamers swelled the sea traffic, taking the well-off citizens of Edinburgh to their summer retreats in southern Fife. All along the eastern coast of Scotland, from Berwick on the border north to Stonehaven, trade, transport, whaling, fisheries and heavy industry sustained the coastal population. Though people were rich in initiative, learning and tradition, many had a life of hardship.

The Lighthouse Builders

More gratitude is owed by the people of the Scottish coast to one family of engineers than to all the great personalities of Georgian Edinburgh. Over five generations the Stevenson family was responsible for the design of almost every lighthouse built around the treacherous shores of Scotland. Robert Stevenson trained at Edinburgh University and in 1807 succeeded his stepfather as engineer to the Commissioners of Northern Lighthouses, the Scottish equivalent of Trinity House. That year, he started work on a lighthouse for Bell Rock, a treacherous reef lying 11 miles off Arbroath, in the middle of the navigation channels for both the Tay and the Forth. The monastery of Arbroath had at one point placed a bell on the rock – hence its name. The bell was stolen by a heartless pirate, who received his just desserts when he later came to grief on the rock.

Today, oil-rig supply boats and tankers still

The bright colours of the day-flying Six-spot Burnet moth warn birds that it is distasteful. It flies in sunny, open grassy places, including sand dunes and sea cliffs, where its caterpillars feed on Bird's Foot Trefoil.

Known to many people by its most famous product, 'smokies' – haddock smoked over oak-wood chips – the town of Arbroath (right) still has an active fishing harbour, as well as various light industries, including boat-building, although the spinning mills and other large factories that sprang up in the 19th century are now abandoned.

This coastal track between Crail and Anstruther (right) was a familiar route for the women of the fishing villages. At Stonehaven (centre right), over fifty miles to the north, a contemporary fisherman's wife keeps the steps of her house as shipshape as the dinghies in the harbour.

navigate past Bell Rock by the beam from Stevenson's lighthouse, built of beautifully dove-tailed granite blocks and towering 115 feet above the sea. It is the oldest working lighthouse in Britain. Another rock threatening ships at the entrance of Stonehaven harbour, south of Aberdeen, was dynamited out of existence by Stevenson, and many coastal villages received new harbours, breakwaters and docks constructed to his designs and under his supervision. The first intermittent flashing lights, the mast lantern of light vessels and the establishment of the first Admiralty survey of British waters were further significant achievements of this remarkable and energetic man.

Stevenson's sons, Alan, David and Thomas, followed in their father's footsteps, extending the network of family lighthouses from Muckle Flugga off the Shetlands to India and Japan. Long-distance travel was to play a large part in the life of Thomas's son, who trained as an engineer, serving his apprenticeship at Anstruther, but whose ill health led him to break with family tradition. He was Robert Louis Stevenson, author of the classic seafaring adventures *Treasure Island* and *Kidnapped*, in which reefs, rocks, merchant shipping and treachery on the high seas play vital roles. Unable to tolerate the Scottish climate, he spent the last few years of his life on his adopted treasure island of Samoa.

Whaling and its Consequences

In Dundee's Broughty Castle Museum, among numerous other mementoes of the whaling trade, there is a photograph of a Polar Bear cub on deck. Crouching behind the prostrate body of its mother, the frightened cub stares at the camera. Collecting zoological specimens was a sideline to the whalers' business – this adult bear is thought to have died on the voyage and the cub, if it survived, would have ended up in a zoo.

The great whales – the main quarry – were

The high wooden masts in Dundee's large docks belong to Scott's Antarctic exploration ship, *Discovery*, now permanently moored in the city where she was built in 1901. Dundee was famous as a whaling port in the 18th and 19th centuries, and the discovery that whale oil could help the newly discovered jute fibre to be woven easily led to the town's pre-eminence as Britain's chief jute producer – a position it still holds, as well as being a centre of commerce and engineering.

hunted for their oil and whalebone, or baleen, with both Scottish and English ships playing an important part in the international whaling trade between the mid-18th century and the First World War. From the myths and legends surrounding the earth's largest mammals, it would seem that in early times the seas were full of them, their schools a common sight off the northern, western and southern coasts of Britain. But commercial whaling had already started as early as AD 900, when Basque seafarers in small boats hunted Biscayan Right Whales off the western coasts of France and Spain. (They were called 'right' whales because they were the right whales to hunt from open vessels, as, approaching close to the coast, they swam slowly, floated when dead, and yielded large quantities of valuable whalebone and oil.)

By the early 16th century, stocks of the Biscayan Right Whales were so depleted that the Basque whalers moved far to the north, to Iceland and Spitsbergen, in pursuit of a fresh quarry – the Greenland Right Whale (or Bowhead Whale). British whalers, and the more successful Dutch, soon joined them. By the 1630s new stocks of Greenland Right Whales were sought around Greenland and Baffin Island. By 1820, most of the Dutch ships had given up whaling, reluctant to chase the increasingly wary whales into the ice, and the British became pre-eminent in the industry.

With the British government offering generous bounties on whale oil, shipowners in the Scottish East Coast ports of Dundee, Leith, Dunbar, Kirkcaldy, Burntisland and Peterhead were quick to take advantage. Dundee was one of the main Scottish ports to profit from the industry, as its museums, monuments and extensive docks still bear witness today. Together with owners in English ports, especially Hull, they trained their captains and refitted their vessels, employing, as so often in marine matters, Dutch expertise. Unlike the Dutch, the British whalers did not hesitate to pursue the whales into the pack ice.

Paralleling the British industry, American whalers chased Humpback and Grey Whales as well as right whales. By the late 18th century, the Yankee whalers of New England had discovered the rich harvest of Sperm Whales, which provided lighting and heating oil and spermaceti, a waxy substance from the animals' enormous heads that could be used in oil-lamps and candles. By the 1920s they had virtually exhausted the stocks of Sperm Whales in the Atlantic.

Gas and petroleum oil began to replace Sperm Whale oil in the 1830s, so other uses were found for whale oils. Dundee's street lights, like those of so many East Coast ports, had run off whale oil for many years. When they were converted to gas, a market was found for whale oil as an additive in the jute industry. Baleen, or whalebone – the hard plates in the upper jaws of the baleen whales, which they used for filtering plankton from seawater – had an extraordinary

variety of uses. The bristles, part of the sieving mechanism, were made into brushes, nets and stuffing for mattresses and upholstery. The tough and pliable 'bone' itself was used to make such items as trellises, window blinds, corset and umbrella frames, tape measures and weaving instruments – it was the natural plastic of the age. The true bones of the whales' skeletons often ended up as kitchen utensils – when they were not erected as trophies, as on the conical hill of North Berwick Law, south of the Forth, or over the entrance of a whaling captain's house in Anstruther, to the north.

Seals, whose hunting by the British goes back to prehistory, became a major quarry when whale returns were tailing off. For little extra cost, ships could be despatched in February or March instead of April to hunt seals off Newfoundland before heading north after the whales. In one year alone, six Dundee ships took almost 140,000 seals. But whales were still the chief quarry, and the whalers would head towards the ice, going further every season as the dwindling shoals retreated. The heyday of British Arctic whaling lasted from the late 18th century to the mid-19th century, when the whales became increasingly scarce, until by 1912 a Dundee ship returned to her home port without a single whale to show for her voyage.

The advent of steamships and the 19th-century invention of an effective explosive harpoon paved the way for the modern whaling industry. With stocks in the world's northern seas depleted, attention turned to new grounds in the Antarctic, home of the world's largest remaining stocks. Blue, Fin, Sei and Humpback whales became the quarry and, by the 1920s, factory ships the means of processing them. By the 1960s, so few whales were left that many species were deemed commercially extinct.

Today, the International Whaling Commission regulates the depleted whale stocks of the world – though a handful of nations (excluding Britain) continues to hunt them. Many feel that attempts to outlaw the practice may have come too late, but whales can still sometimes be seen off Britain's shores – occasionally, close to the ports of eastern Scotland that once depended for their livelihood on these great creatures of the deep.

Oil, Fishing and Wildlife Today
These days, new coastal industries take their place next to the old all along the eastern Scottish shores. Just to the west of the intricate steel cantilevers of the famous turn-of-the-century Forth railway bridge and the slim strands of the 1960s road suspension bridge, the Fife shore harbours the troubled naval shipyards of Rosyth. Further upstream, two towns on either side of the Forth epitomize the contrasts of this coast. Culross, for all its mining history, has preserved its 17th-century buildings with the crow-stepped gables and red pantiled roofs so distinctive of the old Fife trading ports. The architectural in-

A typical sand dune plant as well as a weed of overgrazed pastures, Ragwort is bright with flowers in late summer, and often bright, too, with the caterpillars of the day-flying Cinnabar Moth.

Opposite: The Forth rail bridge of 1890 (right) provided the industrialized Fife towns with a vital link to the markets of the south. The road bridge (above left), constructed 74 years later, opened up the Fife peninsula to tourism. The dual nature of the Firth of Forth is well illustrated by the contrast between the immaculately preserved little town of Culross (top right) on the northern shore, and a small section of an oil refinery at Grangemouth (centre right), just across the water and clearly visible from Culross.

Among the many historical vessels that can be seen in the Scottish Fisheries Museum at Anstruther (right) are these lifeboats; powered only by oars, they were in service until the 1970s. At Aberdeen (below), rig support vessels moor alongside Shetland ferries, fishing patrol boats and cargo ships beneath the high glass offices of the oil companies, which brought prosperity to the region, but also inflicted scars on the coastal landscape, including oil terminals and rig-building sites.

About twenty-five miles east of Edinburgh, the massive wall of Tantallon Castle (above right) is itself dwarfed by Bass Rock, lying a mile out in the Firth of Forth. The steep sides of this great volcanic mass, sticking abruptly out of the water, make it seem much higher than its 350 feet. Used as a prison island in the 17th century, its only inhabitants today are the lighthouse keepers and the seabirds, including a large gannetry.

fluence is unmistakably Dutch, the cobbled streets leading to the medieval Mercat Cross utterly Scottish, and the whitewashed houses gleam from recent restoration.

Across the Forth, Grangemouth presents a night-time picture of fairy lights strung between silvery, misty shapes, whose true identity is disguised in the semi-darkness. The daytime reality is less attractive, for the site holds the refineries and processing plants of many multi-nationals, behind which, in a gloom of dull concrete and grid-plan streets, are the barrack-like homes of the workforce. The docks handle the lethal loads of chemicals and of crude oil from the North Sea oilfields.

Near Grangemouth, Shelduck dine on tiny marine snails on the upper Forth mudflats. Like all the estuary birds in the Forth, they face the threat of oil pollution. Almost 750 birds were found dead after a minor spill in 1978, including some 200 Great Crested Grebes. Ten years

earlier, a much more serious leak from a tanker in the Tay caused the death of well over a thousand birds, mainly Eider Ducks.

Today, the seafood from the Forth is hardly fit for human consumption, thanks to the input of Edinburgh's waste and the runoff of fertilizers and other substances from farms and industries along the banks. The end of the oysters spelled the end of Prestonpans' fishing history. Cocken-zie's harbour has silted up, Granton's has become a marina and the Fisherrow and Mussel-burgh men now fish from other ports. But the mussels flourish on their unwholesome diet and provide food for the wintering diving ducks – Scaups, Pochard, Common and Velvet Scoters, Longtailed Ducks and Goldeneye – that favour the waters around nearby Leith and Aberlady Bay. The mussels do not seem to harm the birds, but examination of dead Eider Ducks in Aber-lady Bay has shown that many contain alarming levels of heavy metals.

Old Dundee has been almost obliterated. The city's modern high-rise skyline, an oil rig temporarily out of service, and the rich Fife farmlands form this contemporary Tayside panorama.

The dapper Goldeneye is a common winter visitor to reservoirs as well as to estuaries and other sheltered coastal waters. Clumsy on land, it is an efficient diver for its diet of molluscs and crustaceans.

Just beyond the eastern edge of the southern Forth shore, Bass Rock is the offshore stronghold of Scotland's oldest recorded gannetry. The second part of the Gannet's scientific name, *Sula bassana*, refers to this ancient volcanic island, with its sheer cliffs and flattish top. Visitors are greeted with a raucous overture from 40,000 screaming, dagger-like beaks. From afar, the rock's surface is covered with a multitude of white polka dots, the space between each bird no more than the length of its body. The sky is a snowstorm of plummeting, soaring, wheeling and gliding Gannets.

As the coast turns northwards from the Firth of Forth, the oil industry that poses such a hazard to seabirds and which hurtled Aberdeen into the boom town of the 1970s is visible offshore, although today it faces a change in fortune. Huge investments are made temporarily redundant as 'stacked' rigs spread their spider legs through the waves in the Forth off Kirkcaldy and Buck-

haven. There are more in the Firth of Tay. Further north, at Ferryden, an expanse of reclaimed foreshore has swallowed the old harbour to become an oil-rig supply base and Montrose has a drilling rig as a training centre.

As for the fishermen of Fife, the last drifters chugged in and out of Largo Bay some forty years ago which was when the herring shoals deserted the Firth of Forth, taking with them Anstruther's title of 'fishing capital of the East Coast'. The town mourns its loss with a floating museum of Scottish fishing boats. Among the exhibits in the harbour of a 1900s herring drifter and the old North Carr light vessel lies only a handful of small working boats, for lobster, crab and scampi fishing. The empty, redstone harbour of Crail tells the same story, against an equally picturesque setting of a 16th-century town, whose tolbooth is topped by a copper weather vane in the shape of a salmon.

Almost unique along the coast of this eastern

This shrimping boat bringing in its catch to the major shrimp market at Pittenweem, Fife, may have come from as far away as Wick, over 250 miles to the north. Once their vessel has docked, the crew will spend the next few hours cleaning the shrimps.

A silver fish of grace and beauty, the Sea Trout haunts coastal waters. It migrates upriver to spawn, joining the Brown Trout and becoming the same colour; the two fish are one species, but the Brown Trout lacks the Sea Trout's migratory instinct.

corner of Fife, Pittenweem can still boast a fishing community. A boatyard established in 1747 continues to build wooden boats and a daily shrimp market animates the harbour. The remaining boats from Crail, St Monance, Cellardyke and Anstruther unload their catches here or sell the crabs, codlings and lobsters straight off the deck. Further north, the fishermen of Arbroath still create a demand for hand-built wooden boats and supply the country with oak-smoked haddock known as 'smokies'. Gourdon, Johnshaven and Stonehaven have kept their fishing fleets, while the estuary towns and villages around Montrose still work their salmon stations. But Crawton, Fishtown of Usan and Boddin tell of the fishing decline in their dereliction, as do the revamped cottages that house oil-company commuters.

Yet despite the lost communities and polluted seas, there is much to celebrate on this historic coastline. A city as great as Edinburgh can surely find the wherewithal to clean its waters; the remaining fishing towns hold on strongly to their connections with the past; birds continue to gather on the shores, and a wealth of marine life still flourishes.

REGIONAL SUMMARY
EASTERN SCOTLAND

The coast between Berwick and Aberdeen is more than 260 miles (418km) long, excluding estuaries and islands. It is known for its golf links, especially Muirfield, St Andrews and Carnoustie.

PHYSICAL PROFILE

The Central Lowlands of Scotland, a complex rift valley system, lie between Dunbar and Stonehaven. The rocks range from Permian to Devonian, with Carboniferous coal measures in Lothian and Fife. The fracturing was accompanied by volcanic activity and many hills and islands are volcanic in origin. North of Stonehaven are older metamorphic rocks (such as schists and gneisses). The firths were flooded at the end of the Ice Age. Freed of the burden of ice, the land rose in places creating raised beaches.

Climate: Average temperatures are 37°F to 39°F (3°–4°C) in January and 57°F to 59°F (14°–15°C) in July. Rainfall averages 25 inches (635mm) a year in the south and 33 inches (838mm) at Aberdeen. Cold sea mists (haars) occur from spring to midsummer, when winds are in the east.

HUMAN PROFILE

Leading settlements include Eyemouth (17,900), known for its Herring Queen Festival. Edinburgh (420,200), famed for its international festival, has two ports (Leith and Granton) on the Firth of Forth. Kirkcaldy (46,500) is Fife's largest town, while St Andrews (11,300) is the HQ of the Royal and Ancient Golf Club. Perth (43,000) has many historical associations, while Dundee (174,300) is known for its traditional jute and marmalade industries. The granite city of Aberdeen (190,500), Scotland's third largest, serves the North Sea oil industry.

Sites of historic interest: Castles include Edinburgh Castle, which houses the Scottish Crown Jewels. Holyroodhouse is a palace dating from 1500, while more than 40 kings have been crowned at Scone, near Perth. St Andrews has Scotland's oldest university (1410), while Sir Ernest Shackleton's *Terra Nova* and Captain Scott's *Discovery* were built at Dundee. The Forth Rail Bridge was opened in 1890, the Forth Road Bridge (1964) and the Tay Road Bridge (1966).

Museums: Eyemouth Museum; Lifeboat museum, Dunbar; North Berwick Museum; Museum of Antiquities, Edinburgh; Museum and Art Gallery, Kirkcaldy; Scottish Fisheries Museum and North Carr light-vessel, Anstruther; Perth Museum; HMS *Unicorn* and City Museum, Dundee; Arbroath Abbey and Museum; Tolbooth, Stonehaven; Provost Skene's House, Aberdeen, and Museum of Anthropology, Aberdeen University.

Famous personalities: John Muir (born Dunbar), Sir Harry Lauder (born Portobello), Robert Louis Stevenson (born Edinburgh), Adam Smith, Robert Adam (born Kirkcaldy), Alexander Selkirk (born Lower Largo).

Marine industry: Fishing ports: Eyemouth, Dunbar, Port Seton, Musselburgh, Pittenweem, Arbroath, Stonehaven, Aberdeen. Shipbuilding: Dundee. Naval base: Rosyth. Smokies (smoked haddock): Arbroath and Findon (Finnan Haddies).

Commerce/industry: Leith, Dundee and Montrose are major seaports. Cockenzie and Port Seton, Kincardine and Longannet have large power stations. Grangemouth has a huge oil refinery.

NATURAL PROFILE

Wildlife: Habitats include two major estuaries (the Firth of Forth and Firth of Tay), on either side of which are fine sea cliffs, such as at St Abb's Head, which also has clear marine waters and associated kelp forests and zones grazed by sea urchins.

Attractions: In Borders, St Abb's Head has spectacular scenery, rich bird and marine life, and varied flora – it is a voluntary (but proposed statutory) MNR. In Lothian, Dunbar has a rich intertidal platform; the East Lothian Coast, which includes Aberlady Bay (228 bird species recorded); Bass Rock; Forth Islands. In Central, Skinflats. In Fife, Isle of May; Firth of Tay famed for Eider in winter – including threatened dune system of Barry Buddon; Tentsmuir Point. In Tayside, Seaton Cliffs; Montrose Basin. In Grampian, St Cyrus (a reserve with 350 flowering plants and ferns); Fowlsheugh (RSPB). *Footpaths:* St Abb's Head, 6-mile (10km) clifftop walk; geology trail at Barns Ness; nature trail at Dirleton; Arbroath to Carlingheugh Bay; Johnshaven to Inverbervie; Catterline to Crawton. *Beaches in Borders:* Pease Bay. *Beaches in Lothian:* Dunbar, North Berwick, Gullane. *Beaches in Fife:* Aberdour, Kinghorn, St Andrews. *Beaches in Tayside:* Carnoustie, Arbroath, Montrose. *Beaches in Grampian:* Stonehaven, Aberdeen.

CAUSES FOR CONCERN

Direct dumping: Sewage sludge and harbour dredgings dumped in the Firth of Forth.

Pipeline discharges: Heavy metal discharges into Firth of Forth harm shellfish and birds. Acidic, iron-rich run-off from mines has affected marine life in the River Ore. Sewage outfalls cause deoxygenation in Firth of Forth. Industrial discharges are thought to impregnate salmon in River Dee with a yellow dye.

Radioactive discharges: Torness nuclear power station is due to come on stream in spring 1988. A Royal Navy nuclear submarine base is a source of radioactive contamination in the Firth of Forth.

Oil pollution: Grangemouth oil refining complex causes oil pollution in the Firth of Forth.

Beaches: Those contaminated with sewage include Portobello, Broughty Ferry and Arbroath.

Threatened wildlife: Oil and heavy metal pollution threaten seabirds, especially diving ducks, in Firth of Forth. Barry Buddon dune system (with many rare plants), which is now an Army firing range, is threatened by planned building developments. Run-off of highly toxic TBT (tributyl tin) anti-fouling paint on nets used at fish farms has polluted surrounding waters.

The increasing success of the Herring Gull has come about as it has adapted to living with humans. Always a scavenger along the coast, where it breeds, it now haunts rubbish tips everywhere outside the breeding season.

While some areas of Britain's coastline are suffering from disturbance and other threats, a number of plants seem to be immune to the problems. One such is the Sea Campion, which sprawls over grassy cliffs and shingle on all Britain's shores.

Coastal pleasures

Many people still brave Britain's unpredictable climate, but those who can afford it are more likely to spend an annual holiday soaking up the Mediterranean sun – on beaches that these days are often cleaner than many of Britain's.

As for swimming, a quick paddle or dip in the surf is enough for most, although some hardy bathers, togged-up in 1920s costumes, wait for Christmas Day to take an icy plunge

off Brighton beach. Windsurfers and yachters pit their wits against wind and water, while at Padstow a brass band accompanies the local regatta – a far cry from fashionable Cowes, where sailors mingle with other spectators.

Amusement arcades and the thrill of an all-too-rare ship launch provide excitement, too. Tranquillity may be a Mablethorpe 'Sunset Strip' cabin, a solitary game of football on a lonely beach, or a snooze in watery winter sunshine on the end of Yarmouth pier. Whatever the preference, one thing is sure – the seaside is still one of the nation's greatest pleasures, although it will not remain so unless the problems that face it are speedily and effectively resolved.

THE HIGHLANDS AND ISLANDS

GEORGE MACKAY BROWN

The small kings bargain and feud and fight.
Among them, unhindered
Pass the wandering priest and the bard.
I seek, I sing the goodness of this land, said the poet
More lovely to me than a sweetheart.
The kings of Pictland
Gave passage to his harp up the broken waters of the west –
How, being briefly troubled, it returns to purity,
Always the blood and the rust
Are washed by sea and mist and rains.
The kind mother
Cleanses her children from cornsweats and the slime of fish . . .
Therefore this bard
Left the beautiful village of Glasgow.
He passed the Inversnaid torrent,
And he lingered at a beach in Barra,
And at Iona knelt awhile
For the purifying of his harp with meditation and psalms.
In winter, among the mountains,
The harp rejoiced in the whiteness and coldness of snow.
He sat, one week of westerly gale
At fishermen's fires.
He gave them a song for their Minch herring.
Northwards, in Orkney, men piled
A longship with arrows and axes
For venturing (but it was murder, burning, pillage
As far as Man and Scilly).
The seamen stopped their lading. Poets are welcome,
They remind men of the great circle of silence
Where the saga sails forever.

A peaceful ship gave him passage
Through the Pentland Firth, the bow
Thrusting the strenuous waters this way and that.
He saw under a Caithness crag
A fisherman hanging salmon nets to take
Glitterings of sun and wind.
A hawk, in Buchan,
Stooped in a pure plummet.
Later, at a market, at Dee-mouth,
Silver of herring was given for silver mintings.

Harp cried!
    He turned.
        The fruitful sea
Keened, a loathsome hag, at the rock.

Follow the harp, songless one.
Find the bride
Asleep, in a last darkness, among the cleanness of
                    roots and springs.

THE HIGHLANDS AND ISLANDS
ABERDEEN TO THE CLYDE

'FROM THE LONE SHIELING OF THE MISTY ISLAND
MOUNTAINS DIVIDE US, AND THE WASTE OF THE SEAS –
YET STILL THE BLOOD IS STRONG, THE HEART IS HIGHLAND,
AND WE IN DREAMS BEHOLD THE HEBRIDES.'

Anon, *The Canadian Boat Song* (1829)

A journey north
is rather like a journey up
a mountain, as the air
becomes colder and more
moisture-laden.
In the far north of
Scotland, alpine flowers
like the Mountain
Avens descend right down
to the rocky sea coast.

Appreciation by southerners of the Scottish Highlands and of the innumerable islands off the coast of Scotland is a relatively recent phenomenon. That intrepid 18th-century English traveller, Samuel Johnson – while complimentary to the inhabitants – took it for granted that no one else could possibly like the place. The Romantic poets, artists and musicians of the next century disagreed, finding the sublime and divine in every rock, loch and mountain. By the 1920s the myth was of a land untouched by time or history, while today the chief attraction touted by the tourist brochures is of an empty area free from human intrusion, in which to be at one with nature. For Highlanders who know their history, whose families have worked this land for centuries and journeyed back and forth across tumultuous seas, such Sassenach responses are highly provocative – or at best laughable.

Opposite: In contrast to
the bleak, rugged cliffs at
Dunnet Head (right) – the
northernmost point on the
British mainland, where
the lighthouse shines
across the stormy waters of
the Pentland Firth – the
landscape twenty miles to
the west on Kyle of Tongue
(above right) is softer and
more luxuriant, thanks to
its sheltered position and
underlying limestone rock.

Shorelines and Settlements

To Mendelssohn and Wordsworth, the cliffs of eastern Skye and the dark, hexagonal columns of rock in the wave-washed caves of Staffa were proof of divine architecture. But the force that gave this basalt to the waves was more akin to the work of the Devil – some 60 million years ago, molten matter from beneath the earth's crust erupted through volcanoes whose eroded tops now form the islands of Skye, Mull and Rhum. Lava flow and ash created other islands, too, including Canna, Sanday, Eigg and Muck.

As well as volcanic rocks, the north-western Highland coast includes ancient, hard, resistant Torridonian sandstone and even older Lewisian gneiss – the oldest rock of the British Isles, formed some 2,000 million years ago. Off the mainland's northern tip, the old red sandstone of Caithness and Orkney has been chiselled by the sea into tapering stacks that are higher than the cliffs they face. The same red rocks border the Moray Firth; here, evidence of the sea's power of erosion is apparent in the blow-holes, chasms and pinnacles, while signs of human endeavour are apparent in the tiny fishing harbours of the north-facing coast.

Not all the Highland shores present such a stark confrontation, however. Moorlands and forests roll gently down to the sea, and there are long white beaches and great expanses of sand dunes. On both east and west coasts, there are also raised beaches, with their caves and narrow clefts (or 'geos'), suspended far above the present shorelines. At several Highland seaside towns raised beaches form natural esplanades.

Colonization of this region, though continuous, has not been evenly spread. From the Stone Age to the Viking invasions, newcomers left some stretches of the coast well alone, recognizing the limited potential of the soil. But many of the later Highlanders had no such choice. The way of life called 'crofting' first developed almost two hundred years ago as a result of the upheaval and near extinction of the Highlanders. On the coast, crofting involved subsistence tenant farming on land with the least potential, with fishing as a vital supplement.

The ancestor of the
ubiquitous feral town
pigeon, the Rock Dove
now finds its more
successful descendants
returning to invade and
breed into its colonies.
True Rock Doves are now
rare and restricted to the
coasts of remote Scottish
islands.

Sand-eels are an important
food for many seabirds, but
they are also heavily
exploited to make fishmeal
for animal feed. This
overfishing seems to be a
major factor in the recent
serious breeding failures at
many Scottish seabird
colonies.

Crofting still continues, though a few crofters are now owner-occupiers.

A good example of current land use in this area is provided by the Isle of Lewis, in the Outer Hebrides. Crofting townships dot the coast, a NATO airfield and an oil depot envelop Stornoway, and inland, dedicated anglers pay small fortunes to the island's owner for salmon-fishing rights. Gaelic is still spoken in the Hebrides, though not by the landowners. On Shetland and Orkney, however, the influence is Norse and the language, although English, is Scandinavian in accent and vocabulary – as are the place names, both on the islands and the northern mainland coast they face.

The Highland Clearances

The greatest shock that visitors to the Highlands would receive, if they could be transported back in time two centuries, would be to find the land quite heavily populated. But between the late 18th and late 19th centuries, more than half a million people were uprooted and evicted from where they and their families had lived for as long as anyone could remember. This forced removal, in which the destitute population became dispersed to the great cities of the Lowlands, to the harsh Highlands coast or even across the oceans to America and the Colonies, is known as the Highland Clearances.

The beginnings of the Clearances go back to Bonny Prince Charlie's defeat at Culloden after the 1745 uprising against English rule. A rampaging revenge of massacre and pillage ensued and the kilt, bagpipes and Gaelic tongue were outlawed. Loyalists to England and King George III were rewarded with the titles of the Culloden dead and the old clan system was abolished. Tribal lands that had been held by the clan chiefs, who acted as the guardians of their people, were now under the influence of the English aristocracy. The clan chiefs became lairds (private landowners). Seduced into the habits – and debts – of southern gentry, they turned over their estates to new, and highly profitable, forms of land use.

During the late 18th century, the price of wool soared. The lairds introduced great flocks of hardy breeds of sheep, which replaced a native population who knew no other world but the glens which had sustained their myths, music and poetry and a life, which in between bloodthirsty clan wars, was for the most part self-sustaining. More land was taken up by turnips, grown by the lairds as winter feed for the sheep. Vast areas above the sheepwalks were deforested and heather was allowed to grow to provide cover for the grouse that were hunted at a premium by English sportsmen. The old patriarchal ties, whereby the chief looked after his kith and kin and they, in return, would give their lives in battle, were broken. With the end of the clan system, those removed to the coast were forced to turn to crofting, eking out a miserable living from the mostly impoverished soil and often unable to pay their tenant rents to the local laird.

In Sutherland, the vast county of north-west Scotland bordered by three seas, three thousand families were evicted between 1814 and 1820 from 794,000 acres and given a mere 6,000 acres of coastal wasteland. Their crops and villages in the valleys were set on fire, giving the terrified people no time to salvage possessions. With no alternative, they moved to the coast, where none of the promised houses, fishing boats and nets materialized. The hard black cliffs of Scotland's northern coast offered few safe harbours and no shelter from the Arctic winds. Where fishing was possible, or even profitable, as at Helmsdale and Golspie, the refugees were forced to depend on a meagre wage from those who owned the boats and curing houses. Their crofters' rents still had to be paid to the laird, whose control over the people even extended to giving – or refusing – permission for marriages to take place. The same grim story was repeated throughout most of the Highlands and Islands.

In the Outer Hebrides, the new crofters, unable to support themselves on the poor land or pay high rents, were forced to work in the new kelp industry. Great swathes of kelp – giant brown seaweeds – attach themselves by thick rubbery 'holdfasts' to the rock just beyond low-water mark on the sheltered eastern shores. Far bigger than the wrack seaweeds of the intertidal zone, their fronds were hacked off and burned over peat fires to produce a fertilizer rich in iodine, soda and potash. While the lairds sold this to English farmers, the islanders were allowed only the kelp that was washed ashore for their crofts. Elsewhere people were prohibited from using seaweed at all, or forced to pay for it. The collapse of the kelp industry led to new hardships and further clearances.

From the 1870s onwards, the profitable sport of deer-stalking replaced sheep-farming which was no longer giving such satisfactory returns. Another round of evictions of the remaining Highlanders began, and two million acres of fertile soil were laid waste for the sake of sport. Three generations had borne untold sufferings and by the 1880s the Highlanders had had enough. The Crofters' Act 1886 ended the conflict, promising security of tenure and fair rents to the crofters, and establishing a status quo of small farming and fishing communities on the coast and extensive bloodsport estates inland that has changed little to this day.

Coastal Crofting

The coastal lands where many of the victims of the Clearances found themselves were the most barren in the country. Many people huddled in caves beside lochs, and suffered a particularly wretched existence subsisting on a diet of seaweed and shellfish. Bare rocks and waterlogged land held little prospect for cultivation. Other settlers were faced with thin acidic soil, often on

The sheep on the island of Iona (above), in the Inner Hebrides, or on the southern tip of the Shetlands (above right) are not native breeds. From the 1790s onwards, the introduced Cheviot sheep displaced the Highlanders. The depopulation, evident here on Skye by the banks of Loch Greshornish (top right), is apparent everywhere. But the crofting life still survives in places. John Macleod (top left) returned to croft on Skye after years in the Merchant Navy. At Badcall Bay, in the Northwest Highlands, salmon nets (centre) dry in the wind. Crofters have always supplemented their income from the land with small-scale fishing.

such steep inclines that the wind would blow it out to sea along with the newly planted seed.

Only one short stretch of northern Sutherland consisted of fertile ground, based on limestone. The rest of the highland shoreline, of far harder rock, had no lime to enrich the soil. On the west coast, heavy rainfall washed the nutrients from the soil. Sour fibrous peat, vital for fuel, had to be cajoled into growing crops and pastures and many lime-poor areas would only sustain potatoes: when the dreaded blight affected every potato patch in 1847, there was nothing for it but to emigrate, beg or starve. The islands were the worst affected, with Handa losing its last few families. The Highlands and Islands suffered another massive depopulation, and thousands of crofters died in the famine.

Given the stark sterility of most of the land, the treasures of the sea held out the only hope for the crofters. Waves and winds, even unaided by seaweed fertilizer, can produce land that not only blooms with a wealth of flowers but which will fatten sheep and cattle in the spring, grow hay for the winter and sustain a crop of oats.

Known as the *machair* (from the Gaelic word for 'plain'), this strip of land usually lies behind a ridge of dunes and occurs in places throughout Scotland's northern and western coasts. The main constituent of its loamy soil is shellsand – the skeletons of plants and animals from the sea ground up by the surf and blown onshore. These finely ground remnants provide the lime missing from the soil itself and allow a profusion of wild and cultivated plants to flourish, as well as providing nest-sites for a variety of birds, including Corncrakes. Crofters living close to a strip of *machair* took advantage of the rich soil. They also used the wild plants of the *machair* as medicines: Kidney Vetch for cuts and bruises, Spearwort as an anaesthetic, Yarrow as an astringent and Selfheal for ailments of the liver, spleen and kidneys.

The crofters led a hard life, working long hours, and had few comforts in their traditional 'black houses'. Just a few steps separated the cattle's nightly shelter and the hearth. The peat fire was never let out and the only daylight came through one doorway. There was no chimney, so the soot could easily be collected for use as

fertilizer, together with cattle manure and sea-weed. Fish might be hung above the fire to smoke and oil from dogfish liver or seal blubber was used for lamps. Double walls of rough stones supported driftwood timbers on which a layer of sods held the thatch. The excellent insulation and the combined warmth of humans and animals made winters tolerable. These days almost all the crofters' cottages are roofed with corrugated iron. The old black houses are now rarely seen, except on South Uist, and these are equipped with modern amenities and the cattle kept outside. Well beyond retirement age, their inhabitants are still at work with the energy and appearance of people twenty years their junior.

From Fisher Lassies to Factory Ships
The Pentland Firth between Caithness and the Orkneys is one of the most furious stretches of water on earth. Cape Wrath, to the west, is only marginally less dangerous. The notorious Corryvreckan whirlpool spins between Jura and Scarba, and tidal races in the Inner Hebridean sounds threaten every small boat's crossing. The

Outer Hebrides and the Northern Isles face the full force of Atlantic storms. Strong motivation, as well as hefty boats and frequent harbours, were – and still are – prerequisites for setting sail from the north and west Highland coasts. Timber for boat-building was rarely close at hand, and on islands like Eigg or Hoy that rise sheer from the sea, or along the walls of cliff in Sutherland and Caithness, there is no shelter for a model boat, let alone a fishing fleet. For centuries, fish, taken from the lochs and sheltered shores with rod and line or by wading out to nets, sufficed to supplement a meagre diet.

The East Coast, on the other hand, had developed full-time fisheries in the less hazardous North Sea by the early 19th century. In autumn and winter, inshore lines were baited for haddock, whiting and codling. Spring and summer involved longer expeditions for cod and ling, and as the boats grew bigger, the men reached the fringes of the Arctic. There was whaling and sealing, too. Finally, in summer, or whenever they made their appearance, there was the drift-net catch of the herrings – the 'silver darlings'.

Portknockie (top) no longer has a fishing industry, due to competition from foreign trawlers, although only fifty years ago its deep harbour made it the busiest port on the Moray Firth. Meanwhile, Gardenstown (above left), with no such advantages, continues to have a boatbuilding yard and a fishing fleet. In the early 1900s, half the Scottish herring catch was landed at Lerwick, Shetland (above), where men are now more likely to look for jobs in the oil industry than in the fishing trade.

Wick, in the far north-east, was the first port to turn herring fishing into a serious industry, in the early 1800s, with merchants and curers contracting the fishermen and setting up the processing, transport and export necessary to cope with massive catches. Barrels and stores of salt covered every available space and the harbour was jammed with simple-rigged open-decked boats. Women and girls – the 'fisher lassies' – gutted, salted and packed the fish into barrels with immense speed and dexterity – not least because they were paid minimal piecework wages. As the fishery developed, the fisher lassies became itinerant workers following the fleets around the coast. By the mid-19th century, the herring fishery dominated all the Scottish East-Coast fishing ports, but by the turn of the century, the smaller harbours were in decline, while Aberdeen, Peterhead and Fraserburgh cornered all the trade. Today, Peterhead alone thrives as a fishing port, with Aberdeen, once pre-eminent, now a poor second.

There are over seventy villages on the coast between Aberdeen and the Moray Firth whose tiny harbours have hardly withstood the years of decline and neglect. Stone cottages arranged end-on to the sea may still house fishing families, if lived in at all, but the men travel long distances by car to different ports, depending on the movements of the fish. The catch has also changed. By the mid-1970s, a mere 120 years after the initial herring boom, which seemed to one local fisher lassie as if 'man was bent on cleaning the sea of its spawn', this state had almost been reached. Herring quotas are now strictly controlled, so the fleets have diminished and many processing plants closed down.

Yet compared with the fisheries of England's eastern coast, those of Scotland are thriving and, indeed, account for almost three-quarters of the total British catch. Peterhead, on the most easterly point of Scotland's coastline, lands more fish than any other port in Europe, attracting buyers from all over Britain and the Continent. Deckhands, when they are not out at sea, take their gleaming new cars for a Sunday spin. Their weekly wage can top a thousand pounds, due chiefly to the high prices fetched by cod and haddock. The money changing hands in Peterhead's enormous fish market and neighbouring processing plants – some £75 million in 1986 – gives some indication of the continued overfishing of the increasingly scarce stocks.

Of the West-Coast fishing ports, Ullapool, lying on the northern shore of Loch Broom, is the largest. The road into the town was called Destitution Road, after the starving Highlanders who built it in return for food during the 1847 famine. Today, freezer trucks full of fish pound along it, heading for the East-Coast markets. But the greater part of Ullapool's catch — mostly mackerel and herring — is sold direct to Communist bloc factory ships known as 'Klondykers', which anchor in the loch and process the fish.

Ten years ago, the Klondykers caught their own mackerel and herring, but now that non-EEC countries are unable to fish within 200 miles of British territorial waters, they buy their fish from Scottish boats. Working 12-hour shifts seven days a week, the processors aboard the Klondykers gut and fillet 200 tons of fish each day. Most of the fish is exported to Eastern Europe, while the rest goes to the Third World.

Most locals get on well with the Bulgarians, Russians and East Germans who crew and work aboard the Klondykers. Up to 5,000 workers provide a welcome boost to Ullapool's shops and pubs at the end of the tourist season – the Klondykers arrive in September and stay for up to six months. But the situation is precarious. Despite strict quotas, the stocks of herring and mackerel are not increasing. Government departments spend time discussing new ways of taxing the Klondykers, but if they left, many Scottish fishermen – from Ullapool to Aberdeen – would have look elsewhere for business.

At many West-Coast Scottish ports, the decline has already happened. Mallaig, on the Morar

The Dark Green Fritillary butterfly has gone from many of its old haunts. But it survives in north-western Scotland because the steep grassy slopes of the sea cliffs, untouched by agriculture, are bejewelled with Wild Violet, the caterpillar's food plant.

On the north-eastern coast of Scotland, Peterhead's cavernous fish market (above right), the most important in Europe, is filled for the second auction of the day, while over on the western coast, on Loch Broom (right), the crew and fish processors from an East European 'Klondyker' factory ship head for the port of Ullapool, whose shops and pubs benefit from the visitors' money after the tourist season has ended.

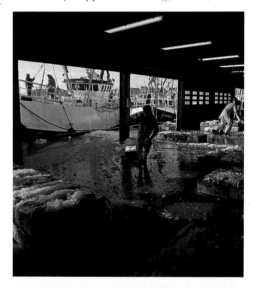

peninsula facing Skye, grew from an evicted crofters' settlement into a thriving fishing port, with rail transport to the Lowlands. The fishermen today are bitter at the fishing industry's plight. Prawns as well as herring and mackerel have become scarce and most of the boats have switched to queen scallops and clams. But illegal trawling for cod, with heavy weights that drag the net across the sea-bed, have damaged the shellfish breeding grounds. Some men go five or six weeks without any income while continuing to pay for diesel fuel and boat repairs. Though optimism for the following season still surfaces with the hope that things may change, many local people have emigrated to the East Coast.

There are too few children now in Mallaig to keep the secondary school open, so they board during the week at the school in the nearest town, Fort William, almost 50 miles away to the southeast. The boys may be able to work on the family boat, but for girls, apart from a job in the processing factory, where the work follows the fortunes of the fishing, the only opportunities lie down south in Glasgow. Life at the other West Coast fishing ports of Kinlochbervie, Lochinver, Oban and Kyle of Lochalsh is much the same.

A very different fish industry has blossomed in the last decade in the sea lochs of the western Scottish coast. Lobster, trout, turbot, plaice, shellfish, and above all salmon, are being farmed on an increasing scale . The system used with the salmon simulates, with freshwater tanks and cages in the loch, the fish's mysterious passage back from the ocean to its place of birth to spawn. The food is dried fish and blood meal, with added doses of pigment, manufactured by a Swiss pharmaceutical company, to give the salmon the colour its wild cousins obtain naturally by eating shellfish. New jobs have been created, but fish farming can damage the environment in two ways. Eutrophication, or overfeeding, of the waters with excess food and fish faeces, results in huge 'blooms' of algae, whose decay imposes a heavy oxygen demand on the water and causes the death of other plants and animals, while impoverishment of the waters, due to large shellfish farms, can deplete the natural resources of plankton, micro-organisms and nutrients.

The Oban ferry leaves for Mull regularly enough, but throughout the western Highlands signposts to harbours with names like Otter Ferry and Stonesferry bear the warning 'No Ferry', and in winter most Hebridean islanders rely on their own boats for transport.

Opposite: The area round Hoy Sound (top left) in the Orkney Islands has suffered serious depopulation since the naval base at Scapa Flow closed in the 1950s. For those who live near Dounreay, the Prototype Fast Reactor (far right) and proposed huge nuclear reprocessing plant may generate jobs, but not without ominous risks.

Although no longer hunted, Otters have undergone a catastrophic decline in the last thirty years. Disturbance has played a part, but the most important cause has probably been pesticide pollution. The remote coasts of northern Scotland are a vital refuge.

Opposite: Oil rigs have intruded into various parts of the wild coastal Highland landscape. Here, rigs are seen being built at Ardersier yard near Inverness (centre left) and 'stacked' – temporarily out of service – in Cromarty Firth (right).

The New Coastal Industries

Along the East Coast of the Highlands, new industries have taken their place alongside the traditional ones – among the most visible manifestations of these new concerns are the giant oil rigs that lie off the coast. Aberdeen is the centre of the North Sea oil and gas industry, with a supply base close beside the yard that once launched the fastest clippers on the seas. In the harbour, rig-support vessels moor alongside Shetland ferries, fishing patrol boats and cargo ships in the shadow of the oil companies' office blocks. Gas arrives at St Fergus Beach, close to Peterhead, and oil at nearby Cruden Bay, from where it is piped to Shetland's huge Sullom Voe terminal to be transferred to tankers.

Lerwick, Shetland's capital, services rigs, Orkney has its own oil terminal and an installation at Stornoway inflates the economy of Lewis. Rig construction works exist on the Cromarty and Moray Firths, on Loch Fyne, Loch Kishorn and the Crowlin Islands and the list does not end there. The industry has been much reduced in recent years, but the damage done by the construction sites is permanent, and abandoned rigs present a huge problem of disposal. Of all the millions of pounds spent, little has gone towards advancing the techniques and readiness to cope with spills and leaks that could at any moment devastate Scottish shores.

Potentially far more devastating than any oil installation, the 1950s experimental fast reactor at Dounreay, on the northern coast of Caithness, has been superseded by a much larger Prototype Fast Reactor. There is a current proposal to build a £300 million Prototype Fast Reactor reprocessing plant ten times the size of the present plant at Dounreay. If the programme goes ahead, ships carrying plutonium will battle through the Pentland Firth or lay up in the Orkneys, and pipelines will disgorge a greater volume of radioactive waste into the sea than at present. Controversy already rages over the local levels of childhood cancers, which the government's own medical statisticians discovered were nearly ten times greater than they had expected.

A Wealth of Wildlife

In the 1960s, *Ring of Bright Water* brought the emerald and azure waters of the Western Isles and one of its best loved creatures to readers and cinema audiences throughout Britain. Gavin Maxwell's animals were of foreign stock, but native Otters still play amongst the rocky reefs, or skerries, off Sandaig, the author's 'Camusfeàrna'. Flexing their sinuous bodies, they swim great distances between rivers and the sea where they hunt crabs, mussels, rock-pool fish, or salmon on their way upstream. Sea caves or evacuated rabbit burrows in the dunes provide their daytime shelter. But like so many animals that were once indigenous to every part of the British Isles, pollution and human persecution and encroachment have banished Otters from

most southern sites. Now fully protected by law, however, Otters still find a refuge in the isolated rivers, lochs and shores of north-western Scotland, which are vital for their survival.

The once-frequent sight of porpoises, whales and dolphins, somersaulting gracefully through the water, has also become rarer, because of pollution from Lowland, Welsh and English shores. But the seas around Orkney and the Shetlands and the north-western coast from Kintyre to Caithness are still visited by these majestic mammals, sometimes chasing shoals of herring to the North Sea.

Other species now rare in the rest of Britain – Red Squirrels, Pine Martens, Polecats and Wild Cats – may make an appearance where Highland forestry plantations reach to the shore. Heavy storms and blizzards force Red Deer down from their favoured slopes to the coast, where they will munch on seaweed as well as grasses in the spray zone. A far less noble creature, the Brown Rat, feeds on shellfish from the rocks or steals eggs and chicks from seabird nests. Another earthbound predator of baby birds, known better as a victim of modern road traffic, is the unassuming Hedgehog. A single pair brought to North Ronaldsay, the northernmost island of Orkney, in 1972 now has a thousand descendants, all growing fat on Arctic Tern and Fulmar chicks. Instead of being killed, the prickly predators are flown to Orkney's Mainland.

The awe-inspiring landscape of Scotland's northern coasts would not be the same without its huge, dramatic colonies of seabirds. On the dizzy cliff-face of Clò Mòr, huge numbers of Kittiwakes as well as Fulmars build their nests. Guillemots colonize the bare ledges, Razorbills nest in smaller groups in crevices and on more sheltered ledges, Shags breed in sea caves and among boulders, and Herring, Great Black-backed and Lesser Black-backed Gulls throng the top of the cliff, while Puffins dig their burrows among the sea pinks on the grassy slopes above.

There are many seabird colonies, each containing tens of thousands of birds, on the cliffs of the Highlands and Islands, but none can compare with those on St Kilda. This small group of islands, whose tiny native population eventually had to be evacuated permanently to the mainland in 1930, to save them from starvation and TB unwittingly introduced by visitors, lies 45 miles beyond the Outer Hebrides. Its mighty cliffs of volcanic rock soar more than 1,300 feet above the angry sea – almost twice the height of those at Clò Mòr. For over a millennium, the St Kildans hunted Gannets, Fulmars and Puffins without exhausting their teeming populations. With hair-raising skill, they scaled the sheer cliffs, using horse-hair nooses on long rods to catch their quarry, which were used to provide food, medicine, bedding, clothing and fuel.

The other creature husbanded by these isolated people was the Soay Sheep. Its diet of seaside vegetation produces a meat rich in iodine

Known to Shetlanders by the Norse name 'Bonxie', the Great Skua is a powerful pirate, harrying other seabirds until they drop their food, and also taking their eggs and chicks. In Britain, it breeds only in the far north of Scotland.

and the St Kildans' dogs were trained to corner each sheep separately, for the Soay – Britain's only truly wild sheep – refuses to be herded. It is thought that the Vikings brought the sheep to St Kilda and it is still the same pure breed: a small, brown, goat-like animal. The rams have impressive coiled horns. Another St Kildan speciality is the St Kildan Field Mouse; the House Mouse did not survive the human-free period before the arrival of the present army station, and the island race of the Field Mouse now often fills its niche. Another singular subspecies of the island is the St Kilda Wren, which lives in holes in the massive cliffs. Of the 28 or more bird species breeding on St Kilda some, like the Lesser Black-backed Gulls, Whimbrels and Red-necked Phalaropes, are newcomers, having colonized St Kilda since the islanders left.

Safe today from human exploitation, the Highland seabirds may still face death from a variety of winged predators, ranging from the Great Black-backed Gulls to the Peregrines.

Undoubtedly, the most spectacular of the birds of prey are the Golden Eagle and White-tailed Sea Eagle. The former species finds sites for its eyries on the cliffs of Jura, Skye and other Hebridean islands. The even larger Sea Eagle became extinct in Britain by 1916, due to human persecution, but chicks from Norway were successfully reintroduced to the island of Rhum, where the species has bred since 1985.

Great and Arctic Skuas are fierce relatives of the gulls that find Shetland, Orkney and the remoter Western Isles much to their liking. Their nests are built on the coastal moorlands and their food is wrested by force from other birds. The Great Skua, known locally as the 'Bonxie', has the habit of harrying gulls, terns and even Gannets in mid-air, forcing them to disgorge their last meal, which the skua then deftly catches. Strong wings enable it to fly hard and fast, and to manoeuvre, even in high winds, so that it gains the advantage over its less agile victims. Skuas also steal many seabird eggs and kill chicks: the Arctic Skuas on Shetland, for instance, have a field day, surrounded by the nests of breeding Eider Ducks, Golden Plovers, Whimbrels and seabirds. The nesting birds on the Shetland island of Fetlar, together with voles and other rodents, have another, much rarer, predator to contend with: the Snowy Owl. A summer visitor from the Arctic, it bred on the island between 1967 and 1975. About twenty young were raised during this period, probably all by the same parents, but these returned to the far north or died. Ornithologists hope, however, that some will one day return to breed.

REGIONAL SUMMARY
THE HIGHLANDS AND ISLANDS

The Highlands and Islands contain about three-quarters of Scotland's coastlines.

PHYSICAL PROFILE

Metamorphic rocks (gneiss, quartzite, schist, slate) and igneous rocks, such as granite, form the dominant rocks of the Highlands and line many coasts. Devonian Old Red Sandstone borders much of the Moray Firth and makes up most of the Orkney Islands. The rocks of the Shetlands, however, are similar to those in the Highlands. Ancient Precambrian rocks occur on the north-western mainland and the Outer Hebrides. Mid-Tertiary volcanic activity in the Inner Hebrides created such basaltic features as Fingal's Cave. Glaciated features include sea lochs (fiords), raised beaches and boulder clay deposits.

Climate: Parts of western Scotland have an average annual rainfall of more than 60 inches (1,524mm), but the eastern coasts have 20–25 inches (508–635mm). The west has milder winters and cooler summers than the east. Northern and western Scotland are exposed to Atlantic storms. Storm waves and high tides produce dangerous seas, with treacherous currents in narrow channels. An impressive maelstrom, caused by a tide race flowing through a narrow channel, can be seen in the Gulf of Corryvreckan between Jura and Scarba. It has claimed many vessels over the years.

HUMAN PROFILE

The region is Great Britain's most thinly populated. Larger settlements include Peterhead (17,000), Inverness (58,300) – the so-called 'capital of the Highlands' – Thurso (26,000) – mainland Scotland's most northerly town – Stornoway (8,000), capital of the Western Isles, and such bustling tourist centres as Kyle of Lochalsh, Fort William and Oban.

Sites of historic interest: Prehistoric sites include a Stone Age village in the Orkneys – Skara Brae – which was buried by dunes 4,500 years ago, and the Callanish stone circle, around 4,000 years old. A monastery founded by St Columba on Iona in AD 563 was the base for converting Scotland to Christianity. Sites associated with Vikings, clan warfare and the 1745 Jacobite Rebellion abound: the Battle of Culloden (1746), when Bonnie Prince Charlie's Highland forces were defeated by the Duke of Cumberland's Army, was the last fought on British soil.

Museums: Arbuthnot Museum, Peterhead; Buckie Maritime Museum; Fishertown Museum, Nairn; Wick Heritage Centre; Thurso Folk Museum; Orkney Natural History Museum, Stromness; Shetland County Museum, Lerwick; Black House Museum, Lewis; Skye Cottage Museum; Colbost Folk Museum, Skye; Rothesay Museum.

Famous personalities: Sir Richard Urqhart and geologist Hugh Miller (born Cromarty), Flora Macdonald (born South Uist).

Marine industry: Aberdeen, Peterhead and Fraserburgh are among Britain's top fishing ports. Smaller fishing ports: Buckie, Macduff, Lossiemouth, Wick, Ullapool, Stornoway, Mallaig, Tarbert.

Commerce/industry: Harris tweed and seaweed are traditional products of the Western Isles. Fair Isle is famed for knitwear.

NATURAL PROFILE

Wildlife: This long and varied coastline is rich in wildlife. It includes all the types of British coastal habitats. There are excellent subtidal and intertidal habitats everywhere with rich algal flora and invertebrate fauna. The Western Isles – comprising the islands of the Outer Hebrides – have Europe's most productive lobster grounds.

Attractions: In Grampian, the Sands of Forvie and Ythan estuary (Britain's fifth largest dunes) have large concentrations of Eider in summer; Longhaven Cliffs; Loch of Strathbeg (RSPB). In the Orkneys, North Hill, Papa Westray (RSPB) is known for its Arctic Terns. In the Shetlands, Fetlar (RSPB), is known for Snowy Owls; Foula has huge seabird colonies. In Highland Region, Loch Fleet, Invernaver, where mountain plants reach sea-level; Handa (RSPB) a rocky isle; St Kilda (proposed World Heritage Site); Eilean na Creige Duibhe (Otters). In Western Isles, the unique *machair*; rich salmon rivers; Loch Druidibeg (South Uist) has Britain's largest surviving colony of native Greylag Geese. In Strathclyde, Loch Gruinart, Islay (RSPB) – famed for wintering geese; Loch Sween is the site of a proposed statutory Marine Nature Reserve. The island of Rhum in the Inner Hebrides is the property of the Nature Conservancy Council. *Footpaths:* There are many magnificent walks, but some are dangerous, especially in the west. *Beauty spots:* Highlights include the Ord of Caithness, the Old Man of Hoy (a stack), the superb Sound of Arisaig, and Fingal's Cave, Staffa. *Beaches in Grampian:* Balmedie, Fraserburgh, Cullen.

CAUSES FOR CONCERN

Pipeline discharges: Untreated sewage is discharged into confined estuaries leading to Cromarty Firth.

Radioactive discharges: Dounreay Prototype Fast Reactor discharges radioactive waste into coastal waters. It is also the site of a proposed Fast Reactor Fuel Reprocessing Plant to which waste will be brought, reprocessed and flown out (200 flights a year).

Agricultural run-off: An estimated 80% of the eutrophication (over-enrichment) in the Ythan estuary between the 1960s and 1980s is the result of run-off of fertilizers.

Inshore overfishing: Mackerel threatened.

Threatened wildlife: Growth of oil industry in the last decade may now present a new threat to Otters in one of the last remaining British strongholds. Prospect of discovery of new oilfields in northern sector of the North Sea raises possible oil contamination of seabird colonies on St Kilda, Flannan Isles, Sula Sgeir, North Rona and Outer Hebrides. Escape of mink from fur farms in Orkney and Shetland may endanger local seabirds.

Pilot Whales are particularly prone to mass stranding, beaching themselves and dying out of water. Few are seen off Scotland now, but until the early 1900s, Shetland and Orkney islanders used to drive the animals onshore, killing them for their blubber.

A bird of traditional hay meadows, the Corncrake has declined as these flower-strewn swards have disappeared from the countryside. The *machair* grassland on the coasts of the Scottish islands is now one of the Corncrake's last haunts in Britain.

THE WESTERN LOWLANDS

ALASDAIR GRAY

He was flying up a wide and winding firth with very different
coasts. To the right lay green farmland with clumps of trees and
reservoirs in hollows linked by quick streams. On the left were
mountain ridges and high bens silvered with snow, the sun
striking gold sparkles off bits of sea loch between them. On both
shores he saw summer resorts with shops, church spires and
crowded esplanades, and clanging ports with harbours full of
shipping. Tankers moved on the water, and freighters and white-
sailed yachts. A long curving feather of smoke pointed up at him
from a paddle steamer churning with audible chunking sounds
toward an island big enough to hold a grouse moor, two woods,
three farms, a golf course and a town fringing a bay. This island
looked like a bright toy he could lift up off the smoothly ribbed,
rippling sea, and he seemed to recognize it. He thought, 'Did I
have a sister once? And did we play together on the grassy top of
that cliff among the yellow gorse-bushes? Yes, on that cliff behind
the marine observatory, on a day like this in the summer holidays.
Did we bury a tin box under a gorse root in a rabbit hole? There
was a half-crown piece in it and a silver sixpence dated from that
year and a piece of our mother's jewellery, and a cheap little
notebook with a message to ourselves when we grew up. Did we
promise to dig it up in twenty-five years? And dug it up two days
later to make sure it hadn't been stolen? And were we not
children then? And was I not happy?'

THE WESTERN LOWLANDS
THE CLYDE TO GRETNA

'NE'ER BY THE RIVULETS I STRAYED, AND NE'ER UPON MY CHILDHOOD WEIGHED
THE SILENCE OF THE GLENS.
INSTEAD OF SHORES WHERE OCEAN BEATS, I HEAR THE EBB AND FLOW OF STREETS.'

Alexander Smith, *Glasgow* (1857)

The Fulmar's phenomenal increase and spread along all British coasts – from the first pairs in Shetland some two hundred years ago to 300,000 pairs today – has been attributed to genetic variation, climatic changes, and the processing of fish at sea, providing plenty of offal for the birds to eat.

The Firth of Clyde lies on the gigantic fault in the rock strata that divides the hard granites, schists and gneisses of the Scottish Highlands from the softer, younger Devonian limestones and sandstones of the Lowlands. To the north of this Highland Boundary Fault lies a harsh, mountainous terrain of poor soil, dissected by a labyrinth of lochs and rivers. To the south, the land changes abruptly to gentler hills and plains, less acidic soils and rocks bearing great seams of coal. The third largest population centre in the British Isles lies on the south-west side of the division, at Glasgow, while most of the Highlands to the north, although fringed with a scattering of settlements around the coast, are almost bereft of human presence.

The Rise and Fall of the Clyde

Before the upper Clyde was dredged in the 18th century, it was shallow and unnavigable. Glasgow's main port was Irvine, almost thirty miles away at the mouth of the river. After the great dredging programme, Glasgow's medieval centre was replaced with solid Georgian mansions built by the tobacco lords who made their fortunes from transatlantic trade in the golden leaves. Then, during the Industrial Revolution, the city experienced a meteoric expansion, as the Ayrshire and Lanarkshire coalfields began to supply the means to power iron and steel furnaces as well as an unrivalled concentration of heavy engineering and shipbuilding.

The impulse that propelled Britain into its world-dominating position no longer has its economic base of docks, yards and factories. Lay-offs are now the order of the day in the Clydeside shipbuilding firms, steel has to be imported and almost all the manufacturing businesses that evolved alongside the key industries have had to follow them to the wall. But the Royal Navy still maintains a strong presence with its nuclear submarine fleet, for which the Firth of Clyde is the gateway to the oceans of the world.

The road to the Clyde from the western Highlands forks at the head of Loch Long. The quicker route follows the bonny, bonny banks of Loch Lomond. The other road and the railway wind along the densely forested shore of Loch Long before cutting across to Gare Loch. From the brooding shadows and claustrophobic atmosphere of Loch Long's narrow fiord, where the wind ruffles the water into angry-looking, choppy waves, the wider, calmer waters of the neighbouring loch seem free from any menace.

It is, however, the land around Gare Loch that is subject to disturbance – felled trees, massive ditches and half-formed embankments, all behind coils of barbed wire set atop electric fences. This is the new extension of the Faslane submarine base, awaiting delivery of the Trident missile system. The Americans, too, have a home for their nuclear submarines in this area – in Holy Loch, which joins the Clyde alongside Loch

Long. A variety of military installations litters these crooked fingers of water that reach towards the most heavily populated region of Scotland.

There are currently more nuclear reactors at sea in submarines than on land in power stations. Since the early 1960s, Western powers have admitted losing seven nuclear submarines be-

Elevators stand idle on Clydeside docks (above) since their decline in recent years. In the 19th century, they exported cotton, then pig-iron, and later steel and machinery, but now very few goods are manufactured on Clydeside.

Between Drummore, on Luce Bay, and the Mull of Galloway, the rich pastoral landscape (left) rolls towards the coast, which is nurtured by the warm Gulf Stream current that gives this part of south-west Scotland its mild climate. This is a largely unspoiled, little-visited area, although intensive farming has obliterated rich grassland communities of plants.

Opposite: Kircudbright Bay, like many of the estuaries along the south-western coast of Scotland, has remained free of development – in contrast to the Clyde. The thousand-foot-high isolated rocky dome of Ailsa Craig (bottom left) is an important breeding site for seabirds, with about 70,000 nesting there each summer, over half of them Gannets.

A gentle giant of the shark world, the Basking Shark eats only plankton. It is in need of protection because it has a low rate of reproduction and suffers from pollution and from hunting – for its rich liver oil.

Opposite: Iron ore and coal destined for Ravenscraig steelworks are conveyed from massive ships at the Firth of Clyde's Hunterston deep-water terminal (centre, far right) to waiting railway trucks. The cooling towers of Chapelcross nuclear power station rise from the Solway Firth's northern saltmarshes (below, far right). The reactor was forced to shut down for two years after an accident in 1967.

At the end of the First World War, British shipbuilders concentrated on what they could still do best – creating one-off, high-quality designs – while other countries started building more profitable types of standardized vessels. British pre-eminence was briefly rekindled after the Second World War, but the family managements' traditional approach failed to stem the competition from the reborn German and Japanese industries. By the mid-1970s, Britain's share of the world's orders for ships was down to a paltry three per cent. Closures had already begun, and the Clyde was ripe for axing.

The Clyde had not lost its militancy, but with the full-scale dismantling of the industry few of the workforce were left to carry on the fight. For many, it is the early years of the struggle that are remembered as heroic. In one of his last speeches, Lord 'Manny' Shinwell, one of the leaders of the 'Forty Hours' strike, said in answer to critics on both right and left that no one could understand the Clydeside spirit – why people fought and risked their lives, and why, too, they accepted only partial gains – unless they had experienced the poverty of Glasgow between the 1890s and the Second World War.

The Clydeside Coast

Not all the Clyde was a harsh world of smog, sweat and grime, however. Among the newly launched ships, the cargo vessels chugging in and out of dock and the fishing fleets were to be seen the cheery funnels and smoke of the paddle steamers. These carried the more fortunate Glaswegians and Clydesiders to the holiday resorts, just a few miles away, off the Cowal peninsula, the Isle of Arran, Kintyre and the gaps between the industrial towns of Ayrshire. Small coastal communities like those of Dunoon, across the firth from Gourock, Rothesay, on the Isle of Bute, and Millport, on Great Cumbrae, expanded rapidly with the introduction of the new ferry services in the 19th century. Of the few remaining piers in this area, Wemyss Bay still has its Edwardian structure, from which the sole surviving paddle steamer, the *Waverley*, continues to do the rounds of the Clydeside resorts.

Few industrial centres in Britain can boast such countryside and coastline on its doorstep. The unyielding heights of cliff and mountain and the open, softly moulded lowlands with abrupt volcanic intrusions are expressions of the complex geology on either side of the Highland Boundary Fault, which cuts through Kintyre, Arran, Bute and Helensburgh. Steep moorland valleys running between mountains whose summits disappear in the mists, gentle hills rising above crescents of red rocks and sand, farmland, forests and shorelines of chasms and caves have for years provided inspection and relaxation for the weary city dwellers of this region.

Ten miles from Girvan on the coast of Ayr, a well-crusted pie of blue-grey speckled granite floats on the horizon. When the islet was owned

by the Marquis of Ailsa, the sole tenant of Ailsa Craig paid his rent by selling feathers gathered from the huge colony of Gannets that to this day breeds on this remnant of an ancient volcano. In the surrounding waters of the Northern Channel, the sleek forms of Basking Sharks, with their large, floppy, triangular dorsal fins, are sometimes seen in late spring. This is when their chief prey, the tiny transparent crustacean *Calanus*, which also forms the herring's staple diet, reaches its peak population, occurring in swarms of countless millions. Harmless to anything bigger than such animal plankton, the Basking Shark is nevertheless under threat from Girvan fishermen, who still hunt it with harpoons for its rich liver oil.

Down the coast at Ballantrae runs a long spit of flat grey stones. Ringed Plovers nest here, both the birds and their eggs superbly camouflaged against the shingle. Terns and Oystercatchers breed here, too. Mats of vegetation draped across the stones are made up of the inevitable Sea Campion, which grows alongside the much scarcer Oyster Plant, a rarity of northern shores.

The Solway Firth

Further south, on the Solway Firth, stands the forlorn unpainted tower of the disused lighthouse at Southerness which once lit the passage to and from Dumfries for the schooners trading with America. The ships eventually grew too large for the River Nith, and Dumfries, like Annan, Creetown and Kirkcudbright, relinquished its quayside business to the Cumbrian ports across the firth. Industries based on water mills flourished and fell, leaving little today to disturb the dunes, sand-flats and saltmarshes in the series of deep bays and inlets that make up the northern Solway coast. True, there is the nuclear power station at Annan, and a scattering of chemical and oil concerns, but the Solway Firth still enjoys the reputation of being Britain's least polluted large estuary.

Fishing on the firth has declined for the lack of local markets but mussel beds and haaf nets for salmon are still tended in the river mouths and bays. Kirkcudbright's harbour gives mooring to as many fishing boats as pleasure craft – though much of the work is taking out visiting sea anglers. Above Kirkcudbright the waters of the Dee have been harnessed by Tongland power station, with a ladder of 29 pools allowing trout and salmon to bypass the dam.

Above all, it is the wealth of wintering geese that makes the Solway such an important site for nature. The mudflats and saltmarshes of Caerlaverock, by the Nith estuary, ring with the wild sounds of the geese that arrive each year from the north to spend the winter on these lonely shores. Visitors include the entire population of some 8,000 Barnacle Geese from Spitsbergen in the Arctic Ocean, up to 5,000 Pinkfooted Geese from Iceland and Greenland and small numbers of Greylag Geese from Iceland.

The graceful arc of Portpatrick's seafront houses is only 21 miles from Ireland. In the late 19th century, storms destroyed the harbour piers and the town's history as a port came to an end. Today, it depends on the holiday trade.

They feed by day on the rich vegetation of grasses, sedges and rushes that covers the six-mile-long strip of pasture just inland. Reclaimed from the water by the natural process of succession, this is one of the largest tracts of saltmarsh in Britain which has not been drained by human hand. Cattle share the rich grazing with the geese. The Barnacle Geese are particularly fond of the clover that grows beneath the other plants. As dusk falls, the geese flight in to roost on the foreshore and are joined there by large numbers of dabbling ducks and waders.

Few people visit the Solway coast. It is on the way to nowhere, save for the shortest crossing from the British mainland, at Stranraer, to Belfast, about 60 miles to the west. The precipitous cliffs of the Mull of Galloway, the sombre shingle of Burrow Head and the mud, sand and marshes of Kirkcudbright and Dumfries are easier to reach by boat than over land and military use has put out of bounds the rocky headlands of Abbey Head and the dunes and warren at the head of Luce Bay.

Often blanketed by grey skies and washed by driving rain, the moors and hills of Galloway descending to the Solway Firth sometimes wear a forsaken air. The merest glimmer of light, however, transforms this southern edge of Scotland into one of the most seductive, unspoilt and varied stretches of coast outside the Highlands.

The Oyster Plant grows on coastal shingle in northern Britain. Always rare, it is now retreating even further north and decreasing, perhaps because of gravel extraction or maybe in response to minor climatic changes.

Stormy weather suits the wild isolation of the Mull of Galloway, whose rugged headland forms Scotland's southernmost point. An RSPB reserve has been established here, with a seabird colony and a wealth of wild flowers.

REGIONAL SUMMARY
THE WESTERN LOWLANDS

The distance between the Clyde estuary and the Scottish-English border near Gretna Green is about 290 miles (467km), excluding estuaries. The head of St Luce Bay is a bombing range. There is also a military zone east of Kirkcudbright Bay.

PHYSICAL PROFILE
From Helensburgh on the Clyde estuary to Girvan, the coast borders Scotland's Central Lowlands. Most of the rocks are of the Devonian and Carboniferous periods, including coal measures in the Ayr coalfield. Beyond Girvan, the coast skirts the Southern Uplands, which are made of older (Ordovician and Silurian) rocks. In the far south there are younger strata and granite intrusions. The island of Ailsa Craig, the remains of an ancient volcano, lies west of Girvan. The sea inlets along the coast were flooded at the end of the Ice Age.

Climate: Because the region faces the Atlantic, it is wetter than eastern Scotland. Glasgow has an average annual rainfall of 37 inches (940mm) and Wigtown 40 inches (1,016mm). Average temperatures in January are around 40°F (4°C); frosts and snow are unusual. July temperatures average 58°–60°F (14°–16°C).

HUMAN PROFILE
The densely populated Clyde estuary includes Glasgow (765,000), Clydebank (51,900), Dumbarton (76,900), Port Glasgow (22,600) and Greenock (59,000). South of Greenock there is a string of ports and resorts, including Irvine (33,000) and Ayr (49,500). The southern coasts are less populated and tourism is generally underdeveloped. The chief centre is Dumfries (32,000), an old border fortress.

Sites of historic interest: St Ninian founded a church on the Isle of Whithorn in AD 397 – the present ruins are 13th-century. Near by is St Ninian's Cave, and the 10th-century Chapel Finian which stands on the shore where Irish pilgrims bound for Whithorn once landed. A major battle in 1263 at Largs, where Alexander III defeated the Vikings, is re-enacted every September. Culzean Castle (1790), one of Robert Adam's finest works, is owned by the NT for Scotland.

Museums: City of Glasgow Art Gallery and Museum; Old Glasgow Museum; McLean Museum, Greenock Maritime Museum, Irvine; Tam O'Shanter Museum Ayr; Burns Cottage and Museum, Alloway; Whithorn Priory and Museum; Gem Rock Museum, Creetown; Stewartry Museum, Kirkcudbright; Dumfries Museum.

Famous personalities: According to legend, St Patrick was born at Old Kilpatrick on the Clyde estuary; James Watt (born Greenock); Robert Burns (born Alloway, now part of Ayr); American naval hero Paul Jones (born Kirkbean).

Marine industry: Though shipbuilding has declined, the Clyde estuary remains famous for its ships, such as the *Cutty Sark*, built at Dumbarton, and the *Lusitania, Queen Mary, Queen Elizabeth* and *Queen Elizabeth 2*, built at Clydeside. Fishing ports include

Stranraer, which has ferry services to Northern Ireland, and Annan.

Commerce/industry: Glasgow and the Clyde estuary form a great industrial conurbation, making engineering products, iron and steel, textiles, chemicals, whisky and oil rigs. There is a huge power station at Inverkip. Hunsterston nuclear power station and an iron-ore complex are located at Fairlie.

NATURAL PROFILE
Wildlife: This short but varied coastline includes sand-flats, dunes, beaches, shingle spits, lochs, mud-flats and saltmarshes. Low-lying habitats are interspersed with rocky islands and sea-shores with rock pools, cliffs, headlands and raised beaches. Many cliffs are rich in flowers; some have caves. The north side of the Solway Firth has extensive sand/silt flats and saltmarshes. The Upper Solway as a whole is of international importance for wintering wildfowl.

Attractions: In Strathclyde, the Clyde islands include Great and Little Cumbrae, while Ailsa Craig is the main seabird site, with a large gannetry; Culzean Country Park (NT for Scotland) includes 3.4 miles (5.5km) of coast; Ballantrae (Scottish Wildlife Trust) has shingle spit and lagoons. In Dumfries and Galloway, sea cliffs of the Mull of Galloway (RSPB) – remarkably rich floristically; Torrs Warren, outstanding acid dunes with important plant and animal life; Caerlaverock and Eastpark (both NCC) are excellent places for viewing wildfowl. *Footpaths:* South of Ayr to the Heads of Ayr; Culzean Castle to Port Carrick; Finnarts Bay to Ballantrae; Jubilee Path (NT) from Kippford to Rockcliffe. *Beaches in Strathclyde:* Ardrossan, Saltcoats, Irvine, Troon, Prestwick, Ayr, Turnberry, Girvan. Care must be taken on some beaches in Solway Firth because of fast-incoming tides.

CAUSES FOR CONCERN
Direct dumping: Clyde estuary has the UK's second biggest sewage dumpsite after the Thames – 1.6 million tons of contaminated sewage sludge is dumped at Garroch Head every year. Garroch Head is also a dumpsite for industrial waste.

Radioactive discharges: Hunterston nuclear power station discharges slightly radioactive cooling water into coastal waters. Currents from Sellafield (Windscale) reprocessing plant, Cumbria, carry plutonium discharges into the Irish Sea, north to Scotland and around the mainland into the North Sea. Plutonium levels off the coast of south-western Scotland are 60 times the average background plutonium level.

Oil pollution: Run-off from both industrial and private users into the Clyde.

Inshore overfishing: Basking Sharks may be over-fished on this coast.

Threatened wildlife: Whisky distillery on Islay once extracted peat from Duich Moss, which threatened wintering Greenland White-fronted Geese (flocks of international importance). This practice has now been abandoned.

In late summer, almost every saltmarsh and sea cliff around Britain's shores is dotted with the pink flowers of Thrift. Its success is perhaps partly a result of the resistance of its soft, springy cushions to trampling.

The Raven was long ago driven from southern and eastern Britain, accused of killing lambs, although it feeds chiefly on sheep carrion. Still widespread in northern and western areas, it often nests on coastal cliffs, especially now that many uplands have lost their sheep due to afforestation.

Food from the sea

Now that fish has become recognized as a healthy alternative to meat, Britain is experiencing a revival of the traditional wet fish shop. Displays of seafood amid mounds of ice combine artistry with a sense of the surreal, as scallops ride on the backs of salmon, prawns appear from the mouths of mullet, and lobsters and crabs wave their claws at passers-by. Despite such bizarre arrangements, the mix of colours, shapes and

textures is superb. So, too, is fish eaten at the seaside within hours of being landed; fresh cod and haddock, or herrings transformed into pale pink kippers by oak-smoking – their flavours are unforgettable.

Today, most fish is processed, but the quayside auctions and wholesale markets, like Billingsgate, where porters bustle to and fro across the slippery floor, ensure the catch reaches inland fishmongers within a couple of days. Specialities, including jellied eels from Cockney London, Arbroath smokies, stall snacks of vinegary cockles, winkles, shrimps and prawns, Colchester and Whitstable oysters, and, above all, the original take-away meal, fish and chips, confirm the importance of seafood to the British palate. The future of this national asset and pleasure is sadly now under considerable pressure from both pollution and overfishing.

CUMBRIA AND
THE ISLE OF MAN

HUNTER DAVIES

That's Whitehaven, though it could be a chunk of any old port, with that dour harbour wall and that boring-looking warehouse. How strange to think that John Paul Jones, founder of the American navy, was an apprentice on a Whitehaven ship and that some years later, in 1778, he tried to capture the harbour for the greater glory of his newly emerging nation. Someone valued Whitehaven – if just for dopey nationalistic reasons.

That's Sellafield. Though don't go too near, my child, even photographs can hurt. How weird to think they picked on such an exquisitely empty coast to frighten us all. Dopey political reasons? Specious economic arguments which appeared to say we have no choice?

That's Barrow, though I don't go too near these days. I made a vow, for purely silly reasons, never to venture into the town again. Oh, just a tease. Stir them up. Annoy them into civic action. I could well have said it about Distington or Workington or Frizington, sad west Cumbrian towns where labour is lost, industry worn out, spirits sagging. Political and economic reasons? Let's forget that nasty stretch up there, they think in Whitehall, then it might go away and not bother us any more.

That's Cumbria. Though who knows Cumbria who only Lakeland knows. All Nature's wonders are there, in miniature, handy for every human, magic for every mortal. But few wonder or wander outside that neat little, snug little Lakeland National Park, so well protected by our heritage, so nicely preserved in our poetry.

Cumbria's coastal life gets forgotten and ignored, though can you call it life, when round the corner death might fall out, while we stand to attention, wrapped up in ourselves. Awed by Grasmere and Rydalwater. Blind to Barrow and Workington. Out on the edges of the map and of the mind, it's all Cumbria.

Hunter Davies

CUMBRIA AND THE ISLE OF MAN
GRETNA TO GRANGE-OVER-SANDS

'... THE COMB OF THE WAVE RICHLY CLUSTERED AND CRISPED IN BREAKING,
THEN ... UNFOLDING TILL IT RUNS IN THREADS AND THRUMS TWITCHING DOWN
THE BACKDRAUGHT TO THE SEA AGAIN.'

Gerard Manley Hopkins, journal (Isle of Man, 19 August 1872)

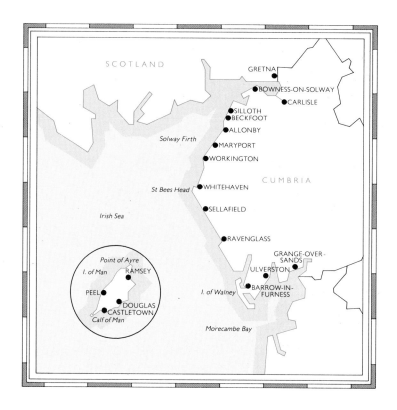

The Black Guillemot is the scarcest of Britain's breeding auks, nesting along northern and western sea cliffs. It is also the most coastal auk outside the breeding season, spending winter close to the rocky cliffs on which it nests.

The north coast of Cumbria is fringed by the saltmarshes of the Solway Firth, across whose choppy waters appear the hills of Galloway, emerging from the mist. Inland lies one of England's loveliest regions, the Lake District. Its mountains approach the sea near Workington and come even closer in the south as the shore retreats before the great golden expanse of sand fringing Morecambe Bay. This can be a magical coast, as alluring as the splendid country behind it. But the old coal and iron ports and the shipbuilding town of Barrow-in-Furness contrast strongly with the lakes and fells which have inspired poets and painters for generations, and the largest and most dramatic intrusion on the British landscape by the nuclear power industry lies on the Cumbrian shoreline.

The origins of the shipbuilding firm of Vickers that still dominates Barrow-in-Furness lie in the town's mid-19th-century industrial boom. Today, the workers, who live on Vickerstown estate, constructed by the company in 1901 on Walney Island opposite Barrow, build nuclear submarines.

A Coast of Contrasts
Descending from Scafell Pike, England's highest summit, along the green banks of Wastwater and the clear, bubbling waters of the River Irt, the view along the coastal plain would once have been of rolling farmland as far as the eye could see. Today, it is dominated by a strange array of concrete, steel and brickwork shapes, covering an area the size of a small town. This is Sellafield, or Windscale as it used to be called, site of Britain's first civil nuclear power station, Calder Hall, built in 1956. It was here that the techniques of reprocessing spent nuclear reactor fuel

were developed, and it is from here that radio-active waste is discharged into the Irish Sea.

Protected by high wire fences and security patrols, about four hundred buildings – flat and low, tall and thin, busy, abandoned or in the process of construction – are scattered between four cooling towers and the sea as if a group of giant children had been squabbling over a box of huge toy building blocks. Rather than lingering in Sellafield's ominous shadow, it is more pleasant to travel north ten miles or so to St Bees Head and the Cumbria Coastal Way. As the path dips along the grassy tops of the weathered red sandstone cliffs, the Isle of Man can be seen from the closest mainland point. There are few trees to break the wind here – only the odd stunted clump of Hawthorn. Yarrow, Knap-weed, Bloody Cranesbill, Thrift and Sea Campion line the path, providing splashes of colour. The coastal way leads into the port of White-haven, a few miles north of St Bees Head.

Above Whitehaven's quayside, a battered iron chute leading from two rain-streaked concrete cylinders awaits the arrival of two small ships bringing phosphates from a bulk carrier an-chored out to sea. The cargo is destined for the largest chemical plant in Western Europe, up on the hill behind the town.

Today, 90 per cent of Whitehaven's harbour dues come from the plant's imports – without them the port would not be viable – although the local population pays a price. Residents living near the factory have learned to tolerate the fumes, but they do complain of suds on their windows – the wastes from the production of toiletry and detergent bases. In the port, a few trawlers from Scotland, Ireland and the Isle of Man and local seine-netters attract the scream-ing gulls, but pollution scares have brought the fishing business to a low ebb. Local people are wary of eating flatfish, which feed on the sea-bed where some of the discharged radioactive ele-ments from Sellafield settle. To the south of the harbour, beside the landscaped park of the disused Wellington coal pit, a notice warns against swimming on account of nearby sewage outfalls.

In the town's old centre, the attractive double-fronted, Georgian terraced houses, built during the heyday of the town, have been restored to their original designs, with graceful pillared porches, wrought iron railings and sash windows

St Bees Head (above) with its seabirds, flowers and remnants of an ancient nunnery, is the most popular coastal beauty spot for local people, and is, thankfully, not yet spoiled. By contrast, other parts of the Cumbrian coast are marred by industrial development, much of it abandoned, and just north of Seascale there is the ugly sprawl of the nuclear reprocessing plant of Sellafield, formerly Windscale (left).

set off by individual pastel colours. Buildings around the harbour – like the old quayside bath house embossed with mermaids and the figure of Neptune – have yet to regain their former splendour.

From Tobacco to Tourism

Whitehaven was once the third largest port in the country, cornering in the 18th century the tobacco trade from the American colonies before Glasgow became pre-eminent in this respect. Having developed colliers with a double-layered hull strong enough to sit aground in the tidal Cumbrian harbours, local shipowners could send their vessels across the Atlantic with a certain amount of confidence. Even so, the eight- or ten-week journey was not without its hazards, for which the merchants would partially cover themselves by withholding wages until the tobacco had been landed and certified.

The outward cargoes included woollen shawls, bonnets, leather boots, saddles and bridles, saucepans, gunpowder, glassware and the odd feather bed. Some of these items were manufactured locally but many were imported along with raw materials from the Lowlands, from Ireland, the Isle of Man, Bristol and Rotterdam, further increasing the traffic at the port. Timber, often brought back with the tobacco, was used to build more ships, and the tobacco itself was usually re-exported, mainly to France.

Various factors contributed to the decline of Whitehaven's tobacco trade. Not least was the conflict of interests between the colliery owners, who needed quayside loading facilities and were content with a tidal harbour, and the merchants, for whom a deep-water harbour was vital for the ever increasing tonnage of trading ships. But it was the American War of Independence that put paid to the easy advantages of colonial trade.

Things that are bad are 'worse than a wet weekend in Workington' in North-west parlance. A steel town of the Victorian age and a steel town still, Workington – unlike its neighbours, Whitehaven and Maryport – has not been favoured by much beautification. But its deep-water port still operates, exporting local open-cast coal and a diminishing cargo of products from the local steelworks.

In recent years, the job of clearing up and landscaping the slag heaps and assorted industrial waste dumped over centuries on the beaches of the Cumbrian ports has begun. Designs for marinas flourish on the drawing boards and visions of cars and coachloads lured from the Lake District down to the coast gleam in planning officers' eyes. A factor that will affect the chances of a thriving tourist trade is the public's confidence in Sellafield.

The Ravenglass Estuary

Three rivers from the Lakeland dales, the Irt, the Mite and the Esk, form the Ravenglass estuary, where a settlement dates from Roman times.

Although only five miles down the coast, the atmosphere of this place is a world away from the ugly sprawl of Sellafield. Shallow creeks wend their way through the lowtide sand-flats, while the peaceful scene is completed by rolling dunes and distant mountains.

Ravenglass is the site of a major breeding colony of Black-headed Gulls, and important research into these noisy, intensely sociable birds has been carried out there at the nature reserve, which is closed to visitors during the birds' breeding season. Although many gulls still nest, there has been a decline in numbers over the past ten years or so. This has puzzled conservationists, who have not ruled out the possibility of pollution as the cause of the decline. Other birds that breed here include Arctic, Common, Sandwich and Little Terns, Oystercatchers, Ringed Plov-

The Coralroot Orchid grows only in a few woods and dune slacks in the north of Britain. It is a saprophyte, living on dead organic matter among the damp peat in which it roots, and thus has little need for the chlorophyll that other plants use to make their food.

Cranes at Workington (above right) load rails from the town's steelworks on to ships for export worldwide, as they have done for over a hundred years, although in ever-diminishing quantities. A striking contrast is provided at Birkrigg Common (right), where the evidence of a pre-industrial age is preserved by the circles of prehistoric stones in their splendid setting above the sands of Morecambe Bay.

ers, Red-breasted Mergansers and Shelduck.

The guano from the gullery acts as a natural fertilizer, encouraging the growth of rich swards of Ragwort, nettles and other plants. On the sand dunes, an impressive variety of plants includes Portland Spurge and Sea Spurge. Spurges have sometimes been dubbed 'the cacti of the Old World'; many have similar adaptations to cacti, with succulent leaves for water storage, which enable them to survive in the dry atmosphere of the dunes. Life on the sand dunes is difficult in other ways, too, with high levels of salt and exposure to strong winds and blowing sand. Interesting plants, such as the scarce Isle of Man Cabbage, grow on the shingle at Ravenglass and animals found there include all six species of Britain's native amphibians – namely, the Natterjack Toad, the Great Crested Newt, the

Common Frog, the Common Toad, the Smooth Newt and the Palmate Newt.

The Isle of Man

Across the Irish Sea, almost half-way to Ulster, lies the Isle of Man, from whose mountainous landscape every country in the British Isles is visible. With its own myths and history, the island has a parliament that goes back for more than a thousand years. Its cultural links are Celtic, with a touch of Viking, but its trading – or, more often, its smuggling – contacts have been with the English mainland.

On the Calf of Man, a wild islet off the southwest tip of the main island, visitors to the bird observatory are rewarded by the sight of a multitude of seabirds – Razorbills, Guillemots, Black Guillemots, Puffins, Storm Petrels and

Douglas, the Isle of Man's largest town and capital since the 1860s, is a graceful though busy place, in the forefront of the island's growing economy. Increasing numbers of ships register here, along with companies seeking the tax advantages, and many of the population are 'comeovers' rather than native-born Manx people.

Separated from the south-western point of the Isle of Man by a narrow, tide-ripped channel, the Calf of Man has a bird observatory where migrant birds are ringed and there is an impressive seabird population.

Two populations of crows, genetically isolated during the last Ice Age, gave rise to the two modern races of the species: Carrion and Hooded Crows. The former is found over most of Britain, while the latter – shown here – haunts the rocky coasts and uplands of the North-west.

St Patrick's Isle, with its ruined medieval castle and cathedral, is joined to the mainland of the Isle of Man by a causeway, forming a natural breakwater for Peel harbour. The large fishing fleet that was based at Peel only a few years ago has dwindled as the herrings have become overfished.

Manx Shearwaters. The last-named, which occur more commonly in Scotland and Wales, returned to the Isle of Man in 1967 after an absence of a hundred and fifty years; they acquired their name because of the fondness of the ancient Lords of Man for their flesh. By the steep slate cliffs where the seabirds build their nests, their cries are drowned by the tidal race round the Chicken Rock and between the Calf and the main island. Choughs speed across the water to return to their nesting caves, while Ravens soar and dive, sometimes mobbed by Hooded Crows.

In contrast to this flourishing life, deformed and damaged fish have been found around the Isle of Man – the culprit is thought to be sewage waste. But the Manx fishing trade is near extinction anyway. Herring fishing in the Irish Sea is restricted to protect against overkill, and only a handful of Manx boats compete with the Scottish or Fleetwood men.

Tourists and multinational business companies – the first seeking a world with different customs and history, the second fiscal independence – come to the Isle of Man. But the island itself is not immune from the activities on the Cumbrian coast and may soon take Britain to the International Court at The Hague to press for the closure of Sellafield.

REGINAL SUMMARY

CUMBRIA AND THE ISLE OF MAN

The distance around Cumbria, excluding estuaries and islands, is about 90 miles (145km). The Isle of Man is about 32 miles (54km) long and 13 miles (21km) wide. The island lies about 30 miles (48km) from the nearest point on the English mainland.

PHYSICAL PROFILE

Most of the coastlands are underlain by Permian to Jurassic rocks. Carboniferous coal seams appear between Maryport and St Bees Head. The Isle of Man, which is geologically similar to the Lake District, consists mainly of Manx Slate (largely Cambrian), with younger rocks on the margins. Most coastal areas are masked by glacial deposits or river alluvium.

Climate: The climate is mild and sunny, with average temperatures of about 41°F (5°C) in January and 59°F (15°C) in July. The annual rainfall generally averages 37–40 inches (940–1,106mm).

HUMAN PROFILE

Carlisle (71,500), the capital of Cumbria, is the largest settlement. Industrial towns include Workington (27,600), Whitehaven (26,700) and Barrow-in-Furness (61,700). Tourist resorts include Silloth, Allonby, St Bees and, on the Isle of Man, the capital Douglas (19,900).

Sites of historic interest: Hadrian's Wall ended at Bowness-on-Solway. Carlisle was a Roman base. Other Roman forts to the south included Beckfoot, Maryport (Roman Alauna) and Ravenglass (Glannaventa). The ruins of Furness Abbey (1127) are a reminder of past ecclesiastical glories.

Museums: Museum and Art Gallery, Carlisle; Maritime Museum, Maryport; Museum and Art Gallery, Whitehaven; Barrow-in-Furness Museum. Isle of Man: Manx Museum, Douglas; Folk Museum, Cregneish; Manx Nautical Museum, Castletown.

Famous personalities: Fletcher Christian (born near Maryport), George Romney (born Dalton-in-Furness), Sir John Barrow (born Ulverston).

Marine industry: Barrow is a shipbuilding centre and port. Workington and Whitehaven are other ports. Fishing is carried on in many towns.

Commerce/industry: West Cumbria produces coal – shafts extend nearly 5 miles (8km) out to sea – and has iron and steel and chemical industries. In Barrow the emphasis is gradually shifting from heavy to light industry. Carlisle has many light industries, ranging from textiles to biscuit-making. Sellafield (Windscale) includes Calder Hall nuclear power station – Britain's first to produce electricity commercially.

NATURAL PROFILE

Wildlife: This coast rises from the great flats of the Solway Firth to the high cliffs of St Bees Head. It falls again to the south. It includes important sand dunes, shingle and saltmarshes. The Isle of Man also has varied coasts, with bird-rich sea cliffs and extensive dunes.

Attractions: In Cumbria, the south side of the Solway Firth, like the north, has extensive sand flats and saltmarsh – the Upper Solway is of international importance for wintering wildfowl; St Bees Head – high sandstone cliffs – breeding sites for various seabirds; Duddon Sands, important for waders – also good saltmarsh; Sandscale Haws and Walney Dunes – the South Walney Dunes are modified by guano from one of Europe's largest gull colonies – also extensive shingle with rich flora. On the Ise of Man, the Ayres in the north; Calf of Man, varied subtidal flora and fauna and a bird sanctuary (Manx National Trust). *Footpaths:* Selker Bay to Annaside. Isle of Man: Ayres Nature Trail; Bradda Head. *Beauty spots:* Solway Coast AONB, 37 miles (60km) of coast from the mouth of the Esk to Maryport, excluding Silloth. The Lake District National Park reaches the coast in the south-east and and south-west. *Beaches in Cumbria:* Silloth, Allonby, Flimby, St Bees, Haverigg, Isle of Walney, Bardsea. *Beaches on the Isle of Man:* Douglas, Laxey, Peel, Port St Mary.

CAUSES FOR CONCERN

Pipeline discharges: Discharges of natural uranium and various heavy metals from a phosphate rock reprocessing plant.

Radioactive discharges: Sellafield (Windscale) reprocessing plant discharges every day 1.5 million gallons (7 million litres) of contaminated, radioactive water (including, over the last 30 years, 0.25–0.5 tons of plutonium) into the Irish Sea, making it the world's most radioactively contaminated sea. This radioactivity has been detected in Scandinavia and Greenland. Scientists thought that radioactive heavy metals would become bound to sea-bed sediments. Instead it seems that plutonium-bearing particles are being stirred up and blown back on to Cumbrian beaches. In some coastal areas, radiation levels are higher than those allowed in many parts of the Sellafield plant. Multiple myeloma (a cancer specifically linked with plutonium contamination) is high in south-western Cumbria; the only other places experiencing equally high levels are Hiroshima and Nagasaki. Rates of childhood leukaemia in Seascale, 1 mile (1½km) south of Sellafield, are ten times the national average. Up to 1984 the radioactive discharges from Sellafield equalled the total discharges from all nuclear power sources in the world. These discharges and the considerable concentration of chemical and other industries on the Cumbrian coast make this a particularly threatened stretch of coastline.

Inshore overfishing: Herring fishing from the Isle of Man is restricted due to overfishing.

Beaches: Serious raw sewage contamination on the Isle of Man coastline.

Threatened wildlife: Some decline in bird populations at Ravenglass Estuary Nature Reserve, including egg desertion by Black-headed Gulls in 1985 at one of Britain's oldest and biggest colonies. Possible causes include predation by other gulls or foxes, and radioactive contamination from Sellafield.

On all but the most exposed shores, Bladder Wrack forms a distinct zone between high and low water. The bladders keep the fronds afloat and are able to capture sunlight – the life source of virtually all plants – at high tide.

The Great Crested Newt is an impressive amphibian, especially in the breeding season, when the male develops a spiky crest. It has gone from much of Britain's countryside as ponds have been drained or polluted, but survives in dune slacks.

LANCASHIRE AND MERSEYSIDE

BERYL BAINBRIDGE

I grew up in Formby, a small village on the Lancashire coast half-way between the city of Liverpool and the holiday resort of Southport. It was wartime and the barbed wire entanglements rolled like tumbleweed across the sand. There was an ancient boathouse on the foreshore, sagging in the wind, and an old recluse lived among the dunes in a shack made out of driftwood.

The pinewoods were so densely planted that you ran hump-backed, zig-zagging beneath the spider webs slung in near darkness, until you burst out into the light and went rolling down the sandbank to where the tadpole ponds, ringed with alder bushes and pussy willow, lay in the hollow below.

Every night of my life, in those far-off days of double summer time, I went down to the shore. Mostly the wind blew and the sea was black, and destroyers crawled along the edge of the grey sky. The sand was littered with bales of salt-encrusted cloth, the sodden pages of log-books from sunken ships, burst melons, ammunition cases, jellyfish as big as bin lids. Nothing since has ever smelt as wild, as pungent as the sea-wrack. Just sometimes, before the sun went down, the whole world turned golden.

In winter I found toads floating, white bellies upward, in the ponds, and I poked them with sticks. In the breeding nights of late April they croaked at the stars, and come June the water was full of tadpoles.

I took it all for granted; the rustlings in the grass, the ploppings in the ditch beside the lane, red squirrels in the woods, the rabbits, the owl hooting near the church, the glimpses of fox and pheasant in the fields, the Natterjack Toads, the dunes that rose and fell before the sea.

Nothing, I thought, would ever change; it was only people who altered or went away.

LANCASHIRE AND MERSEYSIDE

GRANGE-OVER-SANDS TO QUEENSFERRY

. . . WHEN, UPON THE WESTERN SHORES, THE CLOUDS COME BOWLING UP FROM THE HORIZON, MESSENGERS, OUTRIDERS OR COMRADES OF A GALE, IT IS SOMETHING OF THE SEA DETERMINED TO POSSESS THE LAND.'

Hilaire Belloc, *On a Great Wind* (1906)

The Sand Lizard inhabits heaths and sand dunes and is an uncommon and threatened reptile. The small population at the Ainsdale-Formby dunes, on the Lancashire coast, is the most northerly in Britain.

Sand, sand and yet more sand is the dominant feature of this stretch of the British coastline. From the great intertidal flats of Morecambe Bay, the much-vaunted golden beaches fringe the broad, flat peninsula of the Fylde, along which crowd northern seaside resorts. At Lytham, the sand billows over the pavements. On either side of the Ribble estuary it forms vast flats, spreading miles at low tide and creating the dangerous delusion that one could walk from Southport to Blackpool without leaving the beach. Acres of sand dunes tower above the holiday beaches between Southport and Liverpool. The broad wedge of the Wirral peninsula, too, has its fringe of sand, but – largely occupied by sprawling suburbs and bounded by the polluted waters of the Mersey, Dee and Liverpool Bay – it can only look back to happier days. Fortunately, other stretches of the Lancashire coast still retain their wild beauty.

The wild, lonely beauty of Morecambe Bay is captured perfectly in this dawn view of just one small stretch of its vast expanse. One of Britain's largest areas of mud- and sand-flats, it is threatened by pollution from the Mersey and Ribble estuaries.

Estuaries and Sand Dunes

At Morecambe Bay, between Cumbria and Lancashire, huge areas of sand and mud, sculpted by the tides into patterns of tiny waves, descend gently into curling channels that change their courses overnight. Despite the sudden patches of treacherous quicksand, the local fishermen, with an intimate knowledge of the area, drive tractors out on to the bay. Their rows of staked-out nets are reflected in puddles which may turn to ice in the dark days of January. Snow may settle on the sands, concealing tracks and footprints; the wind may whip up the sand into storms or fog may obscure everything.

At low tide, deep water is miles away, invisible even in clear weather, and the River Kent, in the bay's north-east corner, preserves only the shallowest course to join the distant sea. Suddenly, the tide starts to turn, and the sea covers the whole of this great 10-mile-wide plain with alarming speed. During high spring tides, a tidal 'bore' of water roars up the Kent estuary, smashing against the protective walls of Arnside and Grange-over-Sands. A similar wall of water races up the River Lune, in the south of Morecambe Bay. Its course through the sands has been known to alter by half a mile in the space of a year. The only road to Sunderland Point, at the river's mouth, is immersed twice a day. Inhabitants still live by boat, netting salmon or sea

The broad promenade of the quiet commuter suburb of Widnes is one of the few places on Merseyside where industry past and present can momentarily be forgotten.

trout on the river, but nothing remains to remind one of Sunderland's 18th-century role as a major port for West Indian and American cotton, save for the old kapok or silk-cotton tree that grows beside the quay.

Before the railway bridged the Kent and Leven estuaries, a short cut that provided an alternative to the long land route lay across the sands. Carriages, horses and carts and even travellers on foot would set out from Hest Bank near Morecambe, from Kents Bank on the east side of the Flookburgh peninsula, or from the banks by Ulverston, in the company of an expert guide – without whose knowledge they might literally be sunk. Official guides were originally

appointed by the monasteries, then by the Duchy of Lancaster, part of the Crown estates. The 'Queen's Guides to the Sands', as they are known, still lead those who chose to make this hazardous and unforgettable journey. The guide marks out the route during the previous low tide with bunches of laurels known as 'brobs', but the water has been known to tear them from the sand. A sudden storm may blow up and if any mishap occurs, time for rescue is tight. Gravestones in all the churches round the bay record deaths by drowning.

The everyday occupation of the 'Queen's Guides to the Sands' is fishing, a dwindling trade but one that has its own words and customs,

The dramatic expansion of Merseyside during the 19th century included the building of the mock-Gothic bridge on the right of this picture between Runcorn and Widnes to carry the railway across the Mersey to Liverpool. The soaring 1960s bridge of steel girders alongside it carries road traffic across the river, to an area whose industries have contracted as dramatically as they grew.

Today, a trip on the beautiful Barrow-in-Furness to Morecambe line gives no indication of the difficulty of transport before the arrival of the railway in the late 1850s. Passengers boarding at Grange-over-Sands (right) or crossing the Kent estuary at Arnside on a graceful viaduct (centre right) avoid a long detour inland or a hazardous crossing of the sands of Morecambe Bay. At every turn on their journey, they are greeted by magnificent views, such as this one from Arnside (below right), on the Kent estuary, which includes the distant peaks of the Lake District.

With its winter-brightening, vivid orange berries, the Sea Buckthorn is a native of Britain's eastern coast, but much planted along other shores to hold sand and prevent erosion. Fieldfares and other winter-visiting thrushes feast on the berries.

unique to Morecambe Bay. The local fish, never very popular outside the area, is 'fluke' or flounder, hence the name of Flookburgh. The nets strung across the sands like fences sometimes bring in plaice, a more rewarding catch than flounder, but whatever the content of the nets, they have to be reached before the gulls get to them. Whitebait are caught in similar fashion, and trawlers have sometimes netted conger eels.

But the main harvest is shellfish. It was not so long ago that shrimps were trawled in Ulverston Channel by horse and cart, the water reaching above the axles and almost to the horses' necks. Today, tractors tow the nets along the channels, although 'miring' – getting stuck in the mud – is more frequent than in the days of horses. In the heyday of the shellfish industry, the wives and daughters of the fishermen would do the work of sorting, boiling, and 'picking' or shelling the shrimps, for which there would be record-holders and friendly competitions. Mussel beds near

Heysham have been harvested for six hundred years, and cockles have been a Morecambe Bay staple for just as long. The cocklers use a device called a 'jumbo', resembling an upside-down table, to bring the cockles to the surface. They then scrape up the creatures with a three-pronged fork known as a 'craam', which they use to gather the mussels, too.

The price fetched by cockles hardly justifies the work these days and sewage can contaminate the mussels, which have in any case become difficult to sell. Pollution is also the likely cause for the dwindling stocks of shrimps – the only catch to have kept its price. 'Fluke' is caught solely for local consumption and no one smokes it any more. Co-operatives at Morecambe and Flookburgh stave off the final collapse of the Morecambe Bay fisheries, but few still find it possible to make a living from them.

Increasingly, the miles of sand and mud are left to the huge numbers of birds that come here

The shifting sands at Formby Dunes must be kept in check constantly and much of the work is done by the National Trust. Fences aid Marram Grass in stemming the movement of the sand, and conifers have been planted in some areas to help consolidate the dunes.

to feed on the rich supplies of buried worms and shellfish. In winter, Morecambe Bay is the most important site in Britain for waders, containing about a quarter of the country's entire population of Knot, Bar-tailed Godwits, Turnstones and Oystercatchers, and large numbers of Dunlin, Redshank, Curlew, Grey Plover, Sanderling and other species – over a quarter of a million in all. Around the edges of the sand- and mud-flats are saltmarshes, which provide roosting sites at high tide for the waders – and for wildfowl, too – and breeding grounds for Redshank, Oystercatchers, Lapwings, Skylarks and Meadow Pipits. Despite the existence of a large RSPB bird reserve in the bay, and its status as a Site of Special Scientific Interest, the quest for cheap tidal power may lead to the destruction of this internationally important habitat if a proposal for a tidal barrage goes ahead.

A happier state of affairs exists at the nearby RSPB reserve at Leighton Moss, whose reed-beds attract rare insects and Otters as well as a wealth of birdlife, including Bitterns, Bearded Tits and Garganey.

Some fifteen miles to the south of Morecambe Bay, the Ribble estuary, too, may be threatened by plans for a tidal barrage and marina. A major breeding site for Shelduck, Oystercatchers, Lapwings and Redshank, it also attracts the largest winter gatherings in England of Pink-footed Geese and many ducks and waders, too.

The extensive coastal dune systems at Ainsdale and Formby, south of the Ribble, contain numerous specialized plants, such as Grass of Parnassus and Dune Helleborine, that thrive in the lime-rich sands, and are home to two rare creatures, the Sand Lizard and the Natterjack Toad. Red squirrels introduced from the Continent live in the pine woods at Formby, where some of the older dunes are levelled out for commercial asparagus cultivation – the vegetable has been grown here since the 18th century.

An abundant wintering wader, the Knot is present in huge numbers on many British estuaries, notably on Morecambe Bay, drifting like smoke to and fro across the mud. Even so, it is threatened, like all waders, by reclamation and barrage schemes and by pollution.

The Holiday Coast

The year 1871 saw the introduction of Bank Holidays – paid holidays of a week or more did not become law for another sixty years. Skilled working men with Co-op shares, smart clothes and legal union cards could take their families for a weekend by the sea. Even when wages fell, Blackpool kept on going, adding the famous 518-foot half-height replica of the Eiffel Tower to the piers and promenade in the 1890s. Today, over ten million people visit Blackpool each year – and many come just to enjoy the spectacle of the autumn illuminations.

Take a jumble of popular fictional characters, old and new, including Mrs Tiggy-Winkle and Peter Rabbit, a Hundred and One Dalmatians, Father Christmas, teddy bears having a picnic and mice running up the clock, and set them against an equally bewildering mixture of back-drops, from horns and tubas with faces and feet to windmills, Chinese lanterns, Valentine cards, blue and white teapots, psychedelic peacocks and choirboys at prayer. All these and more are there in the famous Blackpool illuminations, gleaming, flashing, moving in staccato and re-flected in the rain- and spray-soaked pavements of Britain's foremost resort.

The 'greatest free show on earth' runs every year from late August to the beginning of November with each stage of the production, from design and construction to eventual dis-mantlement, undertaken locally by 70 full-time council employees. It all began with a royal visit in May 1912, when a mere 10,000 light bulbs on Princes Parade so struck the public that they demanded a repetition in September. The fol-lowing year the demand was made anew and in 1925 it became – barring wars – an annual event. In all the blighted North it is hard to name anything both as universally popular and as undaunted by recession. Hoteliers, breweries, coach operators, fish-and-chip vans, the funfair rides – everyone involved in the autumn tourist trade can keep their business going, thanks to 375,000 light bulbs, over 75 miles of cable and 3,000 kilowatts of electricity.

As the violent grey sea smacks against the piers and promenades of winter Cleveleys, Blackpool and Lytham St Anne's on the Fylde peninsula, the summer scenes of crowded beaches are unimaginable. Also seemingly unimaginable, to many people in authority, is the fact that the beaches at a number of major resorts are con-taminated with untreated sewage. Further south, the people of Southport comment ironically that the prawns grow so big and strong on their unsavoury diet that they climb off the beaches and dance in the nightclubs. In reality, there are very few prawns left, and the owners of the old army jeeps with home-made amphibious cabins who drive far out onto the sands in search of shellfish scarcely make a living these days.

One town that stands apart, though it is linked to Blackpool by Britain's first and last electric

Blackpool (below) remains Britain's most popular seaside resort, despite its polluted beaches. Its electric trams (right) still run along its seven-mile-long promenade, as they have done for the last hundred years, providing superb views of the best light show on the British coast (below). But the tourist industry may decline if the pollution is not dealt with effectively.

A summery sight is provided on a winter's day by this boarded-up ice-cream booth (right) on Morecambe's seafront.

tramway, is Fleetwood, on the north of the Fylde peninsula, an important fishing port, and ferry and container terminal. The Arctic trawler fleet has long since gone, but the packing bays around the port still echo to the greedy squawks of overfed gulls as the latest catch of plaice, cod, dogfish, whiting or shellfish is unloaded. The number of offshore boats has halved in the last few years, and in the last three, the decline has accelerated. As one fisherman explained, 'It's survival of the fittest – you either have a better boat or you work twice as hard. This government only cares for farmers.' Today, the Fleetwood fishermen catch anything the Irish Sea can offer.

Gateway to the World

Graham Greene's assertion that 'no one goes to Liverpool for pleasure' creates an image that the Merseyside Development Corporation tries hard to dispel. What is certainly true is that nobody goes to Liverpool for work any more. Like all ports in decline, it wears a sad cloak of once-important, though still splendid, buildings. Its special place in popular culture leaves legends, like that of the Beatles, but no leads to follow. The television 'soap opera' *Brookside* can set its story in the city without any hint that the docks were once Liverpool's lifeblood and the pivot to its relatively recent history.

A 'London in miniature' was how Liverpool was described in 1698 when its population was around 5,000. It rivalled Bristol as the greatest port outside the capital and built its wealth on a similar three-way trade of cloth, spices and slaves. In the 1720s, the writer Daniel Defoe remarked that if trade went on at that level, the city would soon be as big as Dublin. By then shipbuilding was at its height, with the entire population taking the day off work to celebrate the launch of a multi-masted wooden ship.

As the cotton industry gathered pace, transforming the villages in Lancashire to mill-towns and generating more capital than any business hitherto, so the sea ports transformed themselves too. Sunderland, Preston, and especially Liverpool expanded dramatically to manage the import of raw cotton and the export of cotton cloth. By the 1820s, Liverpool's docks outstripped London's, canals had been dug to Manchester and Leeds and the optimism of the city was summed up in the words of the poet and historian Robert Southey that here 'money and activity work wonders'. William Laird, whose firm was later to merge to become the famous Cammell-Laird shipyards, was building iron steamships and the expansion of Birkenhead was under way. By the end of the 19th century there were over seven miles of docks at Liverpool, said by an American admirer to be 'built as if they were intended to endure as long as the pyramids'. The floating quay forming the landing stage on the pierhead was the largest in existence and almost half the world's trade was being carried in ships that set out from Liverpool.

The deep boom of the Bittern, carrying far across the reed-beds, was once a familiar sound in many counties. Now, with its habitat mostly drained, the Bittern is a rare bird, breeding only in a few coastal reed-beds in East Anglia and Lancashire.

Virtually all Britain's domestic ducks, regardless of their shape and colour, are descended from the Mallard. This is Britain's commonest duck, familiar on ponds, lakes and rivers. But in winter, particularly when fresh water freezes, many head for the coast.

Built in the late 19th century to carry deep-sea ships all the way from the Mersey estuary to Manchester Docks, the 36-mile-long Manchester Ship Canal now only carries just over half the tonnage that it carried during its heyday in the 1940s and 1950s. Today the activity is concentrated at the canal's western end and the docks at Manchester are closed.

Symbols of the city's former glory, the Liver Birds atop the Royal Liver Insurance building on Liverpool's waterfront (above) now survey an area of acute economic depression and the most polluted estuary in Britain.

Men with no jobs to go to fish the murky waters of the Mersey (above), where great ships were once launched and one of the world's greatest ports flourished at Liverpool.

Millions of emigrants, from Ireland and all over Europe, arrived in the city to secure a wretched passage to Australia or North America. The cheapest ticket was for 'steerage' – a place in the open hold where there was no escape from seasickness and from the cholera and typhoid that so many carried. Conditions improved and the chance of shipwreck diminished with the introduction of the steamship liners, and a new class of entrepreneurial passengers developed with the discoveries of gold in Australia and California. Throughout the great emigration period of 1830–1930, the Liverpudlians profited, from the porters and lodging house landlords to the brokers and shipowners. Cunard was one of the Liverpool shipping lines, as was the White Star Line, owners of the ill-fated *Titanic*.

Take the ferry now across the Mersey from Birkenhead, blinkering your eyes to the grey expanses of shipless water, and see the glory of this faded city – the Royal Liver Insurance building with its two legendary birds of stone, Cunard's main offices and the neo-classical headquarters of the Mersey Docks and Harbour Company – the most famous port façade in Britain. Just downstream, Albert Dock had the most modern system of loading and unloading ships when it opened in 1846. Red brick warehouses rise straight above the quays with none of the fancy designs of the later Victorian age. Today, they contain expensive restaurants,

shops and flats, and a Maritime Museum. To the north, dock entrances like medieval castle towers are dwarfed by demolition cranes. Acres of rubble give way to empty warehouses large enough to house the three famous pierhead buildings. Only the container terminal at Seaforth carries on any real trade.

Fifty years ago, the port already in decline, industrial expansion began to take its place. Petrochemical plants, engineering firms, paper mills and food processing factories sprang up along the Mersey banks and flushed their waste untreated down the estuary. Today, the Mersey is largely dead or dying. The port of Liverpool is terminally ill. Birkenhead docks present a ghostly face and the ship-building yards offer a fraction of their former employment. On his visit to Liverpool in the aftermath of the 1981 inner-city riots at Toxteth, the then Secretary of State for the Environment, Michael Heseltine, spoke of the Mersey as 'the single most deplorable feature of this critical part of England'.

Little has been done to remedy this sad situation, and now a barrage project threatens to remove the tidal flow without cleaning up the water. The resources that may go to cleaning Blackpool's beach are likely to be subtracted from the budgets for other environmental programmes, including the urgently-needed clean-up of the Mersey. Real commitment is needed to solve the problems of this historic coastal area.

A tug and a lone tanker by the canal-side refineries and chemical plants symbolize the comparative quietness of the once-busy Manchester Ship Canal, seen here at Ellesmere Port, a few miles before it joins the Mersey at Eastham.

REGIONAL SUMMARY
LANCASHIRE AND MERSEYSIDE

The distance between the Kent and Dee estuaries, excluding inlets, is about 70 miles (113km).

PHYSICAL PROFILE
Carboniferous rocks occur in the north, with Triassic sandstones south of Heysham. Nearly everywhere the underlying rocks are masked by glacial and post-glacial deposits. Reclamation since the 18th century has transformed many marshy coastlands (locally known as 'mosses') in the Fylde peninsula and much of south-western Lancashire into fertile farmland. In the south, the Mersey estuary is kept deep by a strong tidal scour.

Climate: The climate is mild and sunny with average temperatures of 39°F (4°C) in January and 59°–61°F (15°–16°C) in July. The average annual rainfall varies between 35 inches (889mm) in the north and 26 inches (660mm) in the south.

HUMAN PROFILE
This coast was sparsely populated until the end of the 18th century, when land reclamation and the onset of the Industrial Revolution brought people to the area. Resorts include Grange-over-Sands (3,600), Morecambe and Heysham (41,200), Thornton Cleveleys (26,100), Blackpool (147,200), Lytham St Anne's (39,700) and Southport (89,700). Manufacturing is important in Lancaster (46,300), while Fleetwood (28,500) was formerly a great fishing port. Major ports and industrial centres include Preston (143,700), Liverpool (510,000), Ellesmere Port (63,100) and Birkenhead (123,900). Other industrial towns in Merseyside are Widnes (54,400), Runcorn (64,400), Bebington (including Port Sunlight, 64,200) and Wallasey (90,100).

Sites of historic interest: Lancaster, once a Roman camp, has a Norman castle, where ten Lancastrian witches were hanged in 1612. Only a few fragments of the once prosperous Cockersand Abbey on the Lune estuary have survived.

Museums: Lancaster City Museum; Museum of Childhood, Lancaster; Harris Museum and Art Gallery, Preston; Merseyside Maritime and County Museums, Liverpool; Ellesmere Port Boat Museum.

Famous personalities: Laurence Binyon (born Lancaster), Richard Arkwright (born Preston), William Ewart Gladstone, Arthur Clough (born Liverpool), Lady Hamilton (born Neston).

Marine industry: Merseyside has extensive dockyards – the chief container docks are at Seaforth. Heysham and Fleetwood have ferry services to the Isle of Man; Liverpool has services to Ireland.

Commerce/industry: Merseyside has oil refineries and industries making textiles, chocolate, soap and chemicals; marine engineering and shipbuilding have declined. Preston is known for its engineering industries. Lancaster produces, among other things, linoleum, plastics and textiles.

NATURAL PROFILE
Wildlife: This mainly low coast is the western edge of a plain that sweeps down from the edge of the Pennines. Major estuarine habitats are at Morecambe Bay, the Ribble, Mersey and Dee, with sand dunes of great value at Ainsdale and Formby.

Attractions: Between Cumbria and Lancashire, Morecambe Bay is possibly Britain's finest site for waders in winter – saltmarshes rich in flora are behind the sand flats. Also in Lancashire, Leighton Moss (RSPB); Ribble Marshes (NCC). In Merseyside, Ainsdale and Formby dunes, rich in flora with populations of Red Squirrels; Mersey estuary, important intertidal mudflats for wildfowl despite nearby conurbations. *Footpaths:* Morecambe Bay – guides lead walks because fast tides make the area dangerous; Ainsdale dunes – 6 miles (10km) of paths and a nature trail; coastal walks, Wallasey-Hoylake. *Beauty Spots:* Arnside and Silverdale AONB in the north adjoins the Lake District National Park. *Beaches in Lancashire:* Morecambe, Heysham, Fleetwood, Cleveleys, Blackpool, Lytham and St Anne's. *Beaches in Merseyside:* Southport, Ainsdale, Formby, New Brighton.

CAUSES FOR CONCERN
Direct dumping: More than 2.9 million tons (3 million tonnes) of contaminated dredging spoil, with high mercury concentrations, are dumped into Morecambe Bay every year. Mercury levels in fish are approaching the EEC permitted maximum limit for human consumption. High concentrations of PCBs (polychlorinated biphenyls) and heavy metals in sewage sludge have been detected in fish and shellfish from Liverpool Bay, into which thousands of tons of contaminated sewage sludge and industrial wastes are dumped every year.

Pipeline discharges: The Mersey is the UK's most polluted estuary. More than 300 pipelines discharge millions of gallons of highly polluting effluents of all types. There is an alarming possibility of a major accident during the manufacture and transport of highly toxic organic lead petrol additive.

Radioactive discharges: Heysham nuclear power station (Lancs) discharges slightly radioactive cooling water into Morecambe Bay; a second nuclear power station is being built there. Capenhurst (Cheshire) uranium enrichment plant discharges radioactive effluent into Liverpool Bay.

Oil pollution: Large quantities of oil entering in sewage and by direct industrial discharges.

Inshore overfishing: Shrimps in Morecambe and Liverpool bays.

Beaches: Blackpool, Britain's most popular bathing resort, has concentrations of faecal bacteria which are five times in excess of the EEC limits as a result of raw sewage pollution.

Threatened wildlife: Wintering populations of Dunlin and Redshank have declined by more than 20% over the last 15 years – probable causes are disturbance, pollution and loss of habitat due to land reclamation schemes. Possible barrage (water storage) scheme for Morecambe Bay would have serious effects on Britain's largest wintering population of waders.

The Natterjack Toad breeds in the shallow, sun-warmed pools of dune slacks. Once widespread on warm sandy heaths, it is now chiefly restricted to sand dunes as many of the heaths have disappeared.

The Common Shrimp is the basis of many local fisheries all around Britain's coast. But in Morecambe Bay, shrimp fishing has almost come to a halt as the shrimps have been poisoned by polluted waters.

WALES

ALICE THOMAS ELLIS

Alice Thomas Ellis

Dylan Thomas wrote of it in *Under Milk Wood* – as 'Penmaenmawr defiant'; Dr Johnson spoke disparagingly of the road which ran round it; it is on an ancient historical site. But apart from that my favourite country town isn't very well known. Not widely known, that is. It has long been popular as a holiday resort with people from Liverpool and the Midlands who descend in the summer months to take advantage of the miles of safe beach and ramble round the mountains.

Soon however they should cease to constitute a problem since there will be little point in visiting the place at all. The planners have made a plan which, as far as I can see (perhaps they will correct me if I am wrong), will carry a ceaseless tide of traffic along the North Wales littoral and then tip it into the sea. This new road, it is rumoured, will run along the beaches and, surely, render them redundant; for who will want to paddle under a flyover or suck lollies on the verge of the equivalent of the M1? I admit that the coast road has always been a problem and Dr Johnson was quite correct in his estimation of its dangers. It has been improved since his time, but it is still undeniably narrow. Traffic jams stretch for miles and there is no way round them. Crossing the road you take your life in your hands, and all in all things aren't what they used to be.

When I was little my mother and I lived near the local laundry where the laundry girls used to hang the sheets to dry in the field behind. Further along in the same field stood Graiglwyd Farm and above that was the site of a stone axe factory. To the left was the quarry, a source of illicit adventure with trucks left unattended in the evening, derelict huts and great heaps of chippings to slide down. You could once follow the quarry and its workings right down to the sea and the jetty beyond where the quarry boats used to come in to collect the granite, but the boats no longer call and now the jetty has gone too. I expect it would have interfered with the flyover so perhaps it is just as well.

There are other changes. The Beach Café where we used to get home-made ice cream has changed hands and I don't think I'll be going there any more. It's too sad. There is no Silver Prize Band any longer, and the trains don't stop there. I daresay the new road (I believe it's known as the Expressway) will facilitate arrival, but it will destroy the town I knew and I don't think I'll be availing myself of it. I think I shall content myself with memory – of the stone farmhouses, and the terraced quarrymen's cottages; the villas with their monkey-puzzle trees and sword grass; the chapels and the churches which were once always full of singers.

The bust of Gladstone has gone too. First someone stole the head leaving only the base. Now the base has gone as well, and there is only a patch of earth. I expect they'll plant begonias in it eventually, but I shan't go there to see them. I shall wait for some future lifetime when the Expressway has crumbled and only the mountains and the sea are left, with the Great Orme on one side and Anglesey on the other, and Puffin Island out in the bay with the sun setting in glory behind it.

WALES
QUEENSFERRY TO THE MUMBLES

'EVENING ON THE OLDEN, GOLDEN SEA OF WALES,
WHEN THE FIRST STAR SHIVERS AND THE LAST WAVE PALES:
O EVENING DREAMS!'

James Elroy Flecker, *The Dying Patriot* (1906)

Common on all Britain's rocky shores, Purple Laver is traditionally fried in oatmeal and eaten with bacon for breakfast in South Wales. It has said to have a high protein content and be rich in vitamins B and C.

In the seascapes of Wales, what appears on the horizon is so often another piece of land. The curving shape of this coast is the secret of its beauty. From the low stone walls and windswept fields of Anglesey, the snow-capped mountains of Snowdonia across the narrow Menai Strait soar majestically into the mist. From Tremadog right round the curve of Cardigan Bay to its southern end, the Llŷn peninsula always lies in view, its hills rolling out to the western outpost of Bardsey Island. In the south-western part of the Principality, too, the sculpted headlands of Pembrokeshire greet each other, while the soft gold and green of Gower's downs are visible from Tenby.

Opposite: The wild expanse of sand dunes at Rhosneigr (left) on Anglesey have attracted many housebuyers, including second-home owners, from England, despite the nearby RAF base at Valley that sends jets screaming overhead. The western end of the Llŷn peninsula (above right), though still relatively remote and almost entirely unspoiled, is also starting to feel the increasing pressure of tourism.

Coastal Impressions

The great beauty of this curving coastline is not, however, without its darker side. Scars from 19th-century industries are evident and there are ugly modern developments – mostly for the tourist trade. Two nuclear power stations are sited in North Wales, while huge oil refineries overshadow the deep-water port of Milford Haven in Pembroke. The record on sewage disposal at many popular Welsh beaches is far from exemplary and the surrounding seas are not noted for their cleanliness.

In spite of problems such as these, the Welsh coast is still a treasure among the shores of Britain. There are no great industrial ports or cities, apart from Milford Haven, and those serving the South Wales coal belt (see pages 137–8). Instead, the little towns of grey slate and granite almost merge into the skies and hillsides, while rivers, fresh from Snowdonia, run into Cardigan Bay through the drowned valleys of the last great Ice Age to estuaries as lovely as any in Britain: the Glaslyn, the old slate-exporting estuary; the Mawddach, where hopeful locals still pan for gold; and the Dyfi, forming the border of the Welsh princes' stronghold, Gwynedd. Behind Aberystwyth, the mountain backdrop leads to the softer, rounded shapes of Plynlimon mountain, where the Severn, Wye and Rheidol rivers have their source.

Sand Dunes and Seabirds

As well as beautiful estuaries and splendid rocky shores, the Welsh coastline includes many fine stretches of sand dunes. Some have suffered from the tramping of countless feet, but the tourist trade is seasonal and localized, so many of the dunes still bear a rich flora. Newborough Warren, on Anglesey, despite having suffered somewhat from afforestation, remains one of Britain's largest dune systems. In spring, the open sandy areas sparkle with tiny annual plants like Whitlow Grass and Corn Salad. Later, on the more

popular sites, beach-nesting birds, such as the Little Tern and Ringed Plover, have been forced to seek the sanctuary of nature reserves, where they are free to nest in peace and their eggs are safe from visitors' feet.

Wales is nevertheless a fine place for the coastal birdwatcher. The Dee estuary, through which runs the northern boundary between Wales and England, is a favourite winter haunt of waders. The annual total of over 140,000 – more than 10 per cent of the entire British population – includes huge numbers of Knot,

stable dunes, Lady's Bedstraw and Carline Thistle appear, while in the damp hollows, or 'slacks', between the dunes a secret garden of scarce orchids blooms. At the other end of the country, on the south coast of the Gower peninsula, are the equally impressive dunes of Oxwich. Nestling within them is a peaty fen with extensive reed-beds, among which flower Bogbean, Red Rattle, Marsh Arrow Grass and Twayblade.

On many of the Welsh beaches, the gorgeous Yellow Horned-poppy and pink Sea Bindweed grow, while the white heads of Sea Kale often run riot across the shingle. At a number of the more

Dunlin and Oystercatchers. At one of their chief roosting sites, on the rocky islands of Hilbre in the estuary, the commoner waders may be so densely packed that they have to stand on one another's backs as they jostle for a resting place. Most British species of wildfowl can also be seen here, including some of the largest flocks of Pintail in Europe. Grey Seals disport themselves on the estuary's sandbanks in summer, while porpoises, dolphins and Killer Whales can occasionally be spotted swimming offshore.

Another magnet for wintering birds, including Great Crested Grebes, Red-throated Divers,

Tenby's fishing harbour, its ruined castle and near-complete town walls predate its Georgian and Regency terraces by several centuries. Together, they form one of the most beautiful harbour views in Britain, which still attracts many tourists.

terns and ducks, is Traeth Lafan, in the Menai Strait, between Anglesey and the mainland. On these islands, where disturbance and pollution (barring oil disasters) are minimal, it is the breeding seabirds, such as Razorbills and other auks, that claim attention. Across tide-racing sounds, a great variety of seabirds – Manx Shearwaters, Storm Petrels, Fulmars, Cormorants, Shags, Gannets, Guillemots, Razorbills and Puffins, as well as Kittiwakes and other gulls – breed in noisy, teeming colonies on the rocky offshore islands. Off the west coast of Anglesey, at Holy Island, the South Stack Cliffs RSPB Reserve boasts large breeding colonies of nine species of seabirds, as well as Peregrines, Choughs and Ravens. The silver-studded Blue Butterfly flits among the Bee Orchids, Field Fleaworts and buckler ferns of this reserve.

Wildlife in the Balance

Nature is not always so harmonious, however. Brown Rats, unwittingly introduced from boats, may have been one of the causes of the drastic decline in the population of birds that gave

Puffin Island, off the south-east coast of Anglesey, its name. Ramsey and Cardigan Island, both off the Pembroke coast, have been affected similarly. After the rats on Cardigan Island were exterminated, wooden replicas of the birds were erected to persuade the Puffins to return to their nesting burrows. Ramsey makes up for its dearth of Puffins by having Wales's biggest population of Choughs, together with the largest Welsh breeding colony of Grey Seals.

On Bardsey, off the Llŷn peninsula, the constant presence of people ensures that no stowaway rat can jump ashore. Even so, the Puffins have left – for reasons unknown. On Grassholm, one of the Pembroke islands, the cause of their disappearance is perhaps more certain – they seem to have undermined their breeding grounds through excessive burrowing. The heavy tread of human feet can also cause burrows to cave in, and this, along with the ever-growing colony of predatory gulls, may explain the reduction in Puffin numbers on Skomer, another of the Pembroke islands. The decline of this endearing, comical-looking bird is not restricted to Wales,

Gateholm, west of Milford Haven, is cut off from Marloes Sands (right) every high tide, and has been uninhabited since the demise of a Celtic monastic settlement. Near by, the farming community of Skomer (below) left the island in the mid-1950s. Frequent exposure to strong gales and the short but difficult passage to and from Pembrokeshire were forsaken for the advantages of mainland life. Today, the island is a nature reserve, with impressive seabird breeding colonies.

For the full drama of wind, rock and salt spray, South Stack lighthouse (below right) on its tiny promontory west of Holyhead, can be approached via 400 steps cut in the cliffs leading to a suspended footbridge. The drama is heightened by the teeming seabirds and aerobatic Choughs and Ravens that breed on South Stack Cliffs, an RSPB reserve.

however. The entire North Atlantic population has been affected – although numbers seem to have stabilized recently – and it is thought that a main cause of the decline may in fact relate to some change in the distribution of the birds' chief diet of small fish, rather than being connected with their nesting habits.

On Skomer and on Bardsey Manx Shearwaters, packed tightly together on the water, wait for the daylight to fade before taking off for their island burrows. The one illumination on Bardsey that is never extinguished – the beam of the lighthouse – has caused the death of many migrant birds forced to fly low on cloudy nights. In the last few years the hazard has been decreased by floodlighting a patch of gorse to divert the birds. Nevertheless, the island's bird observatory can claim a long list of rare visitors, including Sora Rail and Summer Tanager from America, and Penduline Tit and Crested Lark from southern Europe.

The springtime colours on Skomer are as brilliant as the bills and feet of the remaining Puffins. The strong pink of Sea Thrift, inter-spersed with white Sea Campion and Common Scurvygrass, adorns the cliffs, while away from the edge among swathes of Bracken, broad carpets of Bluebells cover the ground. As darkness falls, and the Manx Shearwaters start up their crooning, wailing and screaming song while they busy round their burrows, another nocturnal creature scampers about – the Skomer Bank Vole, larger, tamer and quite distinct from the mainland race.

Close to Skomer lies the island of Skokholm. Above its red cliffs – site of Britain's first bird observatory, established in 1933 by the pioneering naturalist Ronald Lockley – the turf is kept crew-cut by rabbits, once bred on Skokholm, as on Skomer, for food and for their skins. The Skokholm rabbits have the unique distinction of being flea-less and for this reason immune to myxomatosis. Puffins, Manx Shearwaters and Storm Petrels sometimes take over old rabbit burrows, or lay their eggs in openings in the rocks; the first two are also capable of digging their own burrows.

Grassholm, further out to sea, is the Gannet

Killed by Great Black-backed Gulls, their eggs eaten by rats and their plump young once prized as human delicacies, Manx Shearwaters breed on offshore islands in Wales, the Isle of Man, Scotland and Ireland, returning to their burrow nests only at night.

The most perfectly planned resort in Wales, Llandudno had earned an international reputation by the end of the 19th century. Its fine Victorian hotels and shopping parades exert as great a charm today – although it now faces contemporary problems, ranging from sewage and litter disposal to the difficulty of providing for an increasingly elderly population.

So many pilgrims were buried on Bardsey Island (right) that their bones provided fencing material in the mid-19th century. Today, this unspoiled haven is owned by a trust that protects it from exploitation and maintains an important observatory for monitoring migrant birds and those that breed on the island.

Newgale Sands (centre), at the northern end of St Bride's Bay, have a somewhat misleading name, for although they do reveal some sand at low tide, they are dominated by a long ridge of pebbles, forming a miniature version of Dorset's Chesil Beach.

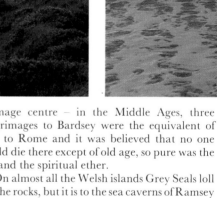

The Chough is a master of aerobatics. Outside Ireland, its stronghold, this red-billed crow now breeds only on the wilder coasts of Wales and western Scotland. Once widespread, its decline seems to be due partly to disturbance and persecution.

capital of Wales, its rock hardly visible for the great gleaming white creatures and their bulky seaweed nests, and the sea around full of more wheeling and diving birds. Although only 250 pairs bred on Grassholm in 1893, today some 22,000 pairs can be seen there in summer, making Grassholm the third largest gannetry in the North Atlantic.

Many of these islands around the coast of Wales provided excellent farming land, their soil being richer than that of the mainland. Cattle were even floated across from Giltar Point, near Tenby, to graze on Caldey, an island which is still cultivated by Catholic monks. On Bardsey, tiny fields between gorse- and bramble-topped ditches are a reminder of what the farmland looked like before the days of mechanization. Bardsey was always difficult to reach – its Welsh name, Ynys Enlli, meaning 'Island in the Tides', is indicative of the hazardous journey. Twenty-seven separate, and potentially lethal, currents form ominous whirlpools in the sound between the island and the mainland. Despite the hazards of the crossing Bardsey was once a major pil-

grimage centre – in the Middle Ages, three pilgrimages to Bardsey were the equivalent of one to Rome and it was believed that no one could die there except of old age, so pure was the air and the spiritual ether.

On almost all the Welsh islands Grey Seals loll on the rocks, but it is to the sea caverns of Ramsey that the largest colony goes to rear its pups. The seals' neighbours in the caves or cliff crevices above may well be Choughs. These handsome red-billed crows, which dazzle with their aerobatic skills, are now restricted to only a few western coasts, but they can be seen wheeling and diving over Anglesey and the cliffs of the Llŷn peninsula and Bardsey, and also along Wales's south-western coast.

Work on the Water
As for the people of Wales, life on the sea has always formed an inevitable and integral part of their existence. All round the world – from Caracas to Quebec, from Melbourne to Dakar, not to mention Liverpool and Bristol – the Welsh have been known for centuries as great seafarers

with exceptional skills of navigation and a knack for building speedy schooners. Their ships carried slate and ore from the mountain quarries, and wool from the huge flocks of sheep, as well as coal from South Wales. They returned home only after long voyages delivering anything to anybody at numerous ports of call. Passengers were ferried to Ireland or America, and on a smaller, busier scale, across the many estuaries of the Welsh coast. The great ships of neighbouring English ports often had Welsh skippers, and almost every little seaside town, from the Dee to the Bristol Channel, had its fleet of cargo vessels as well as fishing boats.

The story of Solva, on St Bride's Bay, in Pembroke, is typical. A tiny settlement on a steep and winding inlet on a coast renowned for its dangerous rocks, it ran packets to New York and conducted a busy cargo trade. Kilns stood ready to burn incoming limestone which was then loaded onto drays and sent inland to neutralize the acidic soil. Warehouses for other commodities from foreign ports or neighbouring towns lined the quay. The last steamship built in

Solva sank during the First World War – as if an omen of what was to come. The little town that had so successfully fought off Viking raids centuries before could not compete in the recession of the 1930s. Life of a sort has now returned to Solva with the warehouses converted to restaurants and chandlers for leisure sailors, and the ancient quayside generating income from weekend yachters' mooring fees.

In the past, the rivers, too, provided wealth from the water. The River Teifi was said to be the best-stocked river with the finest salmon in the 12th century. There are still Atlantic salmon in almost every river of Wales but their feeding grounds across the ocean have been ravaged by overfishing, and raids by poachers using nets, poison and even explosives have taken a severe toll. The traditional Welsh method of catching the fish, with a net slung between two coracles, is still practised on the Teifi and the Taff. The tension rises when a salmon is landed in the boat since a flick of the fish's tail is enough to capsize a coracle. The rights to fish in this way – along with the use of seine nets at the river mouth and

Llanddwyn Bay, where Anglesey meets the southern mouth of the Menai Strait, was once backed by a vast dune system that swallowed up acres of farmland before it was limited by conifer plantations. Work still has to be done after the tourists depart in autumn to repair damage to the dune fences and Marram Grass that help keep the dunes stable.

Opposite: Pleasure boats are the main occupants of Fishguard's old fishing harbour (left) today. On Anglesey, too, the boats that tie up in the old copper port at Amlwch (right) are now mainly pleasure craft, though tankers moor offshore to discharge oil direct into an underwater pipeline.

Wild Sea Kale, with its great fleshy leaves, is a scarce sight today. Once common, it has never recovered from over-exploitation; its tender young shoots were collected to be eaten as a vegetable and plants were uprooted for growing in gardens.

Opposite: This apparently lonely waterside scene at Rhos-on-Sea (left) is deceptive. From Colwyn Bay in the distance, the North Wales coast to the east wears an almost continuous fringe of houses, bungalows, caravans and chalets for miles; a further long stretch of largely industrialized coastline continues to the border near Queensferry.

wading mid-stream – are all hereditary and held by very few people only. Though the practice still continues, coracling is becoming rarer every year – indeed, it may die out altogether in a few years, given the high cost of licences, which rose by 300 per cent between 1986 and 1987, and which are set at £432 for 1988. Carmarthen's River Tywi has alas no salmon or trout to fish – indeed much of its water life has been lost. Only in the last few years has the cause of death in this cleanest of rivers been discovered – acid rain.

The sea presents a less depressing picture. Wales has never had enormous trawling fleets and a factory ship in Welsh waters is a rare sight. Sea bass, as expensive now as salmon, abounds in Welsh coastal waters. Fishing boats from Aberaeron, a delightful town of pastel-coloured houses on Cardigan Bay, and its village neighbour, New Quay, catch plaice, sole and coley as well as sea bass. But the fishing contribution to local economies is significant only in Milford Haven and even there, despite the mackerel of Carmarthen Bay, it is on a minor scale – for fishing in Wales has always been supplementary to farming and quarrying. In Conwy and Caernarfon the search for whiting, dab or tope has been handed over to the tourist trade. Mussel cultivation is no longer viable and insistent notices on the Menai Strait attempt to protect the dwindling stocks of oysters, clams and mussels.

Work on the Shore

Sheltered in the angle between the Llŷn peninsula and Cardigan Bay is Porthmadog, created in the mid-19th century to be the exclusive port for Snowdonian slate. Acres of mudflat were reclaimed and an embankment, upon which the narrow-gauge railway to the quarries could run, built across the Glaslyn estuary. The magical view of mountains rising in russets, smokey greys and mauves above the funnelling river was henceforth to have an industrial foreground. Just further south, a similar railway was laid up the valley from Tywyn to the Nant Gwernol slate quarries. These and other railways of the dead slate trade now carry tourist trains, which chuff up the steep, wooded valleys, through tunnels and villages of slate to the silent quarries, hewn terraces and scree coated green by the fronds of the Parsley Fern.

In Pembroke, the sands of Abereiddi Bay are black from the pounded slate that was worked on the land's edge, while one old pit, channelled to the sea, is known as the Blue Lagoon because of the colour of the reflection of its slate walls in the water. There are abandoned quarries and edges of hills cut like the corners of stepped pyramids all along the Welsh coast. Some of the quarries are completely abandoned, some are now museums, and one, near Porth y Nant on the north side of the Llŷn peninsula, has had its deserted offices and quarriers' cottages turned into a centre for Celtic languages.

Slate was not the only commodity to be extracted from Welsh mountains. One of the prime motives for the conquest of Britain by the Romans was their interest in the mineral wealth – in Wales they found gold in quantities almost unrivalled within their empire. In the Cothi Valley near Carmarthen a seven-mile long aqueduct was built to supply the water needed to pan mined rock. The precious metal turned up again in veins within quartz crystals in the lower slopes of Cader Idris ('Arthur's Seat'), the high mountain throne of mid-Wales.

The area around Bontddu on the Mawddach estuary was a gold speculators' paradise in the 19th century – it still provides gold for the wedding rings of the British royal family. Occasionally, a cry of delight rebounds across the water of the estuary as someone washes out or scratches from the ground a bit of gold clinging to a chunk of quartz. The vast mining conglomerate of Rio Tinto Zinc even proposed to barrage the Mawddach in an effort to dredge and pan all the silt. Plans were shelved when concerned locals informed the company what kind of reception it was likely to receive.

In medieval times, silver was mined by the River Clwyd on the north-east coast of Wales. In various centuries up to the present, the hinterland of Aberystwyth was worked not just for silver but also for copper and lead. This last, and most lethal, substance was mined along the River Rheidol. When lead mining finally ceased in 1927, the river was dead. Nothing survived – no fish, no flies, no worms, no plants – except one lead-resistant alga. After twenty years, life returned with the arrival of sea trout and salmon marking the end of a painstaking process of regeneration.

In Anglesey, Purple Moor-grass was the only plant to survive the effects of smelting copper from the Parys Mountain mines. The last miner was laid off in 1815. Today, at the nearby port of Amlwch, from which the copper was exported, pleasure craft bob about beside the old quays, warehouses and shipyards, while the light plays on the pitted piles of rust- and dun-coloured spoil that resemble desert scenery. Mammoth tankers anchor offshore now, waiting for their oil to be siphoned into terminals via an underwater pipeline while south-easterly winds still waft the sour and unmistakable odour that emanates from the old Parys mines.

A far greater concentration of oil tankers is to be seen at Milford Haven, a large natural harbour guarded by high red sandstone cliffs, and said by Nelson to be unrivalled on the British coast. It was renowned for its miles of deep and sheltered water as much as for its beauty, but the one has been the undoing of the other. Around the green and gentle hills, a steel barricade of storage tanks, cooling towers and refineries claims these waters for the oil industry. Ships that used to carry goods to and from the docks on every branch of this drowned river valley, fishing trawlers, 12th-century troop carriers for the first

The attractive town of
Aberaeron, with its wide
harbour and Regency
houses built by a wealthy
local clergyman, was busy
in the 19th century with
coastal industry. Today,
tourism augments incomes
derived from fishing.

Although Aberystwyth still has its imposing seafront (right), the cultural capital of Welsh Wales also has a beach contaminated with sewage. Milford Haven, with its glistening mooring buoys and oil refineries in the distance (centre), comes as something of a shock to the visitor travelling the generally undeveloped coast of West Wales. It is one of Britain's main oil-tanker ports.

Having survived the depredations of 19th-century collectors, the Small Blue butterfly has now been hit by the loss of its chalk downland habitat. Virtually all the remaining Welsh colonies are found along Wales's south coast.

English invasion of Ireland, Atlantic freighters of the Second World War – all the boats that have ever sailed or steamed into Milford Haven – could be lost inside the holds of the present fleets.

Castles of the Coast

Samuel Johnson remarked that one Welsh castle could contain all the castles he had seen in Scotland. By European standards, the fortresses of Wales are not enormous, but their density in such a small area would be hard to match. Built by Normans, Welsh, Plantagenets or Tudors, restored, in ruins or half way in between, they have become the most resplendent man-made element of Wales and of its coast. While villages and ports huddle round their hills and harbours, the castles smite the landscape, seascape or skyline as if they had erupted, with claps of thunder and attendant dragons. The reality, of

course, was that many, like Edward I's great ring of castles, were built by the English to crush Welsh independence.

Of all the 'Edwardian' castles, Caernarfon alone has received the full restoration treatment – a hundred years ago. Its remarkable state of preservation and its non-circular towers (unique among the fortresses built by Edward) make it appear particularly powerful, even menacing, to this day. In total contrast, Beaumaris, on Anglesey at the eastern end of the Menai Strait, is a fairytale dream of a moated castle of the Middle Ages. Conwy is the most dramatic of Edward I's castles, its effect enhanced by Thomas Telford's suspension bridge. With towers that imitate the fortress's medieval turrets, it spans the river mouth which the castle once guarded as if it was the drawbridge.

Only Criccieth, of all the coastal castles, is

On Cardigan Bay, Barmouth has the appearance of a typical English seaside town, rather than a Welsh one, and is rarely referred to by its Welsh name of Abermaw. Fishing boats still tie up at its harbour on the beautiful Mawddach estuary, but tourism provides most of the town's income – in summer, at least.

A century ago, the quartz-lined slate of Abereiddi's cliffs (above left) was quarried and shipped out from Porthgain, a few miles up the Pembroke coast. Both places bear the scars of their industrial past in an area renowned for its miles of unspoiled coastline.

Welsh in origin; though used by Edward I, it was later sacked, in 1404 by Owain Glyndŵr, last of the Welsh national leaders. Its design as a domestic and defensive fort is clear from its high clifftop site facing Tremadog Bay. Seven hundred years ago, the sea lapped at the rock on which Harlech Castle stands. Like Aberystwyth, Harlech's purpose was to guard the coastal passage between the mountains and the sea.

In every town where Edward built one of his iron ring of forts, English settlers were given brand new streets with English names, laid out in grid plans and encompassed by protective walls extending from the castles. The remains of Conwy's citadel are the most impressive, although this attractive feature, now adorning every holiday brochure, was at the time a social, economic and political division forced on the local community by enemy occupation.

From the military to the mystic, from mammoth masonry to minutest retreat, no better contrast of the scope of history and human designs is afforded in Wales than by crossing the southern part of the Pembroke peninsula from Pembroke Castle to St Govan's Chapel. The Norman stronghold of Pembroke Castle, birthplace of Henry VII, is defended by two rivers and a massive circular wall, from which the central keep once rose. Five miles distant, past the treeless waste of an army firing range and the lily ponds of Bosherston, are the clifftop steps leading down to St Govan's Chapel on a shore where bleak, eroded limestone rocks battle with the sea. A 13th-century structure of utter simplicity, its floor the rock on which it stands, no more than half a dozen paces long, it leans against the cliff and overlooks the fallen scree and boulders tossed towards the sea. A single window, an

Harlech Castle (above) was one of several huge coastal fortresses that formed part of Edward I's ring of castles that dashed any hope of an independent Wales. When Llewelyn ap Gruffydd and his people retreated to the mountains of Snowdonia, Edward took the Menai Strait (right), thus cutting off the Welsh prince from the fertile, wheat-growing land of Anglesey, known to the Welsh as the 'Mother of Wales'.

empty bell-tower and a roof of slate are all that distinguish it from the surrounding rock.

All the great buildings on the coast, from Milford Haven's oil refineries to the mighty North Wales castles, speak of foreign intervention. In just one small area, the Menai Strait provides a number of examples. First Roman Segontium, then English Caernarfon and Beaumaris were built on its banks. At the narrow crossing point is the largest iron suspension bridge the world had ever seen, designed by the Scottish engineer Thomas Telford and completed in 1826 to link Holyhead, the port for Ireland, with London. A mile to the west is the Englishman Robert Stephenson's Britannia Tubular Bridge, opened in 1850 to provide a rail link. Just downstream, on the Anglesey shore, a statue of the English lord and landowner, the Marquis of Anglesey, rises above the water. But this is a mere miniature of his statue perching on a column, comparable to Nelson's in Trafalgar Square, on the hill above the bridge. And now today, as if all of that were not enough, pollution from Lancashire and Merseyside threatens the marine life of this peaceful waterway.

Much else threatens Wales, too. There are 'For Sale' signs in every town and buyers will snap up the houses for use as holiday homes, leaving them empty for most of the year. There is little work, save for tourism. Wales the independent nation seems to be a thing of the past, the ancient past – though the independent spirit of its people still burns fiercely.

REGIONAL SUMMARY
WALES

Wales has a coastline of 614 miles (988km). About six-sevenths is covered in this chapter.

PHYSICAL PROFILE
Most of the coastline is made up of Paleozoic rocks, with igneous intrusions and some Precambrian rocks, notably in Anglesey and the Llŷn peninsula. Coal measures occur in the north-east, south-western Dyfed and Carmarthen Bay.

Climate: Average January temperatures range from 40°F (4°C) in the north to 42°F (6°C) in the south-west. Average July temperatures are around 60°F (16°C) in the north and 58°F (14°C) in the south-west. The rainfall is between 30 and 38 inches (762–965mm) a year. The exposed western coasts have gales on about 30 days in the year.

HUMAN PROFILE
The north coast is a resort area, but the west and south-west are thinly populated. Northern resorts include Prestatyn (16,400), Rhyl (22,700) and Llandudno (19,000). Bangor (12,200) and Aberystwyth (8,700) have colleges of the University of Wales. Holyhead (10,500) and Fishguard (4,900) are ports with services to Ireland. West coast resorts include Aberaeron (1,400) and Cardigan (4,200). The south includes the port of Milford Haven (13,900), the market towns of Pembroke (15,600) and Carmarthen (12,300), the attractive resort of Tenby (4,800), and the industrial town of Llanelli (24,100).

Sites of historic interest: Bardsey and Ramsey islands were early Christian shrines. Wales's patron saint founded a monastery at St David's in the 6th century, though the present cathedral dates from the late 11th century. Magnificent castles, including those at Flint, Conwy, Caernarfon and Harlech, date back to the 1280s and the reign of Edward I.

Museums: Museum of Welsh Antiquities, Bangor; Maritime museums at Fort Belan, Porthmadog and Aberdyfi; Arts Centre Gallery and Ceredigion Museum, Aberystwyth; Carmarthen Museum; Parc Howard Museum, Llanelli.

Famous personalities: Henry VII (born Pembroke Castle), Giraldus Cambrensis (born Manorbier), Dylan Thomas lived in Laugharne.

Marine industry: Leading ports: Holyhead, Fishguard and Milford Haven, a former whaling centre. Pembroke Dock was formerly known for shipbuilding. Fishing ports: Pwllheli, New Quay and St Dogmaels. Loughor estuary is famed for cockles.

Commerce/industry: Milford Haven has large oil refineries. Llanelli has tinplate, engineering and many other industries.

NATURAL PROFILE
Wildlife: This long, varied coastline has flats, sand dunes, estuaries, saltmarshes, coastal heaths, islands, cliffs and important marine sites, with a rich wildlife.

Attractions: In Clwyd, the Dee estuary has great flats and saltmarshes – one of the most important winter bird haunts in Britain, including Point of Ayr. In Gwynedd, Great Orme Nature Trails; Menai Strait, with its rich flora and fauna, is a proposed MNR; Cemlyn Bay (NT bird sanctuary); Holy Island coast, including South Stack cliffs (two very rare plants – Spotted Rockrose and maritime form of Field Fleawort); Newborough Warren (dunes); Bardsey Island – voluntary (and proposed statutory) MNR with rich sublittoral communities. In Dyfed, Dyfi estuary and dunes; Penderi (coastal woodlands); Skomer Complex, including Skomer, Skokholm and Midland Island – Skomer is a voluntary (and proposed statutory) MNR; Stackpole Head to Bosherston Ponds – sea cliffs, dunes, drowned valley etc.; Burry Inlet (between Dyfed and Gower peninsula) and including Pembrey Country Park – large sand flats (important for waders), grazing saltmarsh, dunes (calcareous at Whiteford), limestone cliffs. Also in West Glamorgan, the South Gower Coast – wealth of wildlife, cliffs, marshes, woodland, dunes and rocky foreshore; Oxwich (NCC). *Footpaths:* 170-mile (274km) long coastal path in the Pembrokeshire Coast National Park is one of Britain's finest. It runs from St Dogmaels (near Cardigan) to Amroth (north of Tenby). *Beauty spots:* AONBs in Anglesey and the Llŷn and Gower peninsulas, and coastal parts of Snowdonia National Park. *Beaches in Clwyd:* Prestatyn, Kinmel Bay, Colwyn Bay. *Beaches in Gwynedd:* Llandudno, Benllech, Trearddur Bay, Abersoch, Pwllheli, Criccieth, Harlech, Llandanwg, Barmouth, Fairbourne, Tywyn. *Beaches in Dyfed:* Borth, Aberystwyth, Aberaeron, New Quay, Whitesand Bay, Broad Haven, Tenby, Saundersfoot, Amroth, Pendine, Pembrey. *Beaches in West Glamorgan:* Rhossili Bay, Port Eynon Bay, Oxwich, Caswell Bay, Langland Bay, Bracelet Bay.

CAUSES FOR CONCERN
Pipeline discharges: About 5½ miles (9km) of the Tywi estuary (Dyfed) have been deoxygenated by sewage discharge – the DoE rates it Class D (the most polluted category).

Radioactive discharges: Wylfa nuclear power station, Anglesey, discharges slightly radioactive cooling water into the Irish Sea.

Agricultural run-off: Pollution from slurry, silage and fertilizer run-off is threatening many rivers (and drinking water).

Oil pollution: The large oil terminal at Milford Haven, Dyfed, creates a risk of serious pollution.

Inshore overfishing: Lobster fisheries now being restocked after collapse due to overfishing.

Beaches: Most beaches suffer from pollution with untreated sewage, which stays close to the shore because of short outfalls. The beach at Rhyl and South Beach, Aberystwyth, exceed EEC safety levels for faecal contamination.

Threatened wildlife: Increasing sedimentation seems to be occurring in the Menai Strait, possibly due to dumping in Liverpool Bay. This sedimentation threatens the delicate ecology of this important area for marine life and birds.

Although the Red-breasted Merganser has always been persecuted because of its liking for young salmon, it has escaped the worst excesses of vengeful river bailiffs because it spends much of its time in coastal waters.

The typical mini-shrub of saltmarshes in England and Wales, Sea Purslane has never been a rarity. Yet it has declined, like so much of Britain's wildlife, as its habitat has been lost – to reclamation, development and agricultural improvement.

People by the sea

The lure of the sea has always had a powerful effect on Britain's island race. Boys follow in their fathers' footsteps and sign on as trawlermen or join the merchant navy. The Wrens have little problem recruiting girls, and the pay packets on the oil rigs, for those who can get the jobs, are tempting when so many traditional coastal jobs have gone.

Like a crumbling cliff on an eroding coastline, many old maritime skills, too, have

slipped away. For some seafarers, their faces etched with the experiences of a lifetime as surely as the nautical design on a front door at Footdee, Aberdeen, the view is one of silent harbours. For those who sit and gaze across the waves, there may be loss and yearning, but for others delight and fascination are just as likely. Being by the sea – whether playing bowls, feeding seagulls or just chatting to a friend – has a charm of its own and brings a unique sense of space and freedom.

Not all the old ways of coastal life have been forgotten, though. Welsh fishermen continue to use their traditional coracles on rivers and estuaries, the time-honoured method of smoking fish is still practised and nets must be painstakingly mended.

THE SEVERN ESTUARY AND THE BRISTOL CHANNEL

DENNIS POTTER

When the enormous word Sea floats free of any specified location to glitter for a moment in my mind, I do not summon up a lustrous stretch of mimosa-clad coast beneath an unclouded sky, nor hear the ever-swelling roar of some vast and empty ocean. Instead, I catch a sudden sight of it between a bristle of bungalows at the brow of the street, vanquishing the fumes of the rackety blue charabanc used on Salem Chapel's annual outing. The sea! The sea! Not the one of 'O Hear Us When We Cry To Thee', vengeful and capricious, but the honest and goodly servant bearing promises of joy unbounded.

The mud-rimmed estuary of the Severn as it widens into pebble and sand along one flank beyond Barry in South Wales and, on the other, past Clevedon and Weston-super-Mare, was almost always the destination of these long-gone Bank Holiday trips from what were then the mining villages of the Forest of Dean. Rattles of little wooden spades in brightly coloured tin buckets are, in childhood, more exciting than the plangent cries of the gulls; and a crumbling fringe of rock under a lowering sky cannot compete with a Laughing Sailor who has a slot for pennies in his head to make him bellow and chortle and roll his ping-pong eyes.

Even then, though, in that whirl of twopenny-coloured frenzies and penny-plain chip-bags, there was always the moment of un-attributable yearning, as clear and yet intangible as the fleeting ache on a Christmas morning, when suddenly the sea lapped and murmured in an old mystery, and the crowded land tilted to meet it as though it wanted to paddle, but dare not.

The wonder stays long after the red balloon has drifted away along the shore. And then, and for ever, each coast in everyone's imagination becomes once more the rim of the world. The beckoning edge, still brightening at the furthest reaches of the mind.

On what will unknowing child and mortal adult feed, if we fill it with waste, and shrink it back into the ordered boundary of commodities? The Laughing Vandal has a slot for more than pennies in his head to make him bellow and chortle and roll his ping-pong eyes.

THE SEVERN ESTUARY AND THE BRISTOL CHANNEL

THE MUMBLES TO ILFRACOMBE

'AS SEVERNE LATELY IN HER EBBES THAT SANKE,
VAST AND FORSAKEN LEAVES TH'UNCOVERED SANDS,
FETCHING FULL TIDE, LUXURIOUS, HIGH AND RANKE,
SEEMS, IN HER PRIDE T'INVADE THE NEIGHB'RING LANDS . . .'

Michael Drayton, *The Barrons Warres* (1603)

The Eel can live in virtually any body of water and withstand considerable pollution. Young eels, in fresh water, have yellow bellies, but become silvery as they begin their tremendous journey down Britain's rivers towards the Sargasso Sea where they breed.

The mighty Severn – at 220 miles long, Britain's longest river – is already more than a mile wide below the Severn Bridge, with many tributaries still to join its heavy and turbulent waters before it reaches the Bristol Channel. The bridge links Wales and England across the River Wye as it flows into the Severn, after the two rivers' separate journeys from the same mid-Wales mountain of Plynlimon. At low tide, the Severn estuary contracts to a quarter of its width, its water clouded with dense, churning, chocolate-brown mud. Narrow spits of sand and shoals of rock black with seaweed give the false impression that one could walk across them as if they were stepping stones. But in six hours' time, the rocks, sand and mud might never have existed. The thick brown liquid explodes against the ever-changing contours of the banks, bubbling over them and rising to within a foot or so of the top of the sea wall.

At Bristol docks, now being redeveloped as a leisure centre, a working barge still does its rounds, while the *Tower Belle* offers tourist trips. One of the world's greatest ports in the days of sail, Bristol's situation – on the narrow, muddy River Avon – meant it could not handle the largest ocean-going ships, so Avonmouth, downriver on the Bristol Channel, eventually replaced it.

The Power of the Severn

The combination of high spring tides and the funnelling effect of the estuary in speeding the water's flow creates a wall of water, known as a 'bore', that advances up the river like some Old Testament agent of retribution. On average, the Severn Bore reaches its most spectacular speed (about 13mph) and proportions every seven years. Champion surfers ride it all the way north to Gloucester, while every sensible small-boat sailor stays battened down in port. The bore, which may be over nine feet high, can take the tide as high as Tewkesbury, a good 13 miles above the normal tidal head at Gloucester, itself 21 miles from the river's mouth.

Until recent times, even when the Severn was

not breaking its bounds and flooding fields and villages or capsizing boats, it still caused problems by presenting a formidable obstacle. Fishermen with no need to cross it still had to negotiate the mud with speed to tend their salmon baskets or shellfish nets. On Bridgwater Bay in Somerset, the shrimp gatherers devised a wooden sledge they called a 'mud horse' to reach the water's edge before the tide turned. To journey between the Welsh and the English banks meant a long slippery walk and a hair-raising ferry ride at low tide between Sudbrook in Wales and Severn Beach across the water, during which passengers prayed the tide would not turn and send the water pounding up the

tige and profits of the Industrial Revolution, which changed so dramatically the appearance of the coastline of South Wales.

Yet little remains today to remind one of the great coal boom – or to suggest the smog, dust and smoke that blanketed Cardiff and Swansea during the mid-19th century. The tiny hamlet of Barry, with its Celtic hermitage island, later favoured by pirates and then by smugglers, became a major rail-linked coal port almost overnight. Cargoes still unload at Barry beside the disused sidings and rusting hulks of railway trucks, locomotives and other rolling stock scrapped in the wake of the Beeching Report, but these days jobs are to be found in catering and leisure

This tranquil view of the weathered sea wall near Sudbrook, on the Welsh side of the Severn, east of Newport, is very different from the same scene at high tide. Then, the muddy water surges up the shore, battering the wall when strong winds drive the waves onshore.

estuary. The alternative was a 70-mile round-trip to Gloucester, where the river could be crossed, and back down the opposite coast. Thirteen years of setbacks and disasters at the end of the last century finally produced the Severn Tunnel beneath the route of the old ferry. In more recent years, a tiny car ferry plied between the banks now shadowed by the suspension bridge, opened in 1966.

The Industrial Shores

Towards the end of the 19th century, Cardiff, the English-imposed capital of Wales, had increased its inhabitants almost a hundredfold in as many years. Its Coal Exchange – like Swansea's Metal Exchange – symbolizes in stone the power, pres-

on the island's pleasure park.

The decline in the coal trade hit other South Wales ports with greater severity. The transporter bridge at Newport, which carries cars across the River Usk on a hanging platform, is the ingenious solution to a now anachronistic problem. Today, no ships need the headroom at high tide to move around this port that was the first to load ships with coal. Cardiff used to see in a week the ships that now call in a year. A concrete wall blocks Aberthaw, whose harbour has silted up. The gracious façade of Penarth port offices belies their use as a hostel for the homeless.

Despite the impressive clean-up programmes at Swansea, much of the coast of South Wales still presents a dark landscape of corrugated

Despite its decline as a port, Cardiff (above left) still has a cosmopolitan air, with its Russian, Norwegian, Yemeni and other communities who arrived in the late 19th and early 20th centuries, when ships from all over the world docked there. Newport has been less able to weather the decline. Its unusual transporter bridge (above) may soon be dismantled, for lack of traffic – and funds to maintain it.

factory sheds, twisting pipes and towering chimneys, storage tanks and barbed wire compounds from once-busy steelworks, car manufacturers, oil refineries, chemical plants and gasworks. To turn away from this metallic vista is to watch the murky Severn waters gathering up waste-pipe discharges and to see, across the river, the sunset-coloured smoke from the industrial complex at the port of Avonmouth. A wide-angle lens would also take in four nuclear power plants – a whole spectrum of designs of different dates – one each at Berkeley and Oldbury above the Severn Bridge, and two at Hinkley Point, on the edge of Bridgwater Bay.

The Heyday of Bristol

Bristol's heyday as a port came much earlier than that of its counterparts on the South Wales shores. One of the world's major ports from Saxon times until the mid-19th century, it owed much of its fame and riches to the slave trade. It was the Elizabethan privateer, John Hawkins, who in the late 16th century originated, albeit on a small scale, the triangular trade of exporting textiles, knives, swords and other items to West Africa, shipping kidnapped West Africans to work as slaves in the Spanish colonies of the West Indies, and bringing rum, tobacco and sugar back to Bristol.

By the time slavery was outlawed almost three hundred years later, an estimated eight million Africans had been sold to the Americas. Not all were traded from Bristol vessels, but it was during the years of colonization that Bristol reached its pre-eminence as a port. And there are still reminders in the city of the business that built Bristol. The grave of the last 'Negro servant' in England, who died in 1720 at the age of eighteen, stands in Henbury churchyard. The names of Black Boy Hill and Whiteladies Road refer to the viewing of the unfortunate chattels by their prospective mistresses.

The narrow, muddy Avon Gorge between Bristol and the Severn acted as a natural defence but it meant that the sailing ships used by Hawkins, John Cabot and the other Bristol merchant adventurers had to be towed up the river to the city, even at high tide. By 1809, however, the waters of the Avon had been diverted to form a floating harbour, with gates to hold in the high tide and a multitude of quays around the city centre.

In 1838, the largest steamship at the time, SS *Great Western*, embarked on her maiden voyage across the Atlantic, followed some six years later by SS *Great Britain*, the largest ocean-going iron steamship, with her novel screw propeller. Both these pioneering vessels were designed by Bristol's favourite famous son, Isambard Kingdom Brunel. By 1864 Brunel's suspension bridge was spanning the Avon with unwavering grace high above the gorge at Clifton.

But already the port of Liverpool was gaining ground. Thomas Telford, the greatest English engineer of the generation before Brunel, commented that Bristol merchants had lost their enterprising spirit through indolence and riches, and observed drily 'besides, the place is badly situated'. He was referring to the muddy gorge which was eventually circumvented by the building of new docks at Avonmouth.

The Wild Side of the Estuary

On the south coast of the estuary, the famous Severn mud, once marketed for cosmetic face-masks and much favoured by birds, dominates the shoreline as far west as Bridgwater Bay. The great expanses of mudflats are broken only by the resort towns of Weston-super-Mare, Burnham-on-Sea and Clevedon.

The estuary is of national importance for wintering birds. The most valuable area is that of the New Grounds at Slimbridge, near the head of the estuary, a few miles south of Gloucester. The mudflats and reclaimed saltmarshes here are the winter haunt of a variety of waders and up to 20,000 wildfowl, including the largest concentration of European White-fronted Geese in the whole country, several hundred Bewick's Swans and a wide variety of other wildfowl, including the rare Lesser White-fronted Goose. Slimbridge is the headquarters of the Wildfowl Trust, founded by Sir Peter Scott in 1946 to protect, study and conserve swans, geese and ducks from all over the world, and now containing the world's largest collection of wildfowl.

In winter, Somerset's Bridgwater Bay National Nature Reserve is another magnet for birds. The rich ooze attracts large numbers of wildfowl, such as Wigeon, Shoveler and Pintail, and a wide variety of waders, including Black-tailed Godwits, Lapwings and Dunlin. In autumn, several thousand Shelduck undergo their annual moult here (in curious contrast to the great majority of the British Shelduck population, which crosses the North Sea to join vast numbers of European Shelduck on the main moulting-grounds on the north German coast). Bridgwater Bay is also notable for the unusually large numbers of Whimbrel it attracts in autumn, and for the remarkably rapid build-up of Common Cord Grass on its saltmarshes.

Low, crumbling cliffs greet the Bristol Channel at the edge of the Quantocks. Mud appears again at Minehead, where low tides may reveal the tree stumps of ancient forests, around which hazardous tidal currents still swirl this far downstream. To the west, just beyond Porlock's shingle bay, the rising Exmoor moorlands tumble down to meet the coast, clothed here and there with dense woods, and reaching a dramatic climax in the scree-covered bare bulk of the Foreland, Devon's most northerly point. A low lighthouse avoids the mist that often blankets this headland's summit, and with its opposite number across the water – Nash Point – announces the widening of the Mouth of the Severn into the Bristol Channel.

Once a valuable food source, the Allis Shad is now very rare. It has succumbed to overfishing and pollution, while weirs without fish ladders stop it reaching its spawning grounds upriver. The Wye may be its last breeding river in Britain.

Handsome and striking, the Shelduck has increased during this century and now breeds on many of Britain's coasts, usually nesting in burrows in sand dunes and on grazing marshes.

Across the Severn from cosmopolitan Cardiff, Clevedon (above) is part of a different world, an English world of subdued and respectable leisure. The trees on the seafront show the force of the wind on this exposed coast at the mouth of the Severn.

Lynton, on the hill above Devon's Lynmouth Bay (far left), was spared the fate of its lower-lying sister village, Lynmouth, in 1952. Buildings were destroyed and over thirty lives were lost when raging floods, caused by a freak storm, swept through the village at night.

High above the water, Brunel's graceful Clifton Suspension Bridge (above left) connects the cliffs of Avon Gorge at Bristol.

Despite its tranquil appearance, Somerset's Porlock Bay (left) is swept by currents that make bathing very dangerous.

In just a couple of spots on the cliffs of Steep Holm island – well out of reach of the visitor's hand – the Wild Peony flowers. It may originally have come from the gardens of a short-lived medieval monastery on the island.

Two contrasting aspects of the Severn estuary: the bare and often gloomy expanse of pebbles seen from Col-Huw Point, west of Barry, on the Welsh side (right) and the wooded shore at Weston-super-Mare (below right), on the English side, with rows of holiday chalets at Sand Bay in the distance.

Flocks of all six species and subspecies of flamingos are kept and studied at the Wildfowl Trust's headquarters on the Severn at Slimbridge (above), the world's most comprehensive wildfowl collection.

West of Nash Point on the South Wales shore, huge sand dunes have been built up gradually by onshore gales since the Middle Ages. The small town and castle of Kenfig was virtually buried by 1485, and sand is still piling up along this coast at a phenomenal rate. The vast dune systems contain a wealth of animals and plants. To the east of Kenfig, Porthcawl lays claim to Europe's largest caravan site, while to the west, Port Talbot and Briton Ferry, with their steel and chemical plants and shipbreakers' yards, merge into Swansea with little grace. At the far end of the congested sweep of Swansea Bay, the old oyster fleets of Mumbles Head have given way to sailing dinghies.

Midway between the two coasts the island nature reserves of Steep Holm and Flat Holm are breeding sites for gulls and other seabirds, and form one of the few British sites for the rare Wild Leek. The even rarer Wild Peony grows on high-cliffed Steep Holm, owned today by a trust set up in memory of the author and broadcaster Kenneth Allsop, who was a lifelong supporter of conservation. Flat Holm is said to be haunted by a 'white lady' – variously identified as the wife of one of the island's lighthouse keepers or a cholera victim from the days of the isolation hospital. Firmly in the realm of historical fact, Marconi transmitted one of the world's first radio signals, across three-and-a-half miles of water, to a receiver on Flat Holm from Lavernock Point, on the Welsh side of the Bristol Channel, in 1897.

Contemporary technology may have other plans for the two islands; there have been proposals to use them as mid-channel supports for a variety of Severn Barrage schemes to harness the Severn's immense tidal power. First mooted in 1933, such proposals have recently seen a revival of interest, with ideas of running a road crossing along the top of the barrage. But

the construction of a barrage could result in the loss of some 50 per cent of the estuary birds' feeding grounds, affecting some 50,000 waders and almost 14,000 wintering wildfowl.

Fourteen hundred years ago, at Lydney, just north of Chepstow on the Welsh side of the Severn, a temple was built, probably by Romanized Celts, looking south across the Severn, with mosaic decorations of fish and sea monsters. Some say it was for Nodens, a god of the headland whose purpose was to guard the estuary. The great river still needs guarding. It may yet be possible to use the gift of its tidal power, but only after a careful appraisal and understanding of the intricate webs of life that depend on it.

REGIONAL SUMMARY

This stretch of coastline, including the estuary of the River Severn up to its first main bend, is about 200 miles (322km) long.

PHYSICAL PROFILE

The Bristol Channel, a downfolded and faulted depression, is bordered in the west by Paleozoic rocks, with Carboniferous coal measures around Swansea Bay. In the east are younger (Mesozoic) rocks, largely overlain by alluvium. The funnel-shaped Severn estuary has the world's second highest tidal range, after Canada's Bay of Fundy. At spring tide, the Severn bore – a wall of water up to 9 feet (2.7m) high – surges upriver. Sizeable bores occur on 25 days a year.

Climate: The climate is mild, with January temperatures of 40°F to 43°F (4°–6°C) and July temperatures of 60°F (16°C). The rainfall averages 40 inches (1,016mm) or more a year.

HUMAN PROFILE

Several major ports have grown up in South Wales in the last 200 years, including Swansea (167,800), Port Talbot (47,300), Barry (43,800), Cardiff (260,700) and Newport (105,400). The English coast has many resorts, including Weston-super-Mare (58,000), Burnham-on-Sea (14,900), Bridgwater (26,100), Watchet (3,000) and Minehead (11,200).

Sites of historic interest: South-eastern Wales was of strategic importance to the Romans who built forts at Cardiff and Caerleon, near Newport, and a town at Caerwent, west of Chepstow. A 12th-century Norman castle occupies the site of the Roman fort at Cardiff, while Chepstow Castle overlooks the River Wye. The Severn Bridge (opened in 1966) is Britain's third longest suspension bridge with a centre span of 3,240 feet (988m).

Museums: Maritime and Industrial Museum, Swansea; National Museum of Wales and the Welsh Industrial and Maritime Museum, Cardiff; Legionary Museum, Caerleon; Chepstow Museum; Museum and Art Gallery, Weston-super-Mare; Watchet Museum; Lyn and Exmoor Museum, Lynton.

Famous personalities: Dylan Thomas (born Swansea), W. H. Davies (born Newport), Admiral Sir Robert Blake (born Bridgwater).

Marine industry: Seaports: Swansea, Cardiff, Avonmouth. Shrimp fishing: Bridgwater Bay.

Commerce/industry: Swansea and Port Talbot have metal industries and, most recently, varied light industries. Cardiff has a wide range of engineering and other industries.

NATURAL PROFILE

Wildlife: This coast is dominated by the Severn estuary, with dunes, saltmarshes and occasional cliffs. On the Welsh side are the 'Monmouthshire Moors', a strip of grazing marshes separated by a sea wall from large sand/silt flats. To the south are the flats of Bridgwater Bay, while sea cliffs begin to dominate in the south-west.

Attractions: In Mid Glamorgan, Kenfig Pool and Dunes has a wide variety of plants and animals. In South Glamorgan, the island of Flat Holm (with the rare Wild Leek); Aberthaw Shore, with foreshore, saltmarsh and cliff habitats. In Gwent, Peterstone Wentlooge – mudflats and saltmarsh – the haunt of waders and wildfowl. In Avon, the island of Steep Holm. In Somerset, Brean Down Sanctuary (NT); Berrow Dunes; Bridgwater Bay (NCC) – estuary, saltflats and lagoons with wildfowl and waders. *Footpaths:* Britain's longest footpath, the South-West Peninsula Coast Path, runs from Minehead to Poole Harbour. There are many shorter scenic paths in South Glamorgan and Somerset. *Beauty spots:* The Quantock Hills AONB reaches the coast east of Watchet. The Exmoor National Park includes the largely cliff-lined coasts from west of Minehead to Combe Martin, beyond which lies the North Devon AONB. *Beaches in Glamorgan:* Rest Bay, Southern Down, Barry. *Beaches in Avon:* Clevedon, Weston-super-Mare. *Beaches in Somerset:* Brean, Berrow, Burnham-on-Sea, Blue Anchor, Minehead, Porlock Bay. *Beaches in Devon:* Lynmouth, Combe Martin.

CAUSES FOR CONCERN

Direct dumping: 1,960 tons (2,000 tonnes) of contaminated sewage sludge and more than 2,940 tons (3,000 tonnes) of industrial waste (mostly latex from the carpet industry) are dumped every year into the Bristol Channel, 5 miles (8km) off Swansea Bay.

Pipeline discharges: The Severn receives a wide range of pollutants, from pesticides to toxic metals, which disperse only slowly between the Severn Bridge and a line drawn from Brean Down to Lavernock Point. Concentration of zinc is 30 times greater and that of cadmium 250 times greater than in the uncontaminated north-eastern Atlantic. Lead levels at Portishead are 125 times the open ocean value. One local authority has advised people not to eat more than 4oz (113g) of locally caught shellfish or 1lb (454g) of local shrimps per week because their levels of cadmium exceed WHO safety limits. About $4\frac{1}{4}$ miles (7km) of the Ely estuary between Cardiff and Penarth are rated Class D (the most polluted) by the DoE; its waters are deoxygenated by sewage.

Radioactive discharges: Nuclear power stations at Berkeley, Oldbury and two at Hinkley Point discharge slightly contaminated cooling water into the estuary. Hinkley B has had several emergency shutdowns between 1978 and 1987. (A pressurized water reactor is now planned for Hinkley.)

Agricultural run-off: Fertilizer run-off causes deoxygenation in rivers and streams.

Oil pollution: Five tons of oil enter the Severn estuary daily in consented discharges, besides considerable deliberate or accidental input.

Beaches: Beaches around Swansea Bay and Clevedon do not meet EEC public health standards.

Threatened wildlife: Proposed Severn Barrage will reduce feeding time to waders at this, their most important wintering site, by half.

One of the most colourful of British seaside plants, the Yellow Horned-poppy is becoming less common on beach shingle and sand dunes as a result of over-picking.

NORTH DEVON
AND CORNWALL

TED HUGHES

Now the river is rich, but her voice is low.
It is her Mighty Majesty the sea
Travelling among the villages incognito.

Now the river is poor. No song, just a thin mad
    whisper.
The winter floods have ruined her.
She squats between draggled banks, fingering her rags
    and rubbish.

And now the river is rich. A deep choir.
It is the lofty clouds, that work in heaven,
Going on their holiday to the sea.

The river is poor again. All her bones are showing.
Through a dry wig of bleached flotsam she peers up
    ashamed
From her slum of sticks.

Now the river is rich, collecting shawls and minerals.
Rain brought fatness, but she takes ninety-nine percent
Leaving the fields just one percent to survive on.

And now she is poor. Now she is East wind sick.
She huddles in holes and corners. The brassy sun gives
    her a headache.
She has lost all her fish. And she shivers.

But now once more she is rich. She is viewing her lands.
A hoard of king-cups spills from her folds, it blazes, it
    cannot be hidden.
A salmon, a sow of solid silver,

Bulges to glimpse it.

Ted Hughes

NORTH DEVON AND CORNWALL
ILFRACOMBE TO LAND'S END

*'GREAT BLACK, JUTTING CLIFFS AND ROCKS, LIKE THE ORIGINAL DARKNESS,
AND A PALE SEA BREAKING IN LIKE DAWN, IT IS LIKE THE BEGINNING OF THE WORLD,
WONDERFUL, AND SO FREE AND STRONG.'*

D. H. Lawrence, letter to Cynthia Asquith from Cornwall (1916)

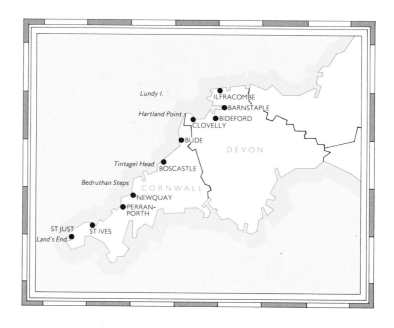

The Common Limpet occurs abundantly around Britain's rocky coasts. Despite its well-deserved reputation for attaching itself with great determination to a chosen rock, it has in the past been harvested for food, although on a fairly small scale.

Gaunt cliffs brace themselves against the ocean's fiercest assaults while the treacherous reefs and mountainous seas can tear a ship apart in minutes and drown the strongest swimmer. The only English shoreline face to face with the fierce Atlantic Ocean, the coast of north Devon and Cornwall is a desolate, and at times uninhabitable, coast. Waterfalls reveal where the grinding power of water and wind and the rocks they toss have gnawed back the sheer headlands, obliterating the gentler valley routes that streams once took to the sea. Where the land slopes more gently, sand dominates, blown by onshore gales and built up into dunes as high as cliffs.

Gradually being worn away by the ceaseless onslaught of the huge Atlantic waves, which can exert a pressure estimated at four tons per square foot, Hartland Point is a dramatic and desolate spot, typical of the rugged north Devon coast. The lighthouse is no longer manned; protected by a sea wall, it depends on automation to keep its light shining.

Hazards and Havens

For all the harsh contours of the cliffs, summer warmth and beauty bestow their favours on this shore. The headland backdrops to sheltered coves glow with the brilliant yellow of gorse and the sensuous pink of thrift, and up above, the fields form a vibrant patchwork of green and gold. But when the skies darken and the temperature drops, or when the glassy sea abruptly changes to boiling white, the mood is set for the harsh tasks that keep – or used to keep – the population fed.

An old seafarers' rhyme warns that 'From Padstow Bar to Lundy Light, is a sailor's grave by day or night'. The coast south from Padstow to Land's End has no less fearsome a reputation, save for the greater chance a stricken vessel had of limping into port. On the coast north from Padstow to Ilfracombe the havens are few and far between, and the hazards many. Off Ilfracombe, sharp rocks and reefs, combined with a vicious tide-race, pose particular dangers to shipping in the Bristol Channel.

At Morte Point, near Ilfracombe, the coast turns abruptly southwards and scree-covered headlands alternate with wide sandy beaches. The huge area of Saunton Sands is backed by the

vast dune system of Braunton Burrows, where the sand, bound by Marram Grass, can tower up to a hundred feet high. This outstanding example of a dune system shows the complete progression from the open sand of the beach through the moist hollows, or 'slacks', with their orchids, Water Germander and other rare plants, to thick scrub. A Site of Special Scientific Interest, much of this unique habitat is protected in a Nature Conservancy Council reserve.

Across the water of the Taw-Torridge estuary, once the haunt of Henry Williamson's *Tarka the Otter*, stands the neat little town of Appledore. Today, its docks and quays are mainly quiet, but it still has a flourishing shipbuilding industry in a covered yard that was the largest in Europe when opened in 1970. Modern vessels take shape alongside replicas of historic vessels, from Drake's *Golden Hinde* to Viking longships and Roman galleys.

Further up the two rivers, the once-thriving ports of Barnstaple, on the Taw, and Bideford, on the Torridge, have long since silted up. Curlews and Oystercatchers still find food in the tidal mud, but salmon rights come cheap these days on the River Torridge, since sewage and slurry from upstream farms have sullied the once clear waters.

West round the curve of Bideford Bay lies the

picturesque village of Clovelly, once an important fishing centre, but now a showcase – an 18th- and 19th-century fishing port in aspic. Nothing could present a greater contrast to this cosy little haven than the mammoth wall of rock that makes up Hartland Point, some six miles to the west. To the Romans this wall was known as the Promontory of Hercules, in recognition of its unceasing labours in resisting the continual pounding of the Atlantic Ocean.

Below Hartland Point, where Devon gives way to Cornwall, the northern stretch of the Cornish coast reveals contorted stress patterns –

With its splendid rock stacks set amid golden sands, Bedruthan Steps (above), on the north coast of Cornwall, attracts so many visitors that plastic matting has had to be laid along the cliff path to prevent further erosion by the tramp of human feet.

The deep valley that ends in the little cove at Trevellas Porth (left) was filled with the noise from tin mines in the 19th century, but the industry was killed off by cheap imports of the metal from abroad.

zigzags of shale and sandstone strata folded when the rocks of the cliffs lay deep underground. The only gap of any size, and even then a tricky one to negotiate, is at Bude. Here, lime-rich sand was delivered to the inland farms by a canal linking Bude with the River Tamar.

South of Bude, near the soaring cliffs of Cambeak Point, where great chunks of quartz-filled rocks slant through the bed of the shore, the misnamed Crackington Haven is a gloomy, frightening place, the squealing and cracking of the pebbles echoing between the sheer, shadowed cliffs. Gorse and Bracken cling on for dear life to the dizzying cliff-tops, gripping the wind-blown turf. Tiny hamlets gain little shelter from the wind, yet Wild Honeysuckle and Red Valerian spill out of the high hedgerows that line the narrow sunken lanes.

The Doom Bar – the Padstow Bar of the old mariners' rhyme – now almost blocks the Camel estuary that once provided a vital link between the fishing port of Padstow and the sea. As the size of ships that could cross the sand-bar diminished, so did the fortunes of Padstow, once north Cornwall's busiest port. When the railway reached the town at the end of the 19th century, Padstow was still exporting local minerals in bulk, but the steady silting-up of the bar soon made large-scale trade impossible.

Tough trawlers and sturdy pleasure cruisers still leave the estuary for the open sea, joined by the more intrepid small-boat sailors. Professional fishermen are out after lemon sole, turbot and dover sole, or busy tending crab and lobster pots. Their catch is displayed in holding tanks in the old quayside fish market. Every month or so, French boats arrive to buy up the stocks of spider crabs. But no one makes the passage in and out without a nose for squalls and an eye on the charts that mark the Doom Bar's position.

Myths and Legends

During the boom of Cornish metal mining in the 19th century the coal to smelt the tin and copper ore came from South Wales. At many a headland or rocky bay with no port to moor the colliers, the coal was dumped overboard at high tide to be collected from the beach when the tide ebbed. Such arrangements left little room for social intercourse, but links between the Cornish people and their fellow Celts in Wales, Ireland and Brittany have always been strong. Languages were similar and many early saints and pre-Saxon legends were common to all. The Irish-born St Ia, who gave her name to St Ives, is said to have journeyed to north Cornwall on a leaf, while St Perran, patron saint of Cornwall, made the crossing on a millstone.

The myth of Arthur, king to Breton, Welsh and Cornish people alike, invokes the lost land of Lyonnesse between Land's End and the Scilly Isles, and the headland fortress of Tintagel. Arthur, it is said, was born at Tintagel and raised there by the magician Merlin. When the sword

held above Dosmary Lake in Bodmin Moor yielded to Arthur's hand, he returned to build a stronghold at Tintagel.

At the end of Arthur's reign, his wounded body was carried to Avalon, the highlands of Lyonnesse – said to survive as the Scilly Isles – pursued by the treacherous Mordred. In a last show of power to his dying king, Merlin sank the lowlands with a salvo of well-aimed earth tremors, drowning Mordred, hundreds of square miles of land, and the capital of Lyonnesse, which some believe still lies close to the surface in the Seven Stones reef off Land's End.

Giants were familiar in these parts, too. According to legend, Bedruthan carved the stacks of granite into the stepping stones named after him that can be seen between Newquay and Padstow. Another Cornish giant, Wrath, did likewise at Basset's Cove, near Portreath. The spherical Bowl Rock above Carbis Bay near St Ives, is said to be a stray ball from a game between local giants and Cormoran, the 'ogre of the Mount', whom Jack the Giant-Killer slew.

The Illicit Trades

Local smugglers embellished such stories to have Wrath and Bedruthan striding out to sea in every storm and snatching ships to devour at their leisure back on shore. Headless passengers in horse-drawn coaches were said to ride on moon-lit nights along the coastal roads. The truth of the matter was much more prosaic.

In return for leaving their stable doors open at night so that the smugglers could borrow horses, the collaborating or coerced villagers were well rewarded with a tin of tea or keg of brandy, which found its way back from the coast with the animals before the sun rose. Sometimes the smugglers' own horses were trained to carry their load to a hiding place while their owners went back to bed.

The graveyards of the coastal churches are full of shipwrecked souls who might have lived had those on land led a less wretched existence. Local boats were known to fight off attempts to rescue ships in trouble as well as using lanterns to lure ships to their doom on the lethal rocks. The most notorious wrecker of them all was 'Cruel' Coppinger, a Dane who swam ashore from his sinking ship at Welcombe Mouth, on the Devon border, in the 1750s, and formed a gang of expert cut-throats. Torture, terror and extortion kept the village people and their vicar quiet while murder on the seas brought in the gains.

The ancient stronghold of smugglers, wreckers and pirates alike was Lundy Island, lying eleven miles out from the north Devon coast, and protected from intruders by rough seas, strong currents and a wall of granite cliffs.

In the Middle Ages four generations of the Marisco family held sway here, their exploits little different from those of the Viking raiders who named the island 'Lundy' – Norse for 'Puffin Island'. Today, few Puffins remain but Kitti-

The Puffin has suffered a serious decline recently, due partly to pollution and overfishing. But it seems that this dumpy, comical auk has suffered population crashes in the past; perhaps the recent decrease is part of this historical picture.

The progressive silting-up of the Torridge estuary at Bideford (above) led to the decline of the town's once prosperous harbour. The congestion of today's road traffic crossing the Torridge by the 24-arched medieval bridge has recently been relieved by a new bridge downstream (bottom).

One of the few sheltered harbours along the outer reaches of the Bristol Channel, Ilfracombe's port (far left) is still the focus of its steep, winding streets, even if the boats there today are pleasure craft rather than fishing vessels. Appledore (centre), north of Bideford, still has a thriving shipbuilding industry.

At Navax Point east of St Ives Bay, deep caves, accessible only from the sea, shelter a colony of Grey Seals, which breed undisturbed in the winter months.

Ilfracombe's lifeboat station, with its photographic record of launches and rescues, and its neat rows of jackets and boots, is ready and waiting (below). At Clovelly (below right), the lifeboat is out at sea. A sudden change in the weather could see it towing the pleasure craft back to the shelter of the breakwater.

wakes, Fulmars and small numbers of Manx Shearwaters still breed on the steep western cliffs, and Jackdaws and Ravens wheel and dive above the ruins of Marisco Castle. Now a nature reserve owned by the National Trust and administered by the Landmark Trust, the island is visited by over four hundred species of other birds – and birdwatchers. Botanists delight in the Lundy Cabbage, which grows nowhere else in the world and is host to two unique species of beetles.

The underwater world of Lundy below the kelp forest is equally rich. Jewel Anemones spread their tentacles, alongside miniature cities of branching sponges. Devonshire Cup Corals, Yellow Cup Corals and Rose Corals inhabit the base of the submarine cliffs, while above live other creatures that rejoice in such names as Sea Fans and Dead Men's Fingers. With its rich oceanic animal life, Lundy was declared Britain's first Statutory Marine Nature Reserve in November 1986.

The Death of the Coastal Mines

To the seafarer the ruined chimneys and engine houses of abandoned mines are familiar landmarks. Clinging to the very edge of the coastline, they share their positions with Bronze-Age cairns and barrows, whose builders were the first to smelt the tin and copper won from the rock about 5,000 years ago. Some 2,500 years later, Carthaginian traders voyaged north to Cornwall to buy tin and copper. Fifty years before Christ was born, Julius Caesar took an interest in Britain when merchants told him of the metals. After the conquest of Britain by Emperor Claudius' legions in AD 43, the Romans extracted surface tin and copper from the Cornish coast.

For centuries, the open-cast mines were worked and the rust-red streams and rivers panned for the two valuable metals. By 1800, Cornwall supplied three-quarters of the world's demand for copper. By the 1860s, cheaper imported copper spelled the end of the boom, and tin mining took over. By the end of the First

Boscastle has the only secure natural harbour on the rugged coastline between Padstow and Bude. To reach it, boats must manoeuvre round a narrow, twisting channel between high walls of slate.

A native of South Africa, the Hottentot Fig is now fully naturalized in many warm temperate regions, including the south-western peninsula of England, where its fleshy leaves form dense mats on the sea cliffs and its exotic flowers bloom in summer.

World War, however, Cornish tin mining suffered the same fate as the copper, as other countries exported cheaper tin. To this day, however, all along the northern Cornish coast patches of reddish-brown tin ore swirling around in the waves indicate a nearby mine, often extending deep beneath the sea-bed.

In recent years, foreign tin prices rose and the industry revived. Major investments looked set to secure the future of the region's oldest industry, only to witness in 1986 another dramatic crash. Mines such as Geevor, near Pendeen, held on while most of the workers were laid off, keeping pumps going and recouping a portion of the cost by taking tourists down the sea-bed tunnels. But Geevor's ancient symbol of a goat with a mermaid's tail looks likely to become another relic of a once thriving industry. Even St Perran, the patron saint of the 'tinners' – as well as of Cornwall – could not ensure the livelihood of the miners and the ports that had once transported the metals all over the world.

Changing Occupations

The death of the mines, the disappearance of the great pilchard shoals in the 19th century, due to climatic change, and the more recent industrial decline has had a profound effect on this coastline. For most of the former mining communities, fishing villages and disused ports, the only means of survival has come from attracting visitors.

The people of Port Quin gave up and emigrated to Canada two hundred years ago, leaving a ghost town exposed to the wayward force of the winds and rain. Clovelly kept its olde-worlde charm because of its discovery by Victorian tourists. The golden sands from Newquay to St Ives are natural advantages that changed those two small towns from fishing ports to a world of bed-and-breakfasts and caravans and chalets.

Even so, not all the old traditions have been lost. At St Ives, the hurling of the silver ball in early February commemorates its Celtic patron saint St Ia. Bude, too, celebrates its Celtic missionary every year, while Padstow's Hobby

Still caught in large numbers off the Cornish coast, Mackerel can frequently be bought in the fish-and-chip shops of Padstow. But will it survive the likely heavy exploitation as stocks of other fish are exhausted by overfishing?

Trevaunance Cove, near St Agnes; is typical of the beaches along the north Cornwall coasts where the full force of the Atlantic is felt. This bright summer view conceals the dark reality of a sea that has destroyed many attempts to build a harbour at the cove to serve the now silent tin and copper mines.

Cornish coastal ruins span the centuries: at Tintagel (right) the 12th-century castle stands on the site of a 6th-century Celtic monastery, while near St Agnes the gaunt, deserted chimney and engine houses of Wheal Kitty mine (above) add to the desolation of the scene. It is one of many Cornish tin and copper mines that closed about a hundred years ago.

Horse ceremony mixes pagan May-Day rites with memories of medieval raids from France.

For all the miles of sand, seaside bathing is never a certainty, and at some resorts there are hazards other than the natural forces, from sewage pollution to broken bottles and jagged tin cans. The one near-constant delight on this coast belongs to the surfers riding in on the great Atlantic breakers to beach after beach, from Morte Point to Sennen Cove. World amateur championships of the sport were held at Newquay in 1986, and surfers can usually be seen braving the cold water and the crashing surf.

At Perran Bay, a favourite surfers' beach, the troughs and crests of waves in deeper waters are reproduced in giant sand dunes for half a mile inland. The 7th-century oratory of St Perran lies buried beneath a dune. On the Camel estuary, the church of St Enodoc lies in a hollow, its roof level with the surrounding sand. The image of Botallack mine's cliff-edge chimney awaiting the inevitable erosion of its base speaks volumes about the elemental battles and the tales of endurance on this coast. As yet another cliff face tumbles, the graceful seabirds find new ledges for their nests. The surfers and the seals glory in the very stuff that crunches ships, and in the sheltered coves and grassy meadows of the hinterland, 'hedges' of hewn slate and granite keep out the ocean gales. Of all the English coast, this stretch remains the least defaced by modern life.

REGIONAL SUMMARY

NORTH DEVON AND CORNWALL

The coast between Ilfracombe, Devon, and Land's End, Cornwall, excluding estuaries and islands, is about 130 miles (209km) long.

PHYSICAL PROFILE

Sandstones and slates of the Devonian period are the main rocks in the north-west. Near Barnstaple these strata dip beneath Carboniferous Culm Measures, so-called because within the layers of shale, slate, limestone, lava and sandstone are traces of a soft coal, locally called 'culm'. The Culm Measures end at Boscastle. The rocks to the south are again Devonian, with large granitic intrusions, especially around Land's End. Atlantic rollers hammer the coast – the beaches are a surfers' paradise. Wave erosion is wearing back the coast, carving bays, headlands and superb cliffs, some of which have spectacular waterfalls plunging over them.

Climate: Mild, with average January temperatures of 43°F (6°C) in Cornwall, and average July temperatures of about 61°F (16°C). Rainfall averages about 45 inches (1,143mm) a year.

HUMAN PROFILE

Outside the tourist season, the coastline is thinly populated. Major settlements and resorts include Ilfracombe (10,100); Barnstaple (19,000), a busy market town; Bideford (12,200), formerly a major seaport; Bude-Stratton (6,800); Newquay (16,000), Cornwall's biggest resort; St Ives (11,000), a haunt of artists; and St Just (4,000), which is England's westernmost town.

Sites of historic interest: Phoenicians traded for tin in Cornwall as early as the 5th century BC. Derelict mineworkings testify to the last prosperous phase of metal production in the 19th and early 20th centuries. Celtic saints founded several settlements, though some of their churches, such as those at Padstow and Perranporth, were buried by sand dunes. The 12th-century Tintagel Castle is believed by some to occupy the site of an earlier castle of King Arthur's. Stratton, near Bude, was the site of the Civil War Battle of Stamford Hill (1643).

Museums: Ilfracombe Museum; Rock and Shell Museum, Croyde; Braunton and District Museum; Barnstaple Museum; North Devon Maritime Museum, Appledore; Hartland Quay Museum; Bude-Stratton Historical and Folk Exhibition; Museum of Witchcraft, Boscastle; Mineral and Mining Museum, Pendeen; Tin Mining Museum, Trewellard.

Famous personalities: John Gay (born Barnstaple). Westward Ho! was named after Kingsley's novel; it is the site of the United Services College, which Kipling attended and used in *Stalky and Co.* Poet Robert Stephen Hawker was vicar of Morwenstow (1834–75). Tintagel is traditionally regarded as the birthplace of King Arthur.

Marine industry: Fishing ports: Appledore, Bideford, St Ives. Surfboards made at Newquay.

Commerce/industry: Tin, slate and copper were once exported from the area. Appledore is known for shipbuilding.

NATURAL PROFILE

Wildlife: The coast is lined by cliffs, broken by occasional estuaries and dunes. Many cliffs are grassy; others are wooded or topped with maritime heath. At the base of the cliffs is a rock-strewn shoreline. The wooded undercliffs, especially between Clovelly and Boscastle, are rich in butterflies. There are many sites of great marine interest, particularly Lundy Island, about 24 miles (39km) west of Ilfracombe, where warm waters from the south mingle with colder waters from the north.

Attractions: In Devon, Lundy Island (NT), site of the endemic Lundy Cabbage, became Britain's first Marine Nature Reserve in 1986; Braunton Burrows Nature Reserve; Northam Burrows; Welcombe and Marshland Valleys. In Cornwall, Bude Marshes; Camel estuary; Hayle estuary. *Footpaths:* Part of the South-West Peninsula Coast Path extends along the entire course of this magnificent coastline. *Beauty spots:* The North Devon AONB extends down the coast from Ilfracombe. The Cornwall AONB takes in most of Cornwall's north coast, from the scenic Bedruthan Steps northwards, and also most of Land's End peninsula. Many stretches of these coasts are owned by the NT, including Cape Cornwall, north of Land's End, which the food company Heinz gave to the nation in 1987. It is a Site of Special Scientific Interest. *Beaches in Devon:* Ilfracombe, Woolacombe, Croyde Bay, Saunton Sands, Westward Ho! *Beaches in Cornwall:* Bude, Polzeath, Daymer Bay, Harlyn Bay, Tregarnon, Mawgan Porth, Watergate Bay, Newquay, Holywell Bay, Perranporth, Trevaunance Cove, Porthowan, Portreath, The Towans, Port Kidney, Carbis Bay, St Ives.

CAUSES FOR CONCERN

Agricultural run-off: Pollution from intensive livestock rearing, via slurry tank leaks, silage effluent and fertilizer run-off, has caused serious contamination in the River Torridge, Devon, leading to large-scale depletion of salmon stocks. The DoE has downgraded the river from Class 1 to Class 3 in the five-year period 1981–6.

Beaches: The South-West Water Authority has the largest number of beaches polluted by discharges of raw sewage in the UK. Financial constraints prevent any imminent prospect of clean-up operations. Affected beaches include the major resort beach of Ilfracombe. There are high levels of faecal bacteria from raw sewage in Barnstaple Bay.

Threatened wildlife: High levels of TBT (tributyl tin) anti-fouling paint found in marinas have led to the widespread destruction of the populations of Dog Whelks.

Other pollution: Spoil heaps from disused tin and copper mines continue to release toxic materials into the sea. They are absorbed by marine organisms, passed up food chains and hence may be consumed by man. The Red River forms a red slick of metal-rich mining wastes near the beach at Portreath, Cornwall.

The cliffs near Bude were once a major site for the Large Blue, which became extinct in Britain in 1979. The caterpillars feed on Wild Thyme, which flourishes only in short, grazed turf, and are then nurtured underground by Red Ants. 'Undergrazing' of the turf seems to be the cause of the Large Blue's demise.

A brilliantly coloured fish of rocky coasts, the Cuckoo Wrasse is widespread round Britain but most common off the West Coast. Its coloration is variable; older males are markedly blue, while younger males and females are redder. Its main threat is pollution.

SOUTH CORNWALL, DEVON AND DORSET

JOHN FOWLES

I will not write of its variety and beauty. I will not write in harmony with the photographs of it selected here. I will not write that all its length, from Dorset to Cornwall, is not under threat. Countless writers close a blind eye and lie, at tourism's behest, to please the grockles and their own sensitivity. I will not.

The nest was a massive affair, used for many generations, on a wide ledge near the base of a sea-cliff, itself at the Cornish foot of England – not just an ordinary cliff, but one of formidable majesty and an overhanging unclimbability. I went there several times over several years to marvel at its inaccessibility and at the sight, from another huge cliff, of the nesting pair flying to their palace, their cartload of twigs, over the fierce sea. It was the perfect nest; so totally unapproachable that it made one smile.

But that was before the species disappeared from Dorset, where I now live. Ten years have passed since I could last look up here at the sound of a Raven's croak, as it is indeed since I glanced out to sea and saw Basking Sharks or dolphins. If it were only these . . . but it has happened to so much else. Things are in retreat, everywhere man increases and advances. Did it not happen so often, we should be shocked at how much disappears, and perhaps most of all with the South-west's great glory in this increasingly urban age, its solitude and wildness. We already have the worst polluted sea in Britain; now technology, with appalling timing, allows us to catch more fish. If pollution doesn't kill, echo-location and the net will. We have a raging fire, and we pour petrol on it.

Years ago I used to find the excessive caution of those Cornish Ravens amusing; no longer. The wise birds knew better than I, both about Ravens' survival and about men. Nothing can stop man's worst self, his vicious notion of what freedom, his freedom, means. Nothing, either creature or landscape, is so good, so innocent, so pure that it will not be ruined or exterminated if it will bring more money. In another species, we would call it cancer.

Above all, I will not hide man's true profession. It is an ancient one on these shores. He is a wrecker; and what he wrecks now is not just ships. It is all that he once most treasured in the world.

SOUTH CORNWALL, DEVON AND DORSET

LAND'S END TO POOLE; THE ISLES OF SCILLY

'THE SPRAY SPRANG UP ACROSS THE CUSPS OF THE MOON,
AND ALL ITS LIGHT LOOMED GREEN
AS A WITCH-FLAME'S WEIRDSOME SHEEN
AT THE MINUTE OF AN INCANTATION SCENE;
AND IT GREENED OUR GAZE – THAT NIGHT AT DEMILUNE.'

Thomas Hardy, *Once at Swanage* (1925)

Many tourists set off from Cornish holiday ports to fish for Blue Sharks, which migrate north from tropical waters each summer. They also suffer from entanglement in fishermen's nets – both sharks and men hunt mackerel and herring.

A beguiling world of smugglers' coves, deep wooded valleys, or coombes; an intricate network of meandering lanes flanked by high flower-decked banks criss-crossing the rich countryside; sudden views from rounded headlands of a startlingly turquoise sea – the general impression of the south coast of the West Country is of a soft, gentle landscape blessed by a mild and sunny climate, in dramatic contrast to the often harsh, uncompromising storm-lashed north coast.

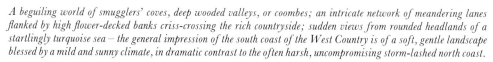

Anatomy of the Coastline

The extreme south-western corner of Cornwall forms the 'foot' of England: the Penwith peninsula, with the wave-battered granite cliffs of Land's End at its tip, making up the toes and the lonely Lizard peninsula forming the heel. From the Lizard to Start Point in Devon, the coastline follows a complex series of tight curves, promontories and indentations, while on the larger scale drawing a great, sweeping semicircle.

Rivers run through narrow creeks and fan out into intricate estuaries like branching fronds of seaweed, while the winding course of the great

Despite the tranquil appearance of the great sweep of Start Bay, south of Brixham, the sea here destroyed the little village of Hallsands seventy years ago after 650,000 tons of its protective barrier of shingle had been removed for building Devonport naval dockyard.

River Tamar virtually separates the whole of Cornwall from its larger neighbour, Devon. A second great semicircle, smoother and less elaborately dissected, carries the coastline eastwards from Start Point to Dorset's Isle of Portland, which juts out like a crooked finger into the English Channel.

For centuries, pilchard and mackerel fishing, smuggling, boatbuilding and farming were the traditional trades of both coasts of the West Country. Although tin and copper extraction was a boom industry in the late 18th and 19th centuries, there were fewer mines on the south coast. A compensation was that the softer rocks of the south could be quarried. Here, human excavations have been superimposed on the work of natural erosion.

Land's End and the Lizard

At Land's End on the south-western extremity, you are constantly aware of being on the edge of our small island; few stretches of the British coastline present such an abrupt encounter between land and sea.

Off Land's End, the sea can be so clear that, with luck, giant but harmless Basking Sharks can be seen beneath the water, from the top of the tough granite cliffs, while the spray hurls itself against the lichen-covered rocks. Nearly vertical,

these dramatic rocky ramparts at the very end of the English mainland are intricately jointed, resembling castle walls in places.

Visited each year by about a million tourists, this famous stretch of headland is not a quiet place in summer, but it requires only a little effort to escape the crowds. Turning your back on the huge hotel and car park perched near the cliffs, you need walk only a short distance to find a place to reflect on the emotive power of this last outpost of the land.

Land's End's status as the south-westerly extremity of the British mainland is matched by Lizard Point's position as the most southerly. Unlike that of Penwith, the Lizard peninsula contains other crystalline rocks besides granite – schists, gabbro and, most abundant and most dramatic, the beautiful serpentine, so-called

because the rich green veins of minerals that run through it give it the appearance of snakeskin.

The name 'Lizard' does not appear to have any connection with serpentine – it is probably derived from the Cornish words for 'court' (*lys*) and 'a height' (*ard*) – but the local inhabitants certainly do. There is a minor industry in quarrying, carving and polishing the dramatic serpentine rock – which is found over much of the southern part of the peninsula – to make ornaments for the tourist trade. It has long been used in local buildings and became fashionable in 1846, when Queen Victoria visited Cornwall and ordered a serpentine table.

The serpentine's high magnesium content yields a thin, poor soil on which the pale pink-flowered Cornish Heath grows, dominating the maritime heaths of the clifftops. Among the

Mevagissey is a typical south Cornwall fishing village, with its sheltered inner and outer harbours. The tall buildings lining the quays are clues to its former prosperity as a fishing port. Today, with the pilchard shoals long gone, due to a change in climate, fishing has declined, and tourism has replaced it as the main source of income.

Lizard's unique flora are many wildflowers such as Wild Chives, Pillwort and Large Lizard Clover, which, like the Cornish Heath, are rarely seen elsewhere. In spring, the grassy places sparkle with the blue of Spring Squill, a typical cliff flower, seen at its finest here. Above this living carpet little intrudes into the view except for the space-age dishes of Goonhilly Downs earth satellite station.

Both coasts of the Lizard have dramatic cliffs, but the east is blessed with better shelter, its secluded coves enabling small fishing communities to establish themselves. Even so, the wind here is strong enough to force inhabitants to tie down the thatched roofs of the whitewashed cottages with chains. Treacherous pinnacles and reefs offshore meant that in the past fisherfolk supplemented their income, as in so many parts of Cornwall, with whatever they could salvage from wrecks. It is not surprising that it was here in this strange, remote part of Cornwall, in Lizard Town, that the last sermon in the Cornish language was delivered in 1678.

The Flower Isles

The Scilly Isles are the last granite outpost of the south-west coast. A splash of tiny rocks and skerries around five main islands that begin 28 miles from Land's End, the Scillies share the gale-ridden exposure of the Hebridean islands with a winter warmth and sunshine more akin to Mediterranean climes. In days gone by, contact with the mainland was limited to fly-by-night smuggling and scavenging operations. Even to the Cornish, the Scillonians were a race apart.

The Victorian age brought the changes to the Scillies that have shaped their subsequent development. The chief catalyst was Augustus Smith, who invested in the leasehold of the islands in 1834 and established a completely new economy. Gradually, the cultivation of early flowers and vegetables became a profitable business. The first regular boat service to the mainland was established to carry produce – today, helicopters share in this task.

From the air, the inward-facing slopes of the main islands present a steeplechase of high evergreen hedges keeping the wind off neat beds of lilies, daffodils, narcissi and irises. Cottages serve as holiday homes and divers hunt out wrecks. Among the visitors are flocks of birdwatchers who come to spot rare vagrant birds from America, Asia or Europe, or to watch the breeding colonies of seabirds that throng the nature reserve on the uninhabited island of Annet. For others, the delight lies in the islands' exciting flora, with several rare natives and a number of subtropical aliens, many of them introduced by the Victorians.

Quarrying and the Coast

The proverbially tough granite, the mottled serpentine and the dark, heavy gabbro are not the only rocks to have attracted the attention of

This view from St Mary's (below) towards the smaller islands of Tresco and Samson epitomizes the wild beauty of the Isles of Scilly. The wrecking of the *Torrey Canyon*, carrying almost 120,000 tons of crude oil, on the Seven Stones reef just north-east of the islands in 1967 provides a stark reminder of the fragile environment of these relatively unspoiled south-western outliers of Britain.

Victorian visitors to the Lizard peninsula gave names to every slab, pinnacle and fissure at Kynance Cove (far right), based on their supposed resemblance to bellows, postboxes and bishops' hats. They also patronized the local trade in ornaments made from carved and polished serpentine, the rock (right) that dominates much of the Lizard. The serpentine trade still thrives, with many small workshops in Lizard Town.

quarriers along the West Country's south coast. China clay – kaolin – from the St Austell region of Cornwall has been loaded onto ships at nearby Charlestown and Fowey since the 18th century, gradually replacing the Cornish copper trade (see pages 148–9) by the end of the 19th century, and becoming one of the United Kingdom's main bulk exports today.

Until recently, the unwanted mica and quartz, together with a coating of kaolin that could not be easily separated, were dumped into rivers near the clay pits. The waters off Pentewan to the west and Par Sands to the east of St Austell, used to be chalky white, while the beach at Carlyon, next to Charlestown, still bears traces of the thick, gritty, greyish clay.

stone which has been used for almost four hundred years in many great buildings throughout the world including St Paul's Cathedral (1675) and the Bank of England (1939) in London and the United Nations Building (1953) in New York. The two areas where the limestone beds produce this tough but easily worked stone are the Isle of Purbeck and the Isle of Portland, the former no island at all, the latter with more claim to the title, but with its own natural causeway in the form of Chesil Beach.

In Purbeck a layer of limestone with a different composition from that of Portland stone is also found. This is Purbeck stone, known as 'Purbeck marble' because it polishes to a beautiful blue, brown or greeny-black sheen. For

A fresh view of Land's End from its seaward edge reveals the gaunt beauty of its granite cliffs, carved by wind and wave erosion so that they resemble castle walls. The immense power of the waves after their long journey across the Atlantic acts like a battering ram against the most westerley point in England, as evidenced by the rocks littering the base of the cliffs.

In Devon, at Teignmouth, dockers used to load the boats with sticky ball clay as well as Dartmoor granite. The latter was used for the old London Bridge, built between 1825 and 1832, and sold to the United States in 1971.

The glowing red sandstone of south Devon, as well as being quarried for use in buildings, has created a beautiful coastline that attracts many visitors. The steep and tumbled terracotta cliffs at Dawlish and Teignmouth are attacked by wind and water along their joint planes, producing fantastic shapes, which make the coastal railway journey unforgettable.

Further east, in Dorset, a different rock base, almost as hard as granite, proved as profitable as china clay. This is the creamy-white Portland

centuries, it was greatly in demand for interior columns and ornamentation – it decorated many of the great English medieval cathedrals and churches. Local quarrying declined in the 1880s and with the concurrent arrival of the railway, the prosperity of Swanage, Purbeck's main town, came to depend on its popularity as a resort.

Purbeck's Arne peninsula, which juts into Poole Harbour, is one of the last vestiges of the heathland that once covered much of southern England. One of the main breeding areas of the scarce Dartford Warbler, the heathland is bordered by mudflats, saltmarshes and reedbeds. Over a thousand acres are protected in an RSPB reserve, though much damage has been done by unwary or uncaring people lighting fires.

Resembling a grass, yet with young leaves curled like watchsprings, Pillwort is a tiny fern. It has become a great rarity as the damp spots it favours have been drained. The Lizard is one of its last British haunts.

Another, long-term, threat to Purbeck's wildlife comes from the recently discovered oilfield that may one day be developed. This could devastate the tangled southern shores of Poole Harbour, including the unique wildlife of Studland Heath National Nature Reserve, which, like Arne, is home to all six species of British reptiles – the Adder, Grass Snake, Slow Worm, Common Lizard and rare Smooth Snake and Sand Lizard – as well as a rich diversity of marine life on the fine sandy shores of Studland Bay.

On the Isle of Portland the effects of human toil are etched in its history. Between its northern edge and Weymouth, a circular harbour, as big as the island itself, was created by the building of three massive breakwaters, the unpaid work of British convicts awaiting transportation to Australia in the 1840s. Before the harbour and the causeway linking the island to the rest of Dorset were built, the Portland islanders were a law unto themselves, retaining old customs and superstitions long after they had been discarded on the mainland. Excluding all outsiders, they arranged their work to suit themselves, hewing

rock and battling with the fierce tide-race round the island in their fishing boats and the ships that carried the quarried stone to other ports.

For generations, the men who worked the quarries negotiated direct with builders or architects without the intervention of middlemen. Even as great an architect as Sir Christopher Wren was unable to claim the rock as the King's property, to be taken without payment. The islanders held angry demonstrations and dropped already quarried stone into the sea, until it was agreed that the Crown would pay a levy to each islander.

Coastal Curiosities

The immeasurable pile of pebbles that attaches Portland to the mainland eight miles away might well provoke superstition. Shingle spits built up by stormy waves are also found on other British shores, but the length and smooth geometric curve of Chesil Beach, in contrast to the curls and points of the far shore of the Fleet lagoon which lies behind it, suggest some strange, otherworldly contrivance.

Many Mute Swans have been affected by lead poisoning. There appears to be little doubt that they have suffered and died from swallowing anglers' lead weights, and it now seems that discarded wildfowlers' shot in coastal areas is also to blame.

Two of the best-known features of the coast of south-western England, Dorset's Lulworth Cove (above right) and Durdle Door (right), are both the result of the relentless power of the waves eroding the limestone rock. At Lulworth, the sea then got to work on the softer clays behind the rock to create a rounded basin.

In 1757, local fishermen claimed to have landed a mermaid on the beach, but that is not the issue that has bemused scientists. Those same fishermen, and their descendants, were more credible when they claimed to know where they had pulled up their boats in the dead of night, to within three hundred yards or so, from the size of the pebbles on the spit. Somehow, the waves manage to sort and grade the pebbles, so that the largest end up at the Isle of Portland, gradually diminishing to the pea-size shingle found at Burton Bradstock.

Whatever the solution to this mystery, it does not seem to bother the specialized animals and plants that make this extraordinary beach and the brackish Fleet lagoon their home. The Scaly Cricket is found nowhere else in the British Isles, while rare plants include the Sea Pea, Shrubby Seablite and Rough Clover. The Fleet also holds the richest concentration of brackish-water plants remaining in Britain. Two species of eel-grass and one of tasselweed – which are flowering plants – grow submerged in the lagoon, providing the staple diet of the large flocks of Gadwall,

Brent Geese and Mute Swans that winter there along with a wealth of other wildfowl.

Chesil Beach is an important breeding site for Common and Little Terns. The beautifully camouflaged eggs of these graceful 'sea swallows' are laid in a shallow scrape in the shingle, and must be protected from disturbance and the shoes or boots of unwary visitors. For this reason, the terns' breeding areas are wardened during summer and the public are denied access.

Since the 13th century, a swannery has been maintained on the edge of the Fleet at Abbotsbury, originally to provide choice feasts for monks with worldly appetites at the now almost vanished Benedictine monastery. Visitors to this rural idyll are kept away from the swans during the breeding season, when some five hundred of these handsome birds nest in peace, and in winter when their numbers swell to a thousand or more, making this the largest concentration in the country. Reeds from the Mute Swans' nesting ground are used to thatch the village houses.

Those who wish to see the many sights on Chesil Beach are obliged to walk, at the retarded

The Isle of Portland (below) achieved fame because its limestone rocks were in great demand for building. The winches used to load the stone on to boats still stand among the rubble of the old quarries.

Viewed here across an idyllic pastoral Dorset landscape, Kimmeridge Bay (left), on the Isle of Purbeck, is one of the few places on the British mainland where oil is found. It is extracted from a 1,500-foot-deep bed of shale on a small scale by a 'nodding donkey' oil pump. If carried out, schemes for large-scale oil drilling in the east Dorset area would create a major pollution threat.

The coastline between Lyme Regis and Charmouth (right) has long been famed for its fossils, found among the unstable, richly varied rocks that formed the cliffs. Here, in the early 19th century, a local girl, Mary Anning, found the first skeleton of an ichthyosaur and other prehistoric reptiles. Ammonites, such as these ones used as decorations in a Lyme Regis wall (below), are common finds today.

Although the Lulworth Skipper occurs along only one stretch of Britain's coast – south Dorset, Devon and Cornwall – it is sometimes very abundant. In good years up to a million of these butterflies may fly on the army ranges east of Lulworth.

pace allowed by the sole-sucking shingle. Access is much easier to the famous beauty spots along the Dorset coast between the isles of Portland and Purbeck. Clifftop car-parks squat above Lulworth Cove, Durdle Door, Burning Cliff and Kimmeridge Bay and relatively few people take advantage of the Dorset Coast Path that climbs five hundred feet above the gleaming chalk of Whitenothe Cliff to look across to Portland and back to Purbeck's St Aldhelm's Head.

Beyond Lulworth Cove the path is interrupted, for most days of the year, by the noisy activities of the army. Despite walkers' complaints about the lack of access, such areas are often better conserved than sites where thousands of visitors dot the coast in summer with their caravans, chalets and litter. It is surprising how much wildlife can turn a deaf ear to exploding shells.

Resorts, Ports and Fishing Villages

Resorts abound along this coast. With their mild climate and their Georgian and Regency seafronts adorned with sub-tropical palms and flowers, Weymouth and Lyme, Sidmouth, Torquay and Exmouth are as popular today as when they were first patronized in the 18th and early 19th centuries.

The ancient borough of Lyme Regis acquired its royal title from Edward I in 1284. Half a mile west of the town is its curving breakwater, called The Cobb, originally constructed in the late 13th or early 14th century. As the only harbour between Portland Sound and the Exe, Lyme thrived off anchorage dues and its own merchant fleet. By the end of the Middle Ages, French raids and the repeated destruction of The Cobb by

storms had contributed to the town's decline.

Scenes from Jane Austen's novel *Persuasion* are set in Georgian Lyme Regis, when the town's fortunes revived as a smart watering place. Most of the seafront houses date from this period, as does the extraordinary natural architecture of the Grand Chasm. This massive landslip of some eight million tons of waterlogged chalk occurred between Seaton and Lyme in 1839, wrenching what is now known as Goat's Island from the cliffs of which it was part. The resulting ravine has become a wilderness of shrubs, trees and animal life, and is protected within a national nature reserve.

The Cobb was rebuilt in Elizabethan times and later joined to the mainland by a causeway. Today it is known to cinema audiences around the world from the film of the best-selling novel *The French Lieutenant's Woman* by John Fowles, who lives locally.

The little fishing villages of the south-west peninsula have always had a particular attraction. Neatly bedded in the coast's curves so that the harbour arm almost completes a circle, the whitewashed stone-built cottages have a snug-

ness that is irresistible. But their very charm has led to the replacement of old local communities by outsiders, as seafront houses in Polperro, Mevagissey or Polkerris come on the second home market at exclusive prices. The local people who are left have little choice but to serve the tourist industry.

But some still take their boats out after the fish, following an ancient and hard way of life. This is no easy coast to navigate, and the huge shoals of pilchards that once swam offshore were no mean feat to catch. Above many a fishing town or village, in the best look-out position, 'huer's huts' still sometimes stand. The huer's job was to spot the shoals and shout down to the harbour for the boats to be launched. By the early decades of this century the pilchards had gone, due chiefly to a change in climate and water temperature. The fishermen switched to mackerel, but numbers of these, too, have dwindled steadily since the early 1980s, due mainly to overfishing by modern freezer trawlers and the effects of pollution.

Gone, too, are the days when Devon could boast the prime fishing-port of England at Brixham, the port where trawling was first developed about two hundred years ago. The Brixham trawlers fished as far afield as the Grand Banks of Newfoundland. The big, strong New-foundland dogs they brought back, along with the fish, were trained to pull boats ashore in rough seas, a sight no longer seen. The excesses of the Dorset sprat feasts at Poole are also a thing of the past. Today, at Newlyn, Cornwall's most important fishing port, strict regulations limit the trawler size to discourage competition from outsiders. Lobsters, crabs and scallops are still profitable catches but in many places the fishing trade is in decline. Many a fishing vessel is kept afloat by taking holidaymakers on sea-angling trips in the summer season.

The much-indented shoreline of the south-west coast has provided numerous pockets for little harbours and fishing villages but the most extensive and impressive havens are in the drowned valleys, or 'rias', that appear on a map as if the surrounding land has been gently torn apart. The soft contours of these estuaries had no dramatic sculpturing by stormy waves, only by the gentler erosion of wind and rain. The sea made its appearance later, when its level rose

The elegant wrought-iron balconies, terraced gardens and splendid views of red marl cliffs at Sidmouth (above and left) are typical of this town which has been a genteel resort for two hundred years. Today, like many of the other resorts along this stretch of coastline, it is increasingly inhabited by the elderly.

In 1864, a local Devon landowner refused to allow the River Dart to be bridged, so the railway had to stop at Kingswear, though a ferry completes the journey across the water to Dartmouth. The local crab fishermen who tie up their boats to the Railway Wharf are suffering the effects of overfishing.

In summer, tourists throng the narrow streets of Polperro – a typical south Cornwall fishing village – that has hardly changed since the 1900s. Though such villages now depend on the visitors for their living, the summer influx creates great pressure on wildlife.

after the last great Ice Age ended and the glaciers melted. The steepness of the former valleys gives depth for heavy ships and the old tributaries that became creeks provide shelter for smaller vessels well away from the open sea.

At both Fowey in Cornwall and Dartmouth in Devon high cliffs border the approach to the rias and provide solid foundations for the castles built for Henry VIII. Defensive booms or chains were fitted across the narrow gap to deter the high-masted foreign or pirate ships from entering the harbours. Today, on the River Fal, mothballed tankers moor beside King Harry's Reach, a good four miles from the open sea. The narrow channel opens into the majestic Carrick Roads alongside the famous port of Falmouth, its wide waters reflecting the two Tudor castles, one by the town and one on the Roseland peninsula. To the south of Falmouth, too close to compete, the serene Helford River has never had a major port, although it does contain important oyster beds and is a favourite haunt of yachtsmen. A tiny twisting creek leads to Gweek, where seals are saved from coastal hazards.

With their densely wooded slopes and unpredictable winding creeks, the drowned valleys have a shrouded seclusion that is best savoured from the water. Hardly accessible from land, the upper reaches of these rias know no roads, shoreside bungalows or factories.

Much of the coastline of Dorset, south Devon and Cornwall has been designated as Heritage Coast, and, to rather more practical effect, many stretches have been bought by the National Trust. However, this did not prevent the *Torrey Canyon* disaster in 1967, the worst oil spill ever in British waters, which covered mile upon mile of Cornish rocks and beaches with oil, destroying whole communities of marine wildlife and sentencing thousands of seabirds to death. Although this catastrophe resulted in stricter controls on oil tankers, the unregulated discharge of oil from ships washing out their tanks or draining from the land continues to pollute the sea and beaches in this area. As well as the oil, there is a host of other pollutants, from hazardous chemicals to raw sewage at Penzance and other popular beaches, belying the tourist brochures with their vistas of clear blue water.

As for the rias, they unfortunately now face their greatest threat. There are a number of proposals to build half-tide barriers across them, so that the wader-beloved mud would disappear under constant water; the better for boating and water-skiing, but bad news for wildlife.

A Chequered Past and a Questionable Future

The naval presence is still strong on this coast, in the training college at Dartmouth, the naval air base on the Lizard, the underwater weapons research centre at Portland, and the HMS *Cambridge* gunnery school just east of Plymouth, at Wembury Point. When ships left Plymouth in April 1982 for the Falklands during the recent

This view from King Harry Ferry down the smooth waters of Carrick Roads – part of Cornwall's largest ria or drowned river valley – towards Falmouth Bay, could be of an inland lake were it not for the tankers and other vessels laid up here.

The impressive Great Green Bush Cricket, nearly two inches long, is restricted to southern England, where it haunts the unspoilt grassland of downs and coastal cliffs. It is particularly noticeable on the Lizard and along the Dorset coast.

Symbolizing Devon's long naval tradition, a replica of Drake's *Golden Hind*, in which he circumnavigated the globe in the 1570s, is moored alongside the fishing boats and pleasure craft in Brixham harbour. Once one of Britain's chief fishing ports, where trawling was first developed, Brixham, like so many other West Country ports, depends as much on tourism as on fishing today.

conflict with Argentina, many felt that national pride in a long naval tradition was upheld. But the enormous Devonport complex, one of only three naval dockyards in the United Kingdom, and builders of battleships for nearly three hundred years, hangs under a shadow as privatization plans progress.

In the jumble of national heritage, the exploits of Drake, the departure of the dissenting Pilgrim Fathers for the New World on the *Mayflower* in 1620, the arrival home of the pardoned Tolpuddle Martyrs in the mid-1800s, the emigration (often forced) of a thousand men and women to Australia in the 19th century, the long history of wrecks on the Eddystone Reef, the Falklands expedition and the recent action by threatened dockyard workers are all bound up with Plymouth, the one metropolis of the south-west coast.

Plymouth is a beautiful city, for all the damage done by bombing in the Second World War and the subsequent rebuilding. Fowey, Dartmouth, Kingsbridge and Falmouth are beautiful, too, not to mention the countless villages of the south-

west peninsula. The fear is that they will become, or have already become, not much more than backdrops for holiday thrills and romances. Switched off after summer, the litter cleared, the boats re-rigged for professional fishing, the cafés and bed-and-breakfasts closed, these towns have still to earn a living between the crowded August breaks and the next Spring Bank Holiday. Winter's compensation is that this lovely coast can be enjoyed at its most natural – both by its people and its wildlife.

Beyond the old stone fences of a coastal field west of Salcombe lies Burgh Island (right), famous for its art deco hotel, which has been restored to its 1920s splendour. It is possible to walk across to the island at low tide. Herring Gulls nest on its cliffs in vast numbers.

Re-erected as a memorial to its designer on Plymouth Hoe, John Smeaton's lighthouse was the third to be built on the treacherous granite teeth of Eddystone Reef, where it lasted longer than its predecessors, guarding shipping from 1759 to 1882. The present Eddystone lighthouse was automated in 1981.

REGIONAL SUMMARY
SOUTH CORNWALL, DEVON AND DORSET

Excluding estuaries and islands, the coast between Land's End and Poole harbour, which is Britain's most popular holiday and retirement area, is about 270 miles (435km) long.

PHYSICAL PROFILE
Land's End and the Isles of Scilly are composed of granite, and the Lizard of serpentine. The sedimentary strata become younger from west to east, with Devonian slates, sandstones and other rocks in the west and Mesozoic chalks, limestones and clays in Dorset. Low offshore reefs, rocky headlands and treacherous local currents are dangers to mariners.

Climate: Average temperatures are 45°F (7°C) in the Isles of Scilly and 41°F (5°C) on the Devon coast. The average July temperature is 61°F (16°C). The rainfall decreases from more than 40 inches (1,016mm) in the west, which has an average of 53 gales a year, to 29 inches (737mm) at Poole.

HUMAN PROFILE
The Isles of Scilly have nearly 2,000 people. Major mainland resorts include Penzance (19,500), Falmouth (18,500), Torbay (115,600, including Brixham, Paignton and Torquay), Teignmouth (16,500), Dawlish (10,800), Exmouth (28,800), Sidmouth (12,400), Lyme Regis (3,400), Weymouth (46,300) and Poole (118,900). The largest city is Plymouth (244,000). Exeter (96,500), on the Exe estuary, is Devon's county town.

Sites of historic interest: Prehistoric sites include Kent's Cavern, Torquay, an Ice Age habitation. Exeter was a Roman town; its cathedral is 12th-century. Swanage Bay was the scene of a naval battle (877), when King Alfred defeated the Danes. Plymouth Hoe is identified with Sir Francis Drake and the defeat of the Armada (1588).

Museums: Benbow Museum of Nautical Art, Penzance; Maritime Museum, Falmouth; Mevagissey Museum; Museum of Smuggling, Polperro; City Art Gallery and Museum, Plymouth; British Fisheries Museum, Brixham; Exeter Maritime Museum; Lyme Regis Museum; Bridport Museum; Maritime Museum, Poole.

Famous personalities: Sir Humphrey Davy (born near Penzance); Sir Walter Raleigh (born near Budleigh Salterton). Literary associations: Daphne du Maurier set *Frenchman's Creek* and *Rebecca* ('Manderley' is Menabilly) in Cornwall; Thomas Hardy wrote about Dorset ('Port Bredy' is Bridport).

Marine industry: Fishing ports: Newlyn, Penzance, Porthleven, Brixham, Plymouth. Boatbuilding: Porthleven, Brixham, Poole, with ship repairs at Falmouth. Devonport, Plymouth, has Royal Navy dockyards. The Britannia Royal Naval College is at Dartmouth.

Commerce/industry: Flowers and early vegetables, Isles of Scilly. Plymouth is the main manufacturing centre, followed by Poole. There is an earth satellite station at the Lizard. China clay: St Austell. Building stone: Portland, Purbeck. Oil extraction: Kimmeridge Bay. Rope making (to 1970): Bridport.

NATURAL PROFILE
Wildlife: A varied coastline, including the rocky Isles of Scilly, maritime heaths at the Lizard, sheltered rias and saltmarshes, slumping cliffs at Axmouth and Lyme Regis, Chesil Beach, a tombolo (a type of spit), and the lagoon behind it, and the chalk and heath of the Isle of Purbeck.

Attractions: Isles of Scilly – rich intertidal and subtidal flora and fauna; Lizard and Kynance Cliffs; Fal-Ruan estuary – mudflats, saltmarsh and alder/willow woodland (now virtually extinct in Europe); Wembury Marine Conservation Area; Slapton Ley; Berry Head; Sugarloaf Hill and Saltern Cove; Dawlish Warren and Exe estuary; Axmouth-Lyme Regis Undercliffs; The Fleet and Chesil Beach; Isle of Portland; Isle of Purbeck, including Purbeck Marine NR, Durlston Country Park and Studland and Arne heaths; Brownsea Island. *Footpaths:* Except for a few interruptions, including firing ranges, the South-West Peninsula Coast Path extends along the entire coast. *Beauty spots:* The Isles of Scilly AONB and parts of the Cornwall, South Devon, East Devon and Dorset AONBs. *Beaches in Cornwall:* Porthcurno, Penzance, Marazion, Praa Sands, Polurrian Cove, Mullion Cove, Kennack Sands, Porthallow, Pendower, Gorran Haven, Porthpean, Par, Polkerris, Looe, Seaton. *Beaches in Devon:* Wembury Bay, Thurlestone, Hope Cove, Salcombe, Paignton, Torquay, Watcombe, Shaldon, Teignmouth, Dawlish, Exmouth, Sandy Bay, Sidmouth. *Beaches in Dorset:* Lyme Regis, Charmouth (fossil-rich), Weymouth, Lulworth Cove, Swanage, Studland, Poole.

CAUSES FOR CONCERN
Direct dumping: 62,000 tons of contaminated sewage sludge each year in Lyme Bay.

Radioactive discharges: Uncontrolled releases occur from nuclear submarines which are based at Devonport, near Plymouth. Potential radioactive waste from Cap de la Hague nuclear reprocessing plant, France.

Agricultural run-off: Affects many estuaries.

Oil pollution: Major spills include *Skopelos Sky* (1978), but frequent discharges from tankers and other vessels are more serious overall.

Beaches: The South-West Peninsula has the worst beaches in Britain – more polluted than most Mediterranean beaches; 50 people advised (1974–1982) to attend hospital as a result of encountering hazardous packages, from drugs to toxic waste.

Threatened wildlife: Great pressure from tourism adds to pollution and coastal development to threaten dolphins and porpoises (now rarely seen), breeding terns and other seabirds, rare reptiles and unique communities of rare plants.

Other pollution: Considerable leaching of tin, copper and other metals from old mines. Tributyl tin (TBT) anti-fouling paint used on boats has led to serious decline in numbers of Dog Whelks and other marine animals.

The Edible Sea Urchin occurs around almost all Britain's coast. In the South-west, it is the basis of the country's only non-food fishery; about half a million urchins are caught for the souvenir trade each year.

At the northern edge of its European distribution, the Smooth Snake is found in Britain only on the warm, sandy heaths of the south, including the Dorset coast. It faces threats from the loss of its habitat, from accidental fires and from persecution.

Safety at sea

Even on a calm day, a strong current or fast tide can pull an unwary bather far from shore with alarming speed. Those who earn their living from the sea face its hazards daily. Despite radar and other modern aids, ships still collide, capsize or run aground – occasionally with heavy loss of life.

Against all odds, however, many are rescued from the cruel sea, thanks to the men of the Royal National Lifeboat Institution and

the RAF's Air-Sea Rescue teams. Ships steer safely past treacherous reefs and sandbanks with the help of Trinity House and its Scottish counterpart, the Northern Lighthouse board; they man and service the lighthouses that sweep reassuring beams or sound booming fog warnings from clifftops, islands or reefs, and also maintain a system of light vessels above shifting banks and a myriad of buoys marking navigation channels and marine hazards all around Britain's shores.

Today, as automation takes over, the lighthouse keeper's lonely life is gradually becoming a thing of the past; ships entering the Port of London, for example, are now guided by computer. But human skills and courage are still vital for saving those in peril on the sea.

THE SOUTH COAST

CLARE FRANCIS

Clare Francis

Boats and bungalows, sprawling towns and rolling downs: Sandown and Shanklin, Bognor and Brighton.

Brighton meant visits to my grandparents. To my seven-year-old eyes it was all houses, steel-grey sea and high chalk cliffs. The cliffs, white and crumbling, looked like rough-cut cheese. Clustered along their treeless wind-blown rims were row after row of villas and bungalows, terraces of tall Regency houses, and massive large-windowed hotels, their faces turned determinedly to the sea, braving winter storms and summer gales, awaiting an exotic southern summer that never seemed to come.

People, people everywhere. Promenading, sitting, eating: patient stoic people, buoyed by the doubtful promise of warmth, of golden light sparkling on a somnolent sea, of well-earned tranquillity; people sustained by the knowledge that, short of crossing the sea itself, they could get no further south, no nearer that elusive sun.

The pier, baroque and resplendent, the fun-fair, the line of once-gaudy beach huts, their paint eroded by the blastings of winter winds, stood reproachful and a little neglected, awaiting the fickle crowds. And at their feet, the sea: a cold grey unwelcoming sea. The waves crashed and hissed on the shingle beach; the surf dragged and tore noisily at the pebbles.

Far out on the corrugated surface of the sea, ships steamed doggedly past. Where were they going? They couldn't stop anywhere along this inhospitable shore. But what would happen if a storm blew up? Would they find harbour?

Later, I discovered that harbours along this coast were few and far between, either crouching uncomfortably at the base of cliffs, ejecting scurrying cross-Channel ferries at regular intervals, or concealing their wide inner waters behind narrow entrances made treacherous by sand bars and racing tides.

Throughout my childhood there were holidays in the Solent: summers of sailing dinghies, hidden anchorages, inaccessible beaches, barbecues, songs around the fire; expeditions to inner harbours and muddy creeks that reached like tentacles into tranquil, untouched places.

The tranquil places are hard to find now. The march of the bungalows and boats is unremitting. Towns spread, villages are engulfed: a massive ribbon development creeps along the shore. Wetlands are dredged for yet more boat-parks, creeks serve as water-highways for boats driven at breakneck speed, marshes are drained for agricultural land surplus to EEC requirements.

Change. Progress. When it wears this face, it's hard to see the point of it all.

THE SOUTH COAST
POOLE TO MARGATE

'... FROM THE LONG LINE OF SPRAY
WHERE THE EBB MEETS THE MOON BLANCH'D SAND,
LISTEN! YOU HEAR THE GRATING ROAR
OF PEBBLES WHICH THE WAVES SUCK BACK AND FLING.'

Matthew Arnold, *Dover Beach* (1867)

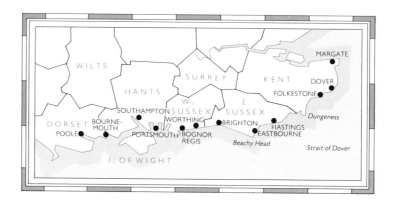

Is the Little Tern doomed to be a bird of nature reserves only? Certainly, its superbly camouflaged eggs are easily trodden on, and disturbance from holidaymakers has driven it from many of its breeding beaches.

To a geographer, the continent of Europe extends beyond the northernmost of the Shetland Islands. Our history and our politics can be labelled European. But in our world and words of daily life, of taking trips abroad and buying unfamiliar French cheeses or German beer, of mingled fascination and mistrust for Latin and Teutonic peoples, Europe begins and ends across the English Channel. The symbolic and strategic value of this stretch of water that at its narrowest is even swimmable, is nowhere better illustrated than at Dover. Passengers returning home from the Continent cling to the ferry rails, battered by freezing winds and drenched with spray, eager for their first glimpse of the famous White Cliffs – the coastal expression of the chalk heartland of England.

This wintry view of a handful of beached fishing boats and tackle on the shore at Hastings (right) is a far cry from the same scene in medieval times, when the town was a powerful Cinque Port, with one of the busiest harbours in Britain.

The Frontline

No matter that in foul weather the indented, scarred chalk raises only a brownish smudge upon the horizon. The cliff-tops of Dover still etch their distinctive scalloped border against the sky and in a sudden burst of sunlight the un-sullied whiteness of the soft rock shines brilliantly. Above the cliffs, commanding the Strait of Dover, stands the castle, its foundations Iron-Age, its military use in known history continuous from Roman times until the Second World War. Today some of its bunkers are open to the public. In fact, many of the forts along England's South Coast – Britain's frontline against invasion – were originally built by the Romans, then taken over and adapted by successive rulers.

The main Roman invasion of England in AD 43 took place along this southern coast. The conquering legions established a fort at Rutupiae (now Richborough) in eastern Kent, which served as a base for their operations in the South-east. They also built two lighthouses – Britain's first – at Dover. One still stands, in a remarkable state of preservation. The lighthouses served a dual purpose, guiding ships into the harbour and providing towers from which look-outs kept watch for possible invaders.

By the 4th century AD, when invasion had become a reality, the Romans built Britain's first system of coastal defences. A line of forts, designed to provide protection against marauding Saxons and other raiders from across the English Channel and the North Sea, ran round the South-east coast from Carisbrooke on the Isle of Wight up to Burgh in Norfolk.

After the Romans left at the beginning of the 5th century, most of their forts fell into disuse, although the Saxon king Alfred used some, including Carisbrooke, and Pevensey, in Sussex, in his struggle against the invading Danes. After the 1066 Conquest, the Normans refurbished and refashioned the old Roman defences and this tradition was continued by the Plantagenet kings from the 12th to the 15th century. New castles were added by Henry VIII, who feared an attack from the combined Roman Catholic powers of Europe after his break with the Church of Rome in 1531.

emplacements. They added tank traps, air bases, dug-outs and pill-boxes to the forts and flooded the coastal marshes.

Traffic across the Sea

Notwithstanding the development of the coastal forts, Britain's historical supremacy has not just been based on sitting tight. The nation needed a navy, as well as a fighting force on land, to protect or expand its trading interests. But a navy was an expense few monarchs could afford. Instead, from the 12th century onwards, they made deals with important coastal towns, in-

The next major phase of coastal fort-building did not come until the early 19th century, when a chain of 74 small, squat Martello towers was built between Seaford, in Sussex, and Folkestone, in Kent, as a precaution against invasion by Napoleon. Today, some of the towers are partly submerged under sand, some have been converted into unusual homes, cafés or museums, while others have been swept away by the sea.

By the Second World War, and the onslaught across the Channel of the Luftwaffe, British military commanders had a choice of Roman, Norman, medieval, Tudor, Napoleonic and Victorian defences for their troops' quarters and gun

cluding the original Cinque Ports of Dover, Sandwich, Romney, Hythe and Hastings, and the Ancient Ports, such as Rye and Winchelsea. In return for providing ships and soldiers, the favoured towns were granted exemption from customs dues, rights over cargoes wrecked on their shores and 'freedom of the seas' – in other words, a licence for piracy.

War and trade went hand in hand, each new campaign bringing fresh markets and commodities. In the Middle Ages, small tub-shaped, single-masted boats plied the Channel, fishing for herring, exporting English wool, salt and tin, and bringing back iron from Spain or Sweden,

The distinctive shape of the famous Seven Sisters, culminating at Beachy Head, has been fashioned over many thousands of years as the sea has steadily eroded the dazzling white chalk of the cliff face, truncating the dry valleys of the chalk downland above. This is one of the very few undeveloped sections of the South Coast; part of the longest stretch of chalk cliffs in Britain, it is protected as a Country Park.

and wine from Bordeaux or the Mediterranean. Sometimes it was more expedient to attack another merchant ship or even raid a foreign port. Retribution usually followed swiftly. Sandwich, Winchelsea, Southampton, Rye and the Isle of Wight were all stormed, burned and pillaged by French pirates during the 14th and 15th centuries. Black ribbons in the robes of the mayor of Sandwich still commemorate these bloody events.

By the late 15th century, ship tonnage was increasing every year. Lymington was one of the biggest ship-building ports on the South Coast, using for its ships the oak from the neighbouring forest that William the Conqueror had planted. When, in the 1490s, Henry VII established the Royal Navy with about eight warships, he chose Portsmouth as its base. The first dry dock was built and the defences dating from the Hundred Years War strengthened. Henry VIII continued his father's work, adding to the dockyards, building new ships and reorganizing the navy. For centuries, trees from the New Forest were felled to build merchant fleets, fishing boats and men-of-war. Portsmouth and Gosport are still the headquarters of the Royal Navy. Submarines now nose about where Henry VIII's famous warship *Mary Rose* was sunk by the French in 1545. Modern missile-carrying cruisers entering the base pass between the same castles that the veterans of Crécy saw.

When iron and steel replaced wood in the 19th century, the ship-building business moved north. But the shipwrights of Bucklers Hard, a little village on the Beaulieu River, which runs into the Solent, were still at work in 1944 – when Operation Overlord was being planned – making wooden minesweepers that were less likely to be sunk by magnetic mines.

The World's Busiest Sea Lane

Seen from on high, the myriad vessels of all shapes and sizes that ply the Channel today appear as congested as the aerial traffic circling above Heathrow. The narrow bottleneck of the Strait of Dover, linking the English Channel with the North Sea, is the busiest sea lane in the world. Ferries and hovercraft crossing the water from seven ports on the South Coast have to weave their way between container ships and other cargo vessels, naval frigates, oil tankers and the odd liner travelling parallel to the coast, not to mention fishing boats and innumerable yachts and other pleasure craft. As well as the great density of shipping, navigation is made difficult by storms, frequent fog, fierce tidal currents, the existence of more than two thousand wrecks and numerous sandbanks.

The most dangerous of all the sandbanks – indeed, one of the greatest hazards of the entire British coast – is Goodwin Sands, which begin four miles off the east Kent coast. Stretching over twelve miles with their furthest point some eight miles out to sea, their shape and position change from day to day. At low tide, patches of the 'Great Ship Swallower', as the sands are known to sailors, are visible from land, along with the masts of two American victims of forty years ago. Other wrecks sometimes surface, but those of scores of older, wooden ships have long since disappeared. Only the ghost of a schooner driven onto the sands with suicidal intent is said to appear every half century.

The stretch of water known as 'The Downs' between the sands and the shore was the making of Ramsgate and Deal, as it provided safe temporary anchorage for sailing ships, which local boats could pilot on the daunting voyage to the Thames as soon as the wind changed in their favour. Today, Goodwin Sands are unfortunately shifting westward – a movement that could eventually spell the death of Ramsgate as a major car-importing port.

Shifting Shorelines

The movements of Goodwin Sands are not the only play of natural forces on this coast. As water is funnelled into the tidal race through the Strait of Dover, silt and shingle are pushed from west to east towards the shore. At the same time, generations of coastal dwellers have worked to reclaim marshland and mudflat, with the sea alternately aiding and hindering the process.

In Roman times, the Isle of Thanet was indeed an island. Ships could take the broad Wantsum Channel, that ran between the island and the mainland to the Thames estuary, without struggling past Goodwin Sands. Romney Marsh was a wide bay sheltering Hythe and Rye, while the headland at Dungeness was nothing but partially submerged sand banks. The wide estuary at Pevensey Levels gave easy anchorage at the port where the Normans disembarked. All the Cinque and Ancient Ports harboured on the sea; today, all but three – Hastings, Hythe and Dover – lie inland.

The partnership of human work and nature, despite occasional quarrels, created Romney and Welland Marshes and the great wilderness of Dungeness. Old Romney and Lydd were known by the Romans as settlements on the sandbanks of Romney Bay. As the sea level lowered, marshy ground appeared between these places and the inland cliffs. From the 9th century onwards, monks who had been granted land rights assisted the draining process by constructing ditches and flood barrier walls. Later landlords called in Dutch experts. Their Dymchurch Wall, rebuilt and reinforced, today protects the reclaimed land from the same storm threat that in 1287 nearly drowned beneath the waves the hard-won marshland.

Lydd lost its harbour to the great ridges of shingle that built up the headland of Dungeness – now the largest accumulation of shingle on the British coast and one of the largest in Europe. Pebbles from the west side are constantly shifted round the corner so that Dungeness as a whole is

Eelgrass
is one of the few flowering marine plants. Although it has decreased during this century, it still forms extensive beds on tidal mudflats and provides an important source of food for wintering wildfowl, especially Brent Geese.

Nothing
is more certain to set most birdwatchers twitching with excitement than an exotic migrant. The Bluethroat is one such bird, although it occurs regularly in small numbers along the south and east coasts of Britain in spring and autumn, at sites such as Dungeness.

Ramsgate's inner harbour (above left) presents a Mediterranean scene of luxury yachts and a sunny promenade, but this view belies its role as one of the busiest commercial ports on the South Coast.

Two winter views of Dungeness show the surreal contrast between the vast, lonely shingle ridge (top) and the area round the hulking buildings of the nuclear power stations (above), which dwarf the fishermen's cottages and the old lighthouse in front of them.

At Portsmouth (left), naval traditions are upheld, as a modern warship noses past the stern of Nelson's flagship *Victory*.

Hamble (right), on Southampton Water, is famous as a yachting centre and many of the sleek boats that grace the Solent are built here. Roman galleys used Christchurch harbour (below right) for a base; today, yachts and other pleasure boats bob gently on its sheltered waters.

Situated on a side creek of Chichester Harbour, Bosham (above), whose 55-foot-high church tower dates from Saxon times, is the fabled site of King Canute's unsuccessful attempt to turn back the waves. Whether the story is true or not, Bosham's waterside streets are sometimes flooded by high tides to this day. Although there has been some redevelopment, the village retains an old-world charm.

slowly moving eastwards. These days, however, the sea's intent is frustrated by the more speedy if laborious tactic of digging up the shingle at the eastern end and dumping it back where it came from. At the similar outcrop of Selsey Bill a concrete wall keeps the shingle at bay. The task at Dungeness is carried out by the Central Electricity Generating Board, who have a vested interest in the area in the form of two great grey nuclear power stations – one a pensionable 1960s Magnox, the other a 1980s advanced gas-cooled reactor – and their associated spider's web of pylons and power lines. Not far away the army has a mock-up of town streets where it practises urban warfare. The rusting debris of old gravel works and smashed-up motor-cars litters the stony ground. Thick fogs often descend as if the sky were ashamed to reveal so grim a place. Yet there is abundant wildlife in this vast triangle of shingle around Dungeness.

A Haven for Wildlife

Among the flooded gravel pits, a small colony of the misnamed Common Gull forms the longest-established English outpost of a species that has its breeding strongholds in Scotland and Ireland. Thanks to co-operation between the gravel extraction companies and the RSPB, Little Terns and Ringed Plovers can bring up their chicks in the solitude of the nature reserve, while Wheat-ears nest in old ammunition boxes half buried in the shingle. The rare Stone Curlew has been known to breed here, too, although the Kentish Plover, always on the northern fringes of its range on the Kent and Sussex coast, has not done so since 1956, having been driven away by disturbance and egg collectors.

In spring and autumn, the winged population soars, as thousands of migrant birds, from fierce Pomarine Skuas to tiny, dainty Firecrests, make a landfall or spend their last hours on British soil here. The skuas and other seabirds are attracted to the abundant supply of fish and other food brought to the surface in the warm water from the nuclear power stations' cooling systems. This area is known to birdwatchers as 'The Patch'. Here, ironically, a technology that has the potential to devastate the whole coastline in-

directly benefits wildlife in the short term.

Summer sees even more delicate creatures arriving from across the Channel – the migrant butterflies, which include Painted Ladies, Clouded Yellows and Red Admirals, and occasional rarities, such as Bath Whites, Monarchs and Pale Clouded Yellows. There are migrant moths, too, such as the abundant annual migrant, the Silver Y. These creatures increase the already impressive range of butterflies and moths – including Essex Skipper butterflies and rare, local moths like the Sussex Emerald, Toadflax Brocade and Pigmy Footman – which breed at Dungeness. The shingle supports the largest British populations of Sea Kale, Dwarf Broom and Fine-leaved Sheep's Fescue. The rare wildflowers that grow here include Stinking Hawksbeard and Nottingham Catchfly. There is an ancient, wind-sculpted scrubland wood, dominated by Holly, which is probably unique in Europe, as well as other shrubs like Blackthorn, Gorse, Bramble and Elder, all of which provide nest-sites for birds, including Magpies and Carrion Crows which usually nest in trees.

Coastal Gains and Losses

Fishermen sell their catch of sole, plaice and squid direct from the boats winched up on the beach below Dungeness. At Hastings, too, the 'luggers' are beached, for this town, like so many others along this coast, lost its medieval harbour to violent storms and the inevitable shingle drift. Dover suffered the same fate but was resurrected with new docks in the 16th century, to which the all-embracing arms of the current outer harbour were added later.

The massive block of the Isle of Wight creates double tides in the Solent and Southampton Water, giving the vast commercial docks at Southampton a long period of high water. Of the South-Coast ports, Southampton alone has been immune to the receding or invading sea. Common Cord Grass, one of the best natural stabilizers of mudflats, was first spotted in Southampton Water in 1870, and soon spread in both directions to play tug-of-war with the sea. One of its earliest successes were the fringes of Chichester Harbour and its neighbour Langstone Harbour, which provide winter refuges for Brent Geese,

The varied shipping that takes advantage of the long period of high tide in Southampton Water includes HMS *Glamorgan*, on royal escort duty after a visit to Southampton by the Queen. Great transatlantic liners no longer sail regularly from the port, however, and much of its container traffic has been lost to Felixstowe, although the oil refinery at Fawley still handles huge tankers.

The Isle of Wight still has many attractions, such as the pleasure pier of Shanklin beach (right) and the wooded shore at Ryde (above), with its fine view across the Solent, but pollution affects its offshore waters.

Dunlin, Sanderling and other wildfowl and waders. A few miles to the south-east, Pagham Harbour is one of the top birdwatching spots in southern England.

Other stretches of the coast have no natural aids to call upon to stem the appetite of the sea. At the centre of the South Downs' abrupt encounter with the water, the cliffs recede at the rate of more than a yard each year. The cottages of Birling Gap are progressively abandoned to join the chunks of powdery rock falling to the beach below. The sharply sloping face of these cliffs between Beachy Head and Seaford, like their counterparts at Dover and on the Isle of Wight, have the appearance of meringue that a child with dirty fingers has crushed to crumbs.

At Beachy Head, the outermost pinnacles may vanish – sometimes within a single lifetime. But people can still walk along the edge of the land to enjoy the breathtaking views and the soft, springy turf, among which grows a rich maritime chalkland flora, including such scarce beauties as the Burnt Orchid, Field Fleawort and Rock Sea Lavender. Sadly, though, the red-billed Choughs that 'wing the midway air' off Dover's Shakespeare Cliff, as described in *King Lear*, are now extinct as breeding birds in England. From the vantage point of Cuckmere Haven or the sea, the Seven Sisters hang a curtain of pure white, velvety chalk, up to five hundred feet high, from their undulating rail of green.

On the Isle of Wight, the scene at Alum Bay is as if barrel-loads of different herbs and spices – turmeric, coriander, sage, white pepper and cayenne – had been emptied over the cliff top. The actual contents of the seven-coloured sands are not vegetable, but the mineral components of the shale, clay and sandstone strata that have been turned on end. The same movement gave greater powers of resistance to the chalk ridge that once linked the western point of the island with the mainland. The extraordinary giant triplet of teeth rearing their 100-foot caps to the sky are all that remains of this lethal causeway known as the Needles.

The Isle of Wight has little in common with the area of low-lying mainland which it shelters so snugly. The white chalk cliffs at either end of the island's central ridge recall the mainland shoreline to the east, while the chines, or coombes, in the clay cliffs looking down the Channel have their counterparts further west across the water. The chalk between St Catherine's Point and Dunnose Head has landslip features, where lush, dense vegetation provides a habitat for numerous colourful creatures, including the rare Glanville Fritillary, found only here and on the Channel Islands.

The most frequent rainbow vision around the Isle of Wight, however, is one of the mainsails, jibs and spinnakers of a thousand sailing boats on their way to or from Cowes, especially during the regattas. The fashionable status of this port was firmly established when Queen Victoria's eldest

Beachy Head's lighthouse (left) was built in 1902 on the sea-bed, using 3,000 tons of Cornish granite. It replaced an earlier one on the clifftop, whose light was often shrouded by mist and whose foundations were threatened by the crumbling chalk. Similarly, the lighthouse on the cliffs above the treacherous Needles (below left), off the Isle of Wight, was abandoned. A new one was built close to sea-level in 1859, positioned on the outermost of the jagged row of chalk teeth. The minaret style of St Catherine's Point lighthouse (far left), on the southern tip of the Isle of Wight, was a creation of the 1830s.

Although common in Central Europe, the Glanville Fritillary is at the very edge of its range in Britain – it occurs only on the southern coast of the Isle of Wight, where its caterpillars feed on the common grassland plant Ribwort Plantain.

The urban sprawl of Bournemouth (right) has taken less than two hundred years to swallow up the ancient heathland that lay between Poole and Christchurch. In recent years, Victorian villas and gardens have been dwarfed by high-rise flats, seen here in this unusual view across a choppy sea, braved by a lone windsurfer.

Brighton's splendid Regency houses (above) and Eastbourne's grand Victorian pier (opposite) were built to cater for the refined tastes of past visitors to these premier South-Coast resorts. Today, modern development has made parts of them less attractive.

The Silver Y moth reaches Britain's shores in large numbers from Europe every summer. On arrival, it is superbly camouflaged on shingle beaches. Its caterpillars feed on almost any plant and the new generation of moths becomes abundant by autumn – although it cannot survive the winters here.

son, later to become King Edward VII, added yachting to his list of princely pleasures.

Pavilions, Promenades and Pensioners

Brighton, once England's most noble resort, received its royal patronage, and a reputation for the curative powers of its waters, long before the Isle of Wight. Brighton sea water was first recommended as a cure for many ills during the 1750s. Thirty years later the profligate Prince Regent took a fancy to this fishing-town spa. As George IV, he cleared the fishermen off the seafront green where they used to repair their boats and nets, and had Henry Holland and John Nash build his extravagant dream palace, the Brighton Pavilion. Ryde's solution to the problem of steam paddleboat passengers arriving at low tide was followed at Brighton with the building of the Chain Pier. The influx of visitors exploded once the rail connection to London was complete, while the population of the town increased tenfold between 1800 and 1850.

Meanwhile, other towns and villages were learning to exploit this new interest in the seafront. The developer of Bognor wanted his resort to be called 'Hothampton', but Queen Victoria was not amused and the old name

survived, with 'Regis' added to it after George V had convalesced there. The tiny fishing port of Worthing grew into five miles of promenade. Water gardens, piers or pavilions and elegant crescents with seaview balconies established Eastbourne and Bournemouth as Brighton's competitors for a rich clientele.

By the time fares to hot foreign beaches were affordable, over half the South Coast of England had become an almost continuous promenade of yacht chandlers, beach huts, fish-and-chip shops, deck chairs, antiques emporia, amusement arcades and brass bands, interspersed by golf courses. Only the ferry ports thrived as the local resorts tried to win people back, despite the rain, licensing laws, and lack of Latin allure. The only people interested were those reaching retirement. New building programmes of villas, bungalows and chalets gobbled up ever greater chunks of the remaining available space. The towns felt the strain of higher social service bills and little job creation from the age-imbalanced population. Incentives were given to London companies to move their offices to the coast, and mammoth conference halls were added to the sea-front skyline. The disastrous Brighton marina drained city funds and failed to attract

the wealthy back to the town. The marina's inner harbour is now to be filled in and covered by a hypermarket.

Without a doubt, a place like Bournemouth with every amenity and the most temperate weather in Britain, is an ideal place to spend old age. But the coast itself is being killed off, and not all the damage is recent. Cobbett in his *Rural Rides* raged about the decline of the New Forest, citing a 95 per cent reduction in oak woods between 1608 and 1783. But he describes both sides of Southampton Water as clothed with trees and having the most beautiful views imaginable. Cranes, oil refineries, storage tanks and power stations form today's landscape.

Parts of the Solent shore of the New Forest, though hardly wooded, are, however, protected. The forest-bred ponies graze amongst heather

plans could easily be dismissed as madmen. And now the well-worn scheme, to bypass the sea from underneath, that hitherto has never been executed, is to be carried through – come what may. No other engineering project could make so radical a break in the traditions of Britain's southern coast. The effects of this immense undertaking on marine and shoreline environments and their human, animal and plant inhabitants are something only time will tell.

Once the tunnelling starts, near Folkstone, a mile-long wall of concrete will form a dump for the dug-up rock on the foreshore below Shakespeare Cliff at Dover. Chalk escaping into the sea may smother the seabed. A proposed link road between Folkestone and Dover may alter forever the skyline of our beloved white cliffs.

Although the tunnel will create employment

Common Cord Grass first came into existence around 1870, when native and introduced American cord grasses hybridized in Southampton Water. Since then, their offspring have invaded, or been introduced to, large areas of tidal mudflats, at once reclaiming, diminishing and threatening this important habitat.

With its round-the-clock departures and arrivals, Dover's busy ferry port nestles in the protective shadow of the great white cliffs. As plans for the Channel Tunnel proceed, the port's future hangs in the balance.

and gorse and Black-headed Gulls gather on the mudflats. The habitats of other marshlands, at Chichester and Pagham harbours, at Romney, and at Newtown on the Isle of Wight, are safe from bricks and concrete, though not from waterborne poisons. For the moment, these areas, Dungeness's shingle ridge and a few stretches of open cliff are all that remain of a south-coast environment that favours wildlife.

The Channel Tunnel

In the 19th century, Channel tunnel projects were usually vetoed by the military. However easy it might seem to guard or block a tunnel entrance in times of war, this was evidently no compensation for watching across the water for the enemy's approach. And when that enemy had been and still was the very country that the tunnel would link with Britain, proponents of the

during its construction, it may well lead to much greater job losses in the long term. It is not just the ferry ports of Dover, Folkestone and Ramsgate that are threatened, but every freight and passenger port from Hull to Plymouth, which are likely to decline when most traffic to the Continent starts to use the tunnel. The link is not in itself an evil. But it will alter our island status, conceptually, not geographically. The history of this southern coast has always been one of movement back and forth across the Channel, ferrying, fishing, trading, building ships and guiding them through the shallow Strait of Dover. When the tunnel is eventually opened, a continuity with the past will be broken – but with the wider perspectives that are opened up, the future of our coast may be ensured, and its unquestionable beauty preserved for future generations to enjoy.

REGIONAL SUMMARY

THE SOUTH COAST

The distance from Poole Harbour to Margate, excluding estuaries and islands, is about 200 miles (322km). The Isle of Wight is 23 miles (37km) long and 11 miles (18km) wide.

PHYSICAL PROFILE

The coast is bordered mainly by Tertiary and Cretaceous rocks, including chalk cliffs and such features as the Needles. The North Downs end at the White Cliffs of Dover; the South Downs at Beachy Head. Between them is a low coast of sandstones and clays. Many old ports now lie inland, cut off by shingle spits. The Goodwin Sands, a danger to shipping, lie 4 miles (6km) off Deal.

Climate: Average temperatures are 40°–41°F (4°–5°C) in January and 62°F (17°C) in July. Rainfall averages 28–29 inches (711–736mm) a year.

HUMAN PROFILE

The coast is a major holiday region. Resorts: Bournemouth (144,800), Ryde (24,300), Sandown-Shanklin (16,900), Ventnor (7,900), Bognor Regis (39,500), Worthing (91,700), Hove (66,600), Brighton (146,100), Eastbourne (77,600), Hastings (74,800) and Ramsgate (39,600). Ports include Southampton (204,400), Portsmouth (179,400), a major naval base, Cowes (19,700), Newhaven (9,900), Folkestone (43,700) and Dover (32,800).

Sites of historic interest: Julius Caesar landed at Deal (55 BC); Dover was HQ of the Roman Northern Fleet. William the Conqueror landed near Pevensey. Fears of invasion led Henry VIII to build castles at Walmer, Deal and Sandown. The Martello Towers between Seaford and Folkestone were meant to protect Britain against Napoleon.

Museums: Rothesay Museum, Bournemouth; Maritime museums at Buckler's Hard, Southampton, Cowes; Museum of Smuggling, Ventnor; Royal Navy Museum and HMS *Victory*, Portsmouth; Art Gallery and Museum, Brighton; Fishermen's Museum, Hastings; Dover Museum; Maritime Museum, Deal; Dickens House Museum, Broadstairs.

Famous personalities: Brighton's Royal Pavilion was built for the Prince Regent (later George IV). Charles Dickens (born Portsmouth, holidays at Broadstairs), William Harvey (born Folkestone).

Marine industry: Southampton is a centre of shipbuilding, including hovercraft. Fishing ports: Hastings, Rye, Folkestone.

Commerce/industry: Southampton and Portsmouth are industrial centres. Fawley on Southampton Water has a huge oil refinery.

NATURAL PROFILE

Wildlife: A region of contrasts, with chalk cliffs and flat, open shores, estuaries, sand dunes and the large floristically rich shingle beach at Dungeness – Britain's largest.

Attractions: Hengistbury Head; Keyhaven-Lymington Marshes; Tennyson Down and the Needles; Fort Victoria Country Park; Newton Harbour – intertidal habitats, saltmarsh and shingle; Hythe Marsh; Chichester Harbour – important intertidal habitats and saltmarshes; Cuckmere Haven; Pagham Harbour (over 200 bird species recorded); Beachy Head and the Seven Sisters; Rye Harbour; Dungeness; Folkestone Warren; Sandwich Bay. *Footpaths:* Part of the South Downs Way runs from Eastbourne to Beachy Head and Cuckmere Haven. Near Dover, parts of the North Downs Way and the Saxon Shore Way. *Beauty spots:* Parts of South Hampshire AONB, Chichester Harbour AONB, the South Downs AONB, and the Kent Downs AONB. *Beaches in Dorset:* Bournemouth, Hengistbury Head, Highcliffe. *Beaches on the Isle of Wight:* Ventnor, Shanklin, Sandown, Ryde. *Beaches in Hampshire:* Southsea, Hayling Island. *Beaches in Sussex:* West Wittering, Bognor Regis, Felpham, Middleton-on-Sea, Littlehampton, Worthing, Lancing, Hove, Brighton, Saltdean, Seaford, Eastbourne, Pevensey Bay, Bexhill, Hastings, Winchelsea. *Beaches in Kent:* St Mary's Bay, Dymchurch, Hythe, Folkestone, Deal, Sandwich Bay, Ramsgate, Broadstairs.

CAUSES FOR CONCERN

Direct dumping: Southampton and Portsmouth harbours receive contaminated dredging spoils; there is also a sewage sludge dump site in the English Channel, east of the Isle of Wight.

Pipeline discharges: Numerous industries cause heavy metal pollution, which is concentrated in the Solent area.

Radioactive discharges: Two nuclear power stations at Dungeness and the Winfrith atomic research establishment and power station discharge slightly radioactive cooling water. A Magnox dissolution plant at Dungeness, expected to come on stream in 1987, will discharge diluted intermediate-level nuclear waste into the English Channel.

Oil pollution: Oil tanker accidents and ballast tank cleaning are the major causes of pollution, together with discharges from the Fawley refinery into Southampton Water.

Inshore overfishing: Small-scale mackerel fishery threatened with collapse by overfishing.

Beaches: TBT (tributyl tin) anti-fouling paint, leaching from harbours, especially in Hampshire, has caused widespread contamination. Sewage contamination of some beaches.

Threatened wildlife: Oil pollution affects seabird populations in the English Channel. Auk populations have still not recovered from heavy oiling during the 1920s and 1930s.

Other causes for concern: The Channel Tunnel will need 2.21 million tons (2.25 million tonnes) of gravel over the 5-year construction period. Most will come from south-eastern England, notably Dungeness, where a massive increase in extraction operations may threaten the wildlife on this, Britain's largest shingle foreshore – internationally important for its rich community of lichens. The shipping density in the English Channel is the world's highest; collisions pose the risk of toxic chemicals, explosives and other hazardous cargoes being washed ashore.

The Common Dog Whelk is one of many shellfish that have been severely affected by the marine anti-fouling paint TBT. This causes female whelks to develop non-functioning male sex organs and thus to become incapable of breeding.

The Redshank is a common wader. Even so, it has suffered from loss of its nesting habitat – coastal grazing marshes and damp grasslands – with the march of modern agriculture.

THE STATE OF THE COASTLINE

CURRENT THREATS AND POSSIBLE SOLUTIONS

DR PAUL JOHNSTON,
Greenpeace Scientist, Queen Mary College, University of London

> 'AT ANY GIVEN MOMENT OF HISTORY
> IT IS THE FUNCTION OF ASSOCIATIONS OF DEVOTED INDIVIDUALS
> TO UNDERTAKE TASKS WHICH CLEAR-SIGHTED PEOPLE PERCEIVE TO BE NECESSARY,
> BUT WHICH NOBODY ELSE IS WILLING TO PERFORM.'
>
> Aldous Huxley, *The Doors of Perception* (1954)

Photo: Bob Edwards

The *Beluga*'s laboratory is well equipped with a gas chromatograph and spectrophotometer, as well as constant monitoring apparatus connected to a small computer. This records results for later analysis. Equipment is constantly upgraded to match the best used in industry and in universities. Greenpeace scientist Paul Johnston is seen here at work in the laboratory.

Rock pools provide a refuge for animals and plants at low tide, but organisms must still be able to withstand extremes of temperature and salinity. These fascinating miniature worlds are particularly vulnerable to oil pollution.

The Victorian author Edmund Gosse, writing in *Father and Son*, described the rock pools of the Devon and Cornwall coast in the 1850s: 'These cups and basins were always full . . . they were living flower beds.' In the space of less than fifty years, this magic world had changed and Gosse sadly observed: 'All this is long over and done with. The ring of living beauty drawn about our shores was a very thin and fragile one . . . The fairy paradise has been violated . . . No one will see again on the shore of England what I saw in my early childhood.' The damage caused by the amateur naturalists of Gosse's time has now been superseded by problems peculiar to the 20th century – but his observations are no less pertinent today.

The sea has long been regarded both as a vital resource, ready to offer up its riches for human benefit, and as an enormous dumping ground, ready to accept some of the huge quantities of waste generated by civilized society. Britain's seas and coastal waters are now threatened by the demands placed upon them by this heavily industrialized and populated island. In part, some of these pressures are unavoidable and constitute the inevitable compromise that accompanies human interaction with the natural environment. However, it may be argued that many of the practices that can threaten coastal waters stem predominantly from economic considerations. These ignore the wishes and needs of all who share in the environment to the advantage of the few who have a direct commercial interest in it.

In assessing the situation, it is important to retain a sense of perspective and to realize that overfishing, for example, may exert as extreme an effect as persistent chemical pollution. The major distinction between these problems lies in the ability of the ecosystem to recover from them. In the case of overfishing, it may be a relatively short time, but it may be several decades or centuries before a chemical pollutant is eliminated from the ecosystem.

It is important to realize, too, that the problems seen around the British coastline are common to a number of European countries – and indeed are found on coasts around the world. Britain, then, serves to exemplify problems that affect – to a greater or lesser extent – all coasts. Given the role of the world's oceans in the determination of climate and weather, and as a rich source of food, it seems clear that any activity that compromises the sea or which has the capacity to do so must be questioned. This does not mean that a lower standard of living has to be accepted. Quite the contrary. By restricting the plethora of man-made chemicals entering the sea, we reduce the risk of unforeseen effects upon ourselves and future generations. Further, by so doing, we restrict the responsibilities of environmental use to the user generation, rather than creating a problem that requires a solution in the future.

In the following pages some of the ways in which the seas around Britain are used, and the ways in which they are threatened, are examined. As will be seen, an unequivocal effort to save and preserve the coastal environment is of urgent importance to us all.

Litter and plastics are commonly found on beaches. They do not decompose, are extremely unsightly, and can be dangerous to animals, especially birds. While the bulk of such materials is thrown overboard from ships, much is discarded by visitors.

THE GREENPEACE COASTAL SURVEY AND CAMPAIGN

The addition of the *Beluga*, with its on-board laboratory, to the Greenpeace fleet in 1986 is a reflection of Greenpeace's increasing concern about levels of pollution in rivers and coastal waters. Of particular interest to Greenpeace are the possible effects of the input of heavy metals and persistent organic compounds.

Although contaminant input into these systems is a result of the industrial activities of several European countries, Britain is responsible for a significant proportion. An increasing number of scientists in Europe subscribe to the view that the current prevalence of necrotic fish diseases, the increase of parasitic infections, the virtual disappearance of coastal dolphin populations in the southern North Sea, and the apparent disturbance of plankton populations are at least partially attributable to contaminant input by man. It is further reasoned by other parties, including Greenpeace, that, in view of the lack of evidence indicating that the disposal of waste into the aquatic environment is completely safe, policy in these matters should err on the side of caution until proof is forthcoming. Large quantities of toxic substances continue to be disposed of in coastal and estuarine waters – the ways in which they enter the natural environment are broadly classifiable as follows: direct dumping, pipeline discharge and atmospheric deposition (see pages 184–9).

The *Beluga* survey aimed to assess and quantify the substances being disposed of around Britain's coast. The boat was equipped during its conversion from a fireboat with a laboratory for the analysis of chemical pollutants and general water quality. The laboratory facility was proven during surveys carried out on the rivers Rhine and Seine. The *Beluga* arrived in Britain in May 1986 and in the following two months travelled around the British coast, visiting many of the major estuaries. Extensive research and public surveys undertaken before the voyage revealed a number of areas of concern, including the following: sewage sludge dumping in the Thames estuary; mercury contamination of Norfolk's River Yare; arsenic and acid iron waste discharge in the Humber; direct dumping of acidic ammonium sulphate waste in the Tees area; the potential threat posed to Tyneside by the ocean incineration base facilities; oil and pesticide pollution in the Forth; heavy metal and chemical contamination in the Mersey; and heavy metal levels in the Severn estuary. Sewage pollution was identified as a major problem at many points around the coast of Britain.

Many of these concerns proved to be justified and provided the inspiration for the continuation of the campaign. Further attention is now being drawn to the current state of Britain's coastline by the Greenpeace vessel *Sirius*'s circumnavigation of Britain, and by other coastal programmes to clean up Britain's beaches and protect threatened wildlife.

Photo: Greenpeace

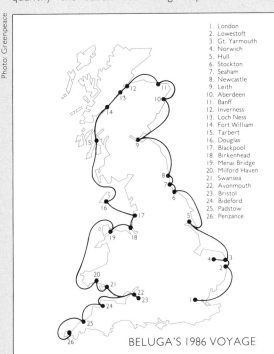

1. London
2. Lowestoft
3. Gt. Yarmouth
4. Norwich
5. Hull
6. Stockton
7. Seaham
8. Newcastle
9. Leith
10. Aberdeen
11. Banff
12. Inverness
13. Loch Ness
14. Fort William
15. Tarbert
16. Douglas
17. Blackpool
18. Birkenhead
19. Menai Bridge
20. Milford Haven
21. Swansea
22. Avonmouth
23. Bristol
24. Bideford
25. Padstow
26. Penzance

BELUGA'S 1986 VOYAGE

The route taken by the *Beluga* around Britain in 1986. The larger, ocean-going Greenpeace vessel, the *Sirius*, is carrying on with the survey work, taking in 1987 much the same route as the *Beluga*'s. But, due to its much greater draught, the *Sirius* can travel round the north of Scotland rather than using the Caledonian Canal.

The Greenpeace research vessel, the *Beluga*, was originally built in 1961 by the Burmester Shipyard in Bremen, West Germany, as a fireboat. *Feuerlöschboot III* was bought by Greenpeace in 1984. The Menzer Shipyard in Hamburg was given the job of refurbishing the boat to serve as a floating laboratory and campaign vessel. Greenpeace renamed the boat the *Beluga* – in memory of the White Whales, or Belugas, that once swam off British coasts. The laboratory facilities enable many of the commonest contaminants found in estuarine and coastal waters to be analysed on board, while the boat's shallow draught and excellent manoeuvrability make sampling in otherwise inaccessible locations possible.

DIRECT DUMPING

This sewage sludge dump-ship is used by the Thames Water Authority to convey sludge to the Barrow Deep dumpsite. The sludge is pumped into the ship from the gantry in the fore-ground – to which a Greenpeace protestor is chained. This was one of the many protests carried out by crew members of the *Beluga* during the 1986 coastal survey.

Prawns are becoming increasingly expensive in the shops as their diminishing stocks are exploited ever more efficiently. Only by using our marine resources with concern for their conservation will we be able to continue enjoying them.

The major sewage sludge and industrial waste dumps found around the shores of Britain are shown here. Areas where dredging spoils are re-deposited are not shown. Containerized wastes are not dumped in the areas shown either – they are taken to deep waters over a hundred and fifty miles from land, where their subsequent recovery is all but impossible.

The disposal of wastes, 'dumped' from ships or barges into the open sea, accounts for a relatively small proportion of the contaminants introduced into the environment. However, the local impact of the practice on fisheries and amenities can be severe – and there are indications of more far-reaching effects. A large variety of materials, including industrial waste, dredgings, munitions, sewage sludge and, until recently, radioactive waste, is dumped at sea. Some waste, like munitions, is contained in drums, but some, like sewage sludge, is dumped 'loose' and uncontained. The areas in which such materials are dumped can be found marked on Admiralty charts as 'spoil grounds' – this name reflects the fact that the bulk of the waste is composed of sediments removed by dredging operations to keep ports and harbours clear. It is unfortunate that the same harbours often support large industrial complexes, for the sediment in the ports and harbours acts as a 'sink' for industrial contaminants, which can then be released when

the sediment is disturbed or moved.

By 1990, Britain will be the only country bordering the North Sea committed to the disposal of waste by direct dumping. Other countries regard the practice as undesirable and, indeed, unnecessary, for, in many cases, chemicals may be recycled or used as a feed-stock in other processes. For example, a dumping operation involving the disposal of 150,000 tons (152,407 tonnes) of ammonium sulphate waste per year will shortly be stopped by using the substance as a raw material in fertilizer manufacture. In Britain, improved recovery of coal from coal waste could significantly reduce the amount of waste generated at Easington colliery where, over the years, a beach dump has blackened many miles of once golden sand.

At present Britain is also the only country in Europe dumping sewage sludge in the North Sea – this is of great concern. Sewage sludge dumping operations have been likened to a massive, unlicensed release of genetically en-gineered bacteria which has profound implica-tions for the health of both human beings and marine life. It is standard practice to treat sewage together with some industrial effluents – the sludge acts as sediment and 'soaks up' contaminants. Bacteria exposed to these con-taminants can become resistant to them and pass on the resistance to naturally ocurring populations of bacteria in the sediment of the dumping ground.

Ironically, the practice of mixing trade and domestic effluent stems from early pollution control measures. The elevated levels of con-taminants in the sludge preclude the use of this potentially valuable resource as a fertilizer. But even where sludge is uncontaminated, effects on animal and plant life may be detected some miles away on the sea-bed.

Sea dumping of the materials described may therefore be seen as undesirable in the short term. In the long term, it represents an unacceptable shifting of responsibility to future generations. Once dumped, even con-tained waste may be difficult or dangerous to recover from the sea-bed – drums may leak and disperse contaminants over a wide area. The best cautionary tale in this connection is the problem currently being experienced with the chemical munitions that were dumped in Baltic waters at the end of the Second World War. The drums have either dispersed from the dumpsite or have started to leak into the surrounding water. No safe means of dealing with them exist at present. The Baltic may be far from Britain, but munitions dumps are found in several areas around the British coast. In view of such problems, dumping must be regarded as a highly irresponsible activity.

FORTH

GARROCH HEAD

TYNE
TEES

LIVERPOOL BAY

SPURN HEAD

HARWICH
SOUTH
FALLS
BARROW DEEP

BRISTOL CHANNEL

PLYMOUTH
EXETER
SOUTHAMPTON

● Industrial waste dumpsites

● Colliery waste dumpsites

● Sewage sludge dumpsites (operational and proposed)

INDUSTRIAL WASTE AND SEWAGE SLUDGE DUMPSITES AROUND BRITAIN

PIPELINE DISCHARGES

The many effluent pipelines around Britain's shores are not conspicuous. As a rule, they run out to the high tide mark, and are only between 6 and 24 inches (15 and 60cm) in diameter. They are nonetheless capable of prodigious feats. One pipeline on the Humber, for example, can disgorge almost 1.96 tons (2 tonnes) of arsenic in a day. Together with a brother pipeline on the Severn estuary, it also discharges some 60 per cent of the highly toxic metal, cadmium, entering coastal waters – that is, if you ignore the 16.72 tons (17 tonnes) entering the sea off Cumbria each year. This Cumbrian pipeline is also responsible for the discharge of some 88 tons (90 tonnes) of natural

Photo: Aero Films

Photo: Bob Edwards

uranium per year, somewhat more than the infamous Sellafield plant discharges. In turn, though, plutonium and other radioactive isotopes are the problem at Sellafield. And it is not just heavy industry which is responsible for these kinds of pipeline discharges – why, for example, does a brewery need to discharge high levels of mercury?

Suffice it to say that a large quantity of various contaminants enters Britain's waters from pipelines and rely on dispersion and dilution in the water to reduce their levels to below those toxic to plants and animals. However, many contaminants are conservative in their behaviour. They persist in the environment and may be accumulated in food chains. There is no guarantee therefore that dilution is an ad-

PIPELINE CONCENTRATIONS
AROUND BRITAIN

equate way of protecting the environment. Ultimately, these materials may be absorbed by human beings through the consumption of fish and shellfish. What was once locked in the earth or confined to the test tube is thus released irresponsibly into the wider environment. In many cases – especially that of the exotic organic compounds – the materials are so new that any long-term effects are as yet uncertain or unknown. But mistakes in the past have shown the potentially devastating effects of some such materials, of which the pesticide DDT is possibly the best known (see page 193). The discharge of toxic metals and chemicals into the sea may have a particularly severe effect upon sea basins with low circulation, hence the concern about the continuing contamination both of the North Sea and of the Irish Sea.

It is often argued that if the discharge of these materials was stopped, the production costs of many items used in modern life would become prohibitive. This view effectively states that the environment – in preference to the producers of such items – should be made to pay the price. This is a short-sighted view, and one that can only be held by those who lack even a basic understanding of the delicate processes of nature. As with other polluting activities, it is crucial that a precautionary approach towards pipeline discharges is adopted to avoid the possibility of unforeseen effects upon natural systems.

The pipelines discharging industrial effluent into British waters are concentrated in the areas shown on this map. The discharges may be direct to the sea or estuary, or part of combined discharges of sewage and industrial waste. A large amount of the contaminants discharged into sewers will eventually be dumped with sewage sludge which – when it is contaminated – cannot be used on land.

- ⬤ Metal discharges (including mechanical, electrical and engineering industries)

- ⬤ Chemical discharges (including production of rubber and plastics)

Taken from the air, this photograph shows a pipeline discharging sewage into coastal waters.

Greenpeace protests at the site of a pipeline on the Humber, which is responsible for the discharge of up to 1.96 tons (2 tonnes) of arsenic into the river in a day. The plant to which this pipeline belongs is also responsible for a great proportion of the cadmium discharged into British waters.

INCINERATION AT SEA

The incineration ship *Vulcanus II* in operation in the North Sea. The wastes being incinerated are not only dangerous in themselves if spilt, but they can also give rise to extremely toxic combustion products, one of which has been linked with birth defects. The recycling of wastes could put an end to ocean incineration, which – by acting as a cheap disposal route – encourages the unnecessary production and use of toxic chemicals.

Photo: Greenpeace/McAllister

Ocean incineration is the process of burning hazardous wastes at sea. Among the wastes treated in this manner are the organo-chlorines – arguably the most toxic substances produced by man. Besides being direct poisons, many exert a suppressive effect upon the central nervous system. The use of ocean incineration stemmed from the realization that burning waste on land might be dangerous to human beings. It was argued that transferring incineration operations to the sea would protect people from possible harm. In essence, this is another example of 'dilution' being used as 'the solution to pollution'. In this instance, the atmosphere is used as the diluent.

So what then is the nature of this particular threat to the marine environment? Any vessel, be it a sailing dinghy or a supertanker, may fall victim to an accident. In the case of an ocean incineration vessel, carrying a medium sized cargo of 106,000 cubic feet (3000 cubic metres) of waste, an accident involving a breach of the storage tanks would cause damage to a large area of the sea. Some of the compounds incinerated out at sea behave in a similar fashion to the pesticide DDT (see page 193), and a spill might result in fish being declared unfit for human consumption for many years and incur enormous monitoring costs. The *Torrey Canyon* and *Amoco Cadiz* accidents have shown the immense damage caused by oil spills. An accident involving the smaller quantities of the more toxic waste carried by an incineration ship would be more damaging.

This is not, however, the only threat posed by ocean incineration vessels. Toxic wastes are not totally destroyed when they are burned, and some escape uncombusted into the atmosphere. Some are even converted by the incineration process into new, perhaps more toxic, compounds, like dioxin. (Dioxin was the chemical released by the accident in 1976 at Seveso in Italy, which resulted in birth defects. It is one of the most potent poisons known and it remains in the environment indefinitely since it is not biodegradable.) The amount of the toxic compounds created depends upon conditions at sea. In rougher weather, which can introduce discontinuities into the incineration process, more toxic compounds will be formed. When the plume from the incineration furnaces touches the sea, the uncombusted and converted substances dissolve in the uppermost layer of the water where many animals, including fish, go through their larval stages and can thus be poisoned. More of these products will be deposited in coastal areas by the atmosphere.

The process of ocean incineration may thus be seen to have several serious drawbacks. In fact, the United States of America's Environmental Protection Agency has refused to allow test burns in United States waters and has observed that if an accident were to occur, clean-up measures might be impossible. The North Sea is the only area in the world where burning on a commercial scale is permitted. There are alternatives to the use of this process and many of the wastes could be recycled using adaptations of present technology. While incineration remains as a cheap means of disposal, however, the equation will continue to be weighted towards the profligate use of these materials.

RADIOACTIVE DISCHARGES

Radioactivity is an emotive subject – with justification. As an agent causing multifarious ills, it is without parallel. The most dangerous radioactive materials emit particles with high energy – if taken into the body, these particles act on cells in the way that a cannonball would act on cardboard. In particular, the effects on the body's genetic material can be very severe. Admittedly, everyone is exposed to natural or 'background' radiation (see page 193) but levels of this have been increasing since the first atomic bomb. Recently, it has been realized that slight increases in background radiation may result in unexpectedly elevated levels of radiation-related disease.

The efforts of Greenpeace were instrumental in halting the dumping of radioactive waste at sea, but pipeline discharges of the waste continue. The nuclear reprocessing plants of Sellafield and Cap de la Hague in Brittany continue to load coastal waters with long-lived products from the reprocessing of nuclear fuels. These products can be taken up by fish and seaweed and thence passed to human beings. Nuclear power stations contribute lesser quantities of radio-nuclides to the marine ecosystem but there is a danger of causing widespread contamination – as demonstrated by the effects of the Soviet Union's Chernobyl disaster in 1986.

Steadily increasing levels of background radiation are not, however, solely due to the nuclear industry. Hospitals and universities use radio-isotopes which often enter the drains and then pass to rivers and estuaries. Even the responsible homeowner may dispose of radioactivity without realizing it – domestic smoke detectors, for example, contain radio-active elements.

The numerous inadequacies in the models constructed by scientists to predict the behaviour of radioactive substances introduced into the environment were also highlighted by the Chernobyl disaster and uncertainties are increasing. It would seem only sensible that processes using radiation should be restricted to land where they may be more easily controlled. This, however, is not the case. In the

BRITISH NUCLEAR ESTABLISHMENTS

way that the submarine revolutionized naval warfare, so the nuclear reactor revolutionized the submarine. Inevitably, some nuclear submarines have been lost at sea, and those that have been found are monitored for radiation leaks. It is not generally known whether any of these wrecks are emitting radiation, but it seems likely in the case of those known to have broken up, like the USS *Thresher*.

There have been three serious accidents involving land-based nuclear reactors – at Windscale (Sellafield), Three Mile Island and Chernobyl – and seven Western nuclear submarines have been lost in circumstances shrouded in secrecy since 1963. Some 37 reactor-based incidents are thought to have occurred aboard Soviet nuclear vessels alone since 1954. Between eighty and a hundred nuclear vessels are at sea at any one time. The potential exists for a marine disaster involving these vessels – which are in many cases armed with nuclear weapons.

Nuclear installations around Britain range from research establishments and military installations to power stations and reprocessing and fuel fabrication facilities. The radioactive caesium-137 discharged from Sellafield – arguably the 'dirtiest' nuclear facility in the world – has been traced as far as the North Sea and the coasts of Norway and Denmark (see map arrow).

- ● British Nuclear Fuels establishments
- ● United Kingdom Atomic Energy Authority establishments
- ▲ Electricity Board nuclear power stations
- ■ Ministry of Defence establishments
- ■ Amersham International establishments (radio-isotope manufacturers)

Radiation – which cannot be seen, smelled, tasted or felt – has been linked with a number of diseases, including cancer and leukaemia. It acts by damaging components of human cells, including DNA, the transmitter of all genetic information. Growing and dividing cells are the most at risk – children may thus be particularly vulnerable to radiation-linked disease as background radiation levels continue to increase.

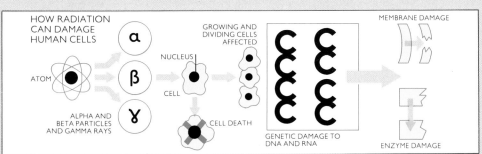

HOW RADIATION CAN DAMAGE HUMAN CELLS

α
β
γ

ATOM

ALPHA AND BETA PARTICLES AND GAMMA RAYS

NUCLEUS

CELL

CELL DEATH

GROWING AND DIVIDING CELLS AFFECTED

GENETIC DAMAGE TO DNA AND RNA

MEMBRANE DAMAGE

ENZYME DAMAGE

AGRICULTURAL POLLUTION

The crop sprayer is a familiar sight in rural areas where chemicals are applied to control pests and enhance crop growth. The exponential increase in the use of nitrate fertilizers since the Second World War has resulted in potentially dangerous levels of nitrate in some drinking water supplies.

During the 1960s the Peregrine suffered infertility and egg breakage through shell thinning – the effects of organo-chlorine pesticides accumulated through its prey. Partial bans on these poisons have allowed a recent slow increase, and small numbers now breed on Britain's northern and western coastal cliffs.

Persistent pesticides, once sprayed, enter a cycle that involves the atmosphere, the rivers and the sea. Small planktonic organisms in the water can accumulate pesticides and pass them to higher animals which may be severely affected. Ultimately, the pesticides may be taken up by human beings – with unknown long-term effects.

Agriculture constitutes the largest industry in Britain and it utilizes great areas of land. Far from being a simple, traditional operation, it depends for efficiency upon all branches of science. The increasing intensity of both arable and livestock agriculture since 1940 has created a large number of attendant problems.

Inorganic fertilizers and pesticides are now used to maximize crop plant yields. Pesticides range from simple substances like copper sulphate to the specialized and complex organophosphate chemicals, which act as nerve poisons to a wide variety of pests. Antibiotics similar to penicillin are added – as are steroid compounds – to the foodstuffs of intensively reared animals to increase their saleable weight. Intensively reared pigs are fed supplements of copper and zinc salts to improve weight gain – these are then present in the large volumes of slurry generated. And the growing practice of silage manufacture can produce highly polluting effluents.

Given the size of Britain's agricultural industry, it is surprising that it does not cause more pollution problems, although recently the number of incidents attributable to farming has grown alarmingly. The exponential increase in the use of nitrate fertilizers over the last forty years has led to undesirable levels of nitrate both in drinking waters and in surface waters, such as the Norfolk Broads. These waters eventually discharge to the sea through estuaries and it is here that further problems are now becoming apparent.

The presence in the sea of excess nitrogen and phosphate from agriculture and sewage can markedly change the nature of the marine plants and animals present through the process of nutrient over-enrichment called 'eutrophication'. Normally, nitrogen and phosphate are present in limiting quantities, and this determines the types of animals and plants present in the water and sediment. While not poisonous as such, increased quantities of these two substances allow different plant and animal communities to establish themselves – given time, there will be a 'knock-on' effect influencing species higher in the system. This process of nutrient over-enrichment is insidious and long-term and it may push an ecosystem into an undesirable state. In areas of low circulation in coastal waters the microscopic plants normally present may be superseded by smaller mobile forms, which produce toxins and appear in such numbers as to colour the sea red. If eaten by shellfish, and the shellfish eaten by human beings, these toxins can cause severe poisoning.

Clearly, the recent initiatives to take areas of agricultural land out of production will help alleviate environmental concern. Most pesticides and fertilizers have only been in use for a relatively short period and the long-term effects upon wildlife and humans are simply not known. Only when techniques became available to detect substances like the chemical pesticides aldrin, dieldrin and DDT, were the dangers realized and the causes of some inexplicable ecological changes unravelled. DDT is no longer manufactured for use in Europe, but every individual has detectable levels of the chemical in his or her body fat – and is likely to pass it on for many generations to come.

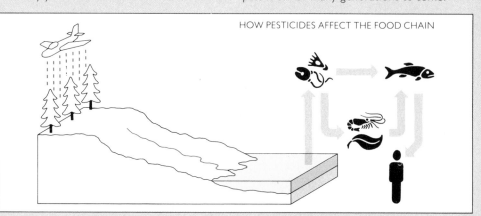

HOW PESTICIDES AFFECT THE FOOD CHAIN

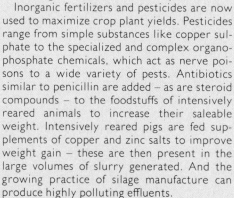

OIL POLLUTION

The exploration and development of the North Sea oilfields since the 1970s has been a valuable boost to Britain's economy and has involved the development of highly advanced technology. On a global scale, offshore oil production is responsible for about 2 per cent of the oil entering the sea – about a quarter of that released by natural seeps and erosion. Even in the highly developed North Sea area, offshore production is only responsible for about 10 per cent of the oil input.

Undoubtedly, there are problems associated with an offshore oil industry, particularly those which relate to the use of diesel oil-based drilling muds (banned from January 1987 in the North Sea) and oily production water from the wells. These two substances can cause noticeable effects on the sea-floor animals up to two miles from a rig. Oil well blowouts present a major problem. That there have been no blowouts during the history of the British fields is fortunate indeed, for the effect on marine life could be catastrophic – as shown by the oil well blowout in the Gulf of Mexico from June 3, 1979 until March 23, 1980.

If the oil industry itself is not a major contributor to oil pollution, where then does the bulk of the oil entering British coastal waters come from? If it is assumed that the sources are locally the same as they are globally, then the greatest contributor is shipping, closely followed by municipal and industrial waste waters. Anyone who has poured used car oil into the drains rather than dispos-

ing of it responsibly has contributed to the problem. A great reduction in output could be achieved simply by care and forethought on the part of the users of petroleum products. It is daunting to realize that an amount of oil equal to a *Torrey Canyon* load may enter the North Sea by such means each year. Because it enters in small amounts it does not attract the attention that a large-scale spill would.

Is oil contamination dangerous? Obviously, it is a highly visible problem which causes damage to fisheries, birdlife and the tourist industry. In some cases, the dispersants used to treat oil spills are even more toxic than the oil itself. After the *Torrey Canyon* disaster, barnacles were found to have been greatly damaged by the dispersants used to clean up the oil. Recently, it has become apparent that oil floating on the surface of the sea may be toxic to the small organisms that live there, while those in the water column may also be affected. The threat to mammals is generally local and the result of gross oil pollution – the reported otter mortalities in the Shetlands for example. Significant effects of oil pollution may result over a long period of time after the contamination has occurred in intertidal areas. Oil inputs to the sea must therefore not be treated with complacency. Shipowners and industry must maximize efforts to conserve a valuable commodity and thus reduce marine damage. The efforts of individuals, too, could significantly reduce the amounts of oil reaching the sea.

Much of the oil reaching the sea comes from land run-off. The disposal of used car oil into drains contributes to the run-off and also causes operational problems at sewage works – which can in turn lead to further pollution problems. Waste oils, including solvents and paints, can now be disposed of through recycling depots in most cities.

This map shows the major oil and gas fields in the North Sea. The drilling of wells and the transportation of oil can lead to catastrophic spills – seabirds are the animals most severely affected, although seals and otters may be killed, too. As yet there have been no oil pollution incidents due to well blowouts in the North Sea, although this is an ever-present risk.

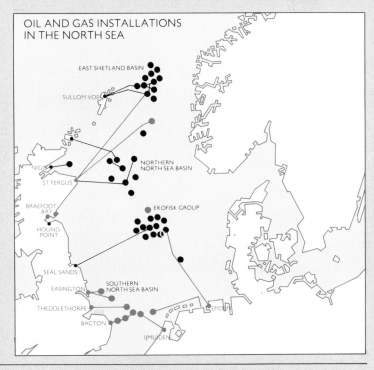

OIL AND GAS INSTALLATIONS IN THE NORTH SEA

EAST SHETLAND BASIN

SULLOM VOE

NIGG

ST FERGUS

BRAEFOOT BAY

HOUND POINT

NORTHERN NORTH SEA BASIN

EKOFISK GROUP

SEAL SANDS

EASINGTON

THEDDLETHORPE

BACTON

IJMUIDEN

SOUTHERN NORTH SEA BASIN

EMDEN

INSHORE OVERFISHING

Purse-seiners, as well as trawlers, bring their catches to sell at Peterhead fish market, now the largest in Europe. The use of the purse-seine net, often accompanied by a giant suction device to scoop the fish out of the net, now makes it possible to catch in a day what was once caught in a month. The numbers of purse-seiners are controlled, but their capacity to catch vast numbers of fish provides a threat to stocks.

The fisherman, an individualist relying on a blend of skill, intuition and technology, is part of Britain's maritime tradition, and the small fishing boat is an integral part of the scenery around Britain's coast. To an extent, this scene is a relic of the past. Sophisticated modern fishing vessels are now the driving force of the fishing industry and the application of more efficient technology has been accompanied by far-reaching changes.

Britain's herring fishery provides one example of these changes. Once, it supported a large number of seasonal workers who, with the boats, followed the herring migration along the coast. In the 1960s, the North Sea catch was some 885,000 tons (900,000 tonnes) shared between the European countries and Russia and Poland. But by 1977 the stock had been so seriously over-exploited that herring fishing in the North Sea was banned, with similar measures introduced in the western Scottish and Celtic Sea fishing grounds. Although the ban has now been lifted, landing tonnages are still strictly controlled. This was not the end of the story. As a result of the collapse in herring stocks, the mackerel fishery underwent rapid development. In turn, it, too, suffered a decline from which it has not recovered.

The failure of those who exploit fish stocks to consider the maximum sustainable yields of their industry has had consequences for fish eaters other than human beings. Recently, problems with seals breaking through fish farm

nets have increased and lack of food in the wild is thought to be at least partially responsible. Serious systemic changes in coastal waters due to overfishing are also likely. The large-scale removal of an important component of the ecosystem can unbalance it profoundly and interfere with natural nutrient recycling.

Shellfish, too, have been over-exploited, but shrimps, crabs and lobsters are now subject to fishing controls. In Britain – but not on the Continent – net mesh sizes are strictly controlled to avoid the destruction of too many juveniles. The fishing industry depends on sufficient breeding and the survival of juvenile fish to maintain populations.

It is appropriate to consider the importance of juvenile populations in relation to the oyster fishery. This depends upon a good 'spatfall', or settlement of larvae, to sustain it. In recent years, a decline in the vigour of oyster fisheries was linked to the use of the tin-based anti-fouling compound TBT, which was highly toxic to juvenile oysters and caused shell malformation in adults. Because of these problems – and in case of any long-term effects on human health – TBT is in the process of being restricted by the government. It was, and still is, used by countless small boatowners to prevent the build-up of barnacles and weeds on the bottoms of their boats. Once the damaging properties were described and confirmed, the manufacturers of the anti-fouling paint adopted a curious attitude. Instead of making efforts to reduce the effects of their product, they proceeded to launch an advertising campaign that effectively encouraged people to stockpile the paint.

Continued harvesting from the sea depends upon the adequate management of stocks, and on the co-operation of diverse groups of people with diverse interests. Perhaps it may be hoped that in the future, upon finding that a product has hitherto unrealized damaging effects, manufacturers will be prepared to work with the interested parties and initiate urgent research on their products.

Overfishing is a threat to even Britain's commonest sea fish, like the plaice. Also, an increasing incidence of diseased plaice has been attributed to pollution. The days when the ocean's wealth could be exploited without a thought are over.

The fishing ports shown here are primarily associated with the deep sea fishing industry. However, the coastal fishing grounds, also shown, support many local fisheries, which vary in importance from year to year. The continued existence of Britain's fishing industry depends on the careful management of both the industry itself and of the waters upon which it depends.

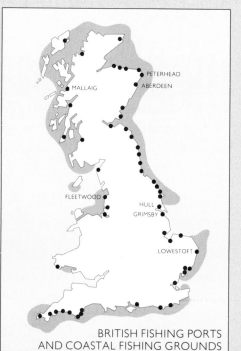

MALLAIG
PETERHEAD
ABERDEEN
FLEETWOOD
HULL
GRIMSBY
LOWESTOFT

BRITISH FISHING PORTS
AND COASTAL FISHING GROUNDS

BEACH POLLUTION

Photo: Bob Edwards

The disposal of sewage directly onto beaches, or in areas where it can be carried back to shore, is not only unsightly but also a health risk. The rock singer Ian Dury contracted polio from a contaminated children's beach pool; other viral and bacterial diseases may also be transmitted through exposure to sewage. Antibiotics present in the sewage can cause bacteria to become resistant, thus making the diseases more difficult to treat. The discharge of combined sewage and industrial waste into the sea can also cause damage to fisheries and marine ecosystems.

It generally comes as something of a surprise to realize that of all the beaches in Britain a mere 27 were originally designated to comply with EEC standards for bathing beaches. For this we have largely the pipelines to thank and, in particular, those that discharge sewage around Britain's coastline. It can be argued that it is safe to discharge sewage into the sea, since it will eventually break down and cause no harm. A moment's consideration of the materials that enter the sewer system suggest that this may be a rather optimistic view. We are, for example, encouraged to dispose of surplus drugs into this system. In some areas, industrial effluent and agricultural effluent are combined with domestic waste waters. On many beaches, this raw cocktail is discharged directly onto the beach or so close to it that the tides and currents bring the mixture back to shore.

Thus Britain's beaches look unsightly and smell unpleasant. But the real danger stems from the large number of bacteria and viruses present in the mixture. These may survive for considerable periods of time in sea water, and retain their power to cause infections ranging from simple stomach upsets to polio and viral hepatitis. This, then, explains our dearth of safe bathing beaches – not even Blackpool, that most famous of resorts, is officially safe.

Industrial waste is also discharged onto beaches. The effect of colliery waste on the beaches of Durham has already been mentioned (see page 184). Other industrial materials are washed up on the shore from time to time, and cause injuries. Oil, too, can pollute beaches. On the Dorset coast, it is quite common to find canisters marked 'Danger: if found, notify Coastguard!'; these are flares or munitions used by the armed forces – they, too, can cause injuries. A whole variety of material is thrown or lost overboard from ships – those translucent pebbles, much prized by young beachcombers, are broken bottle glass.

Plastics are a particularly unsightly pollutant on beaches and, as they are not biodegradable, they can take many years to wear away, as can the assorted steel and aluminium cans that often contrast so starkly with natural forms in rock pools. All these pollutants can be harmful to wildlife, especially seabirds. They are, however, problems that the individual can begin to address by the proper disposal of litter. Perhaps then our beaches will again become places to find and observe nature, rather than passive repositories for the husks of products of our modern existence.

Like so many of Britain's seabirds, the Razorbill has decreased along many coasts, perhaps because of overfishing. It favours remote, rocky cliffs, stacks and islets. British colonies hold a sizeable proportion of the world's total population.

THREATENED WILDLIFE

Dolphins and porpoises are threatened all around Britain's coast by marine pollution, by competition with humans for fish, by disturbance and injury from shipping, by entanglement in fishing nets, and even by deliberate harassment or attack.

The wildlife around Britain's coastline is unique and its diversity is due to the variety of habitats. The marine world owes its riches partly to the interaction of the Gulf Stream and the colder Atlantic waters – places still exist where representatives of up to 13 different phyla of animals may be found. (A phylum is the name given to groups of animals or plants that are grouped according to their broad characteristics.)

The ecology of Britain's shores is naturally dynamic and resilient. But it cannot withstand human ravages: dunes planted with conifers, saltmarshes and estuaries reclaimed for agriculture and industry, and everywhere the twin threats of pollution and disturbance. In the previous pages some of the ways in which people can exert changes unfavourable to animals and plants present in the coastal environment have been considered. Everyone is familiar with the effect of oil slicks on birds – a large oil incident may threaten the viability of an entire breeding population. Seals, too, can be affected and their fur can be fouled by oil with fatal consequences. Otters can also fall victim to oil, though in most parts of the country they have died out due to pesticides present in their food and the ever-increasing disturbance along rivers. In addition, every coastal or estuarine pipeline discharge causes a change in the communities of wildlife living in the mud in the discharge zone.

Over the last fifty years, the numbers of dolphins and whales observed in British waters have declined markedly. The cause is unknown but it is thought to be a combination of overfishing and pollution. Certainly, the decline in reproduction in North Sea seal populations can be related to pollution of the water by the organic chemicals known as PCBs. Direct dumping can cause many changes in the animals living on the sea floor and scientists are now turning their attention to the large number of diseased flatfish being caught in British and foreign seas and estuaries. Again, it is thought that pollution may be responsible. Reclamation schemes can exert a toll on wildlife by reducing areas of suitable wetland and mudflat habitat. For example, the proposed Severn barrage will supply cleanly manufactured electricity but it will also completely change the hydrographic properties of the estuary and affect approximately 23 designated SSSIs (Sites of Special Scientific Interest).

The preservation of wildlife is of enormous importance, but it is the possible impact upon humans of a continued abuse of the environment that seems to be most people's primary concern. The truth of the matter is that we do not know enough about the long-term effects of this abuse on man – but the pressure upon the seas is at an unprecedented level. Obviously, any loss or restriction of our wildlife – apart from reducing the pleasure to be derived from our surroundings – may be taken as a warning that we ourselves are not invulnerable.

The population levels of porpoises and dolphins around Britain's coasts may be regarded as an indication of the general health of the marine ecosystem. The decline of these creatures is therefore of great concern. The reduction in sightings over the last forty years is shown on these maps – only two sightings were recorded by the Beluga on her 1986 coastal survey. Meanwhile, Britain's estuaries and coastal waters continue to deteriorate, perhaps irrevocably.

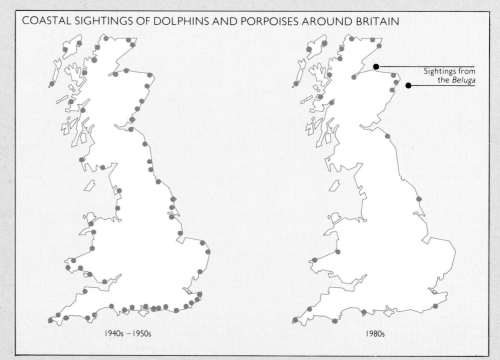

COASTAL SIGHTINGS OF DOLPHINS AND PORPOISES AROUND BRITAIN

Sightings from the Beluga

1940s – 1950s

1980s

THE FUTURE OF BRITAIN'S COASTLINE

The British coastline is under great pressure – many of the coastal riches and features described in this book are threatened by industrial development, waste disposal, persistent pollution and natural processes, and their future hangs in the balance. Once destroyed, then like the ancient British wild wood, it will be impossible to re-create them.

The threats to the sea are in many cases difficult to visualize because of the seeming infinity of the marine system and its superficially unchanging appearance. Nonetheless, the problems are real and we are now perilously close to causing changes from which this finely balanced and harmonized ecosystem may not recover. No longer must the sea be viewed as a convenient communal waste lagoon or the rich and varied estuaries as convenient piplines to convey wastes to it. Those who use this environment to maximize profits for company shareholders must now take into consideration the greater number of shareholders in the natural environment – at whose expense these profits are made – and the future generations, whose historical judgement as inheritors will eventually be voiced.

There exists a responsibility at both the individual and the national level to preserve and nurture this environment for the future. It is this sense of responsibility that Greenpeace seeks – and will continue to seek – to develop. The quotation at the beginning of this section is highly appropriate and Greenpeace may justifiably take the credit for the ending of several

Photo: Bob Edwards

The crew of the *Beluga*, together with Greenpeace scientists and campaigners, at the end of the *Beluga*'s 1986 coastal survey. The dedication and expertise of this group of people – together with the support of those who gave their time to make films, take photographs and participate in the various actions – have played no small part in creating a wider awareness of the current state of Britain's coastline.

The *Beluga* Crew:

Captain:
Bodo Quedenfeldt/
Bene Hoffman

Chief Engineer:
Ronald Bayer

Scientists:
Paul Johnston,
Sigrun Hellman,
Peter Kalensee

Deckhand:
Hamid van Lohuizen

Campaigners:
Andrew Booth,
Beverley Thorpe

environmental abuses and the development of an atmosphere in which the conscientious conservation and restitution of the marine environment may proceed.

Evidence of a new awareness may be found in the growing number of conservation organizations and projects and designated SSSIs. It is important that these are jealously protected from those who would destroy them, deliberately or otherwise. We may then hope to develop a society that works with and for nature rather than in constant conflict with it.

TECHNICAL TERMS

Dredging The removal of sediments from harbour areas in order to preserve navigation channels is known as dredging. Because the sediments act as a 'sink' for chemicals, the removed material or 'spoil' can often release large quantities of heavy metals.

Heavy Metals The heavy metals include lead, arsenic, mercury, cadmium, copper, tin and zinc. While some play a role in the biochemistry of the cell, all are toxic at relatively low levels. They may be accumulated by marine organisms and cause reproductive failure or abnormal growth. An example is the effect of TBT (tributyl tin), an organic chemical containing tin, on shellfish.

Inorganic Chemicals are substances such as calcium carbonate or sodium chloride (salt). Inorganic fertilizers contain simple compounds like potassium nitrate and sodium sulphate. When dissolved, such substances form ions.

Organic Chemicals are substances composed primarily of carbon and hydrogen. The best known are perhaps the constituents of petroleum oils.

Organo-chlorines are organic chemicals that have been manufactured to contain a high chlorine component. Simple organo-chlorines, such as tri-chloroethylene, may be produced when tap water is chlorinated to kill bacteria. The more complex varieties are often centred around a carbon ring structure and they have biocidal properties. The best known are the pesticides DDT, aldrin and dieldrin. None are biodegradable and all can accumulate in food chains – primarily in the body fat. A similar group of chemicals are the PCBs (polychlorinated biphenyls) which were used as electrical insulating oils. They do not break down in the environment, either. These substances are no longer manufactured, but a large stockpile, which will be difficult to dispose of, still exists. The PCBs have been implicated in the reproductive failure of populations of North Sea seals and in the lowered IQs of children exposed to the chemicals.

Organo-phosphates are organic chemicals containing a phosphorous group. These substances are used as pesticides and act as effective nerve poisons to most higher forms of life. Although they are ultimately biodegradable, it may take some time for them to break down; during this period they can pose a threat to aquatic life.

Radio-isotopes and Background Radiation Radio-isotopes are forms of an element that emit radio-activity. Some radio-isotopes occur naturally, but others are produced in large quantities by the nuclear industry. Due to natural radio-isotopes and cosmic radiation, there exists in the natural environment a level of 'background radiation'. Atmospheric weapons tests have caused an increase in the level of this background. The activities of nuclear installations can cause a high elevation of the background level – this, in turn, may cause an increase in radiation-related disease.

Sewage Sludge and Slurry Sewage sludge is the material left in the settling tanks of sewage works; it is similar to the slurry produced by farm animals. Both substances may contain high levels of heavy metals and organo-chlorines, particularly in sewage works which receive these materials in the form of industrial wastes.

THE PRESERVATION OF THE COASTLINE
HOPE FOR THE FUTURE

'WHAT WOULD THE WORLD BE, ONCE BEREFT
OF WET AND WILDNESS? LET THEM BE LEFT,
O LET THEM BE LEFT, WILDNESS AND WET;
LONG LIVE THE WEEDS AND THE WILDERNESS YET.'

Gerard Manley Hopkins, *Invershaid* (1881)

Opposite: This map locates major areas of importance for the conservation of coastal landscape and wildlife. While RSPB and other nature reserves, and stretches of coastline owned by the National Trust, the Ministry of Defence and other bodies, cannot be shown on this scale, many important protected coastal areas (including AONBs) are indicated, together with coastal footpaths of particular interest and beauty.

Thousands of Barnacle Geese winter on the west coast of Scotland, notably on the island of Islay, where numbers have soared over the past thirty years due to protection. The birds feed mainly on farmland, causing conflict between conservationists and local farmers.

As the future of Britain's coastline hangs in the balance, so the need to solve the problems that face it becomes more urgent. The threats to our coastal heritage stem from a multitude of sources, but, equally, there is a variety of organizations, both old and new, that are fighting to save Britain's shores. Ranging from small local naturalists' trusts to major national bodies, like the Royal Society for the Protection of Birds and the National Trust, these groups play a crucial role and require all the help – both practical and financial – they can get to continue their vital work.

Some organizations concentrate mainly on arguing their case by using facts and figures and participating in official policy-making committees, while others rely more on direct action and its ability to influence and gain popular support. Many have local offshoots and run national and regional conservation programmes and activities to which the individual can make a valuable contribution. All these approaches have their place and will appeal to different people. The following listing gives contact details for the major conservation organizations concerned with the preservation of the coastline and indicates their main aims and activities.

Much magnificent work has already been undertaken by many of the organizations: habitats and wildlife species have been protected, reserves created and scientific surveys, such as that conducted by Greenpeace, undertaken; pressure has been brought to bear on the abusers of the coastal environment and progress has been made. As the threats continue, however, so too does the importance of the work done by conservation bodies, and indeed by their numerous members, whose combined efforts and commitment will hopefully ensure the preservation of Britain's rich coastal heritage for generations to come.

Of the many organizations, in addition to Greenpeace, that are actively involved in the fight to preserve Britain's coastline, most of those listed here are specifically concerned with protecting and conserving the marine and coastal environments and their wildlife. The aims and activities of the others are in some instances more varied (encompassing a wide range of concerns), but all work towards protecting our natural heritage; many also run specific coastal campaigns and programmes – such as 'Enterprise Neptune' organized by the National Trust. A number of the groups listed have local branches all over the country and many produce magazines and newsletters for members.

ORGANIZATIONS CONCERNED WITH THE CONSERVATION OF BRITAIN'S COASTAL AND ESTUARINE ENVIRONMENTS

Botanical Society of the British Isles (BSBI)
Dept. of Botany, British Museum (Natural History) Cromwell Road, London SW7 5BD 01-589 6323

Welcomes membership from all those, whether beginners or experts, who are really interested in wild plants and their study and conservation.

British Herpetological Society (BHS)
c/o Zoological Society of London, Regent's Park, London NW1 4RY 01-722 3333

Devoted to the scientific study of reptiles and amphibians, which are well represented on some of Britain's coastline.

British Naturalists' Association
23 Oak Hill Close, Woodford Green, Essex IG8 9PH

Supports schemes and legislation for protection of wildlife and preservation of beautiful landscapes, and works towards extending and popularizing nature study.

British Trust for Conservation Volunteers (BTCV)
36 St Mary's Street, Wallingford, Oxon. OX10 0EU 0491-39766

Organizes and involves people of all ages in practical conservation work. Projects include sand-dune restoration and coastal footpath construction and maintenance.

British Trust for Ornithology (BTO)
Beech Grove, Station Road, Tring, Herts. HP23 5NR 044282-3461

Promotes, encourages, organizes and carries out study and research into all branches of ornithology, particularly relating to the effects of man on wild bird population; long-term projects include the Birds of Estuaries Enquiry (jointly with NCC and RSPB) and Beached Birds Survey (jointly with the RSPB). Welcomes membership from all seriously interested in ornithology.

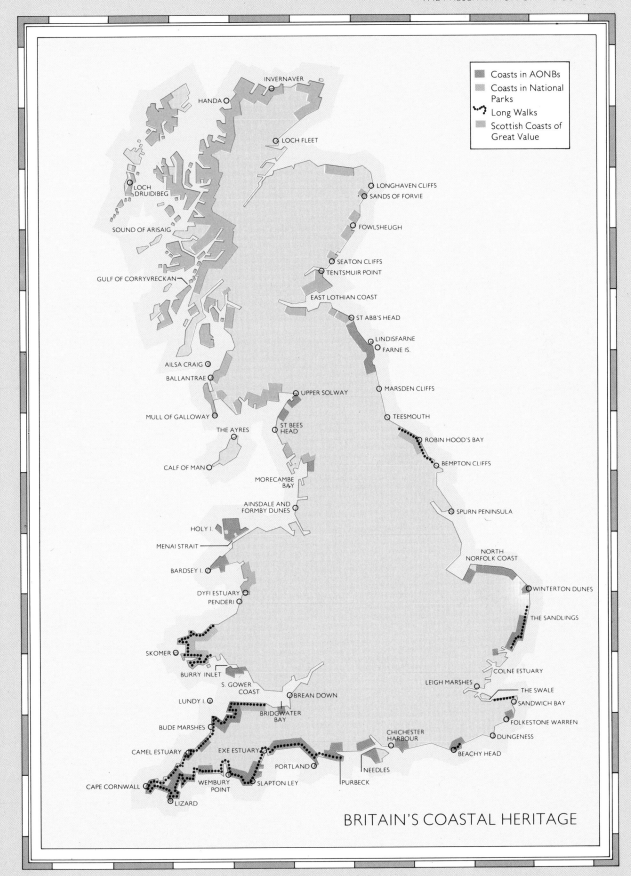

Coasts in AONBs

Coasts in National Parks

Long Walks

Scottish Coasts of Great Value

INVERNAVER

HANDA

LOCH FLEET

LOCH DRUIDIBEG

LONGHAVEN CLIFFS

SANDS OF FORVIE

SOUND OF ARISAIG

FOWLSHEUGH

SEATON CLIFFS

TENTSMUIR POINT

GULF OF CORRYVRECKAN

EAST LOTHIAN COAST

ST ABB'S HEAD

LINDISFARNE

FARNE IS.

AILSA CRAIG

BALLANTRAE

UPPER SOLWAY

MARSDEN CLIFFS

MULL OF GALLOWAY

ST BEES HEAD

TEESMOUTH

THE AYRES

ROBIN HOOD'S BAY

CALF OF MAN

BEMPTON CLIFFS

MORECAMBE BAY

AINSDALE AND FORMBY DUNES

SPURN PENINSULA

HOLY I.

MENAI STRAIT

NORTH NORFOLK COAST

BARDSEY I.

WINTERTON DUNES

DYFI ESTUARY

PENDERI

THE SANDLINGS

SKOMER

BURRY INLET

COLNE ESTUARY

S. GOWER COAST

LEIGH MARSHES

THE SWALE

LUNDY I.

BREAN DOWN

SANDWICH BAY

BRIDGWATER BAY

FOLKESTONE WARREN

BUDE MARSHES

CHICHESTER HARBOUR

DUNGENESS

CAMEL ESTUARY

EXE ESTUARY

BEACHY HEAD

PORTLAND

WEMBURY POINT

SLAPTON LEY

NEEDLES

CAPE CORNWALL

PURBECK

LIZARD

BRITAIN'S COASTAL HERITAGE

Coastal Anti-Pollution League (CAPL)
94 Greenway Lane, Bath, Avon BA2 4LN
0225-317094

Works towards stopping the indiscriminate pollution of Britain's beaches by sewage.

Common Ground
London Ecology Centre, 45 Shelton Street, Covent Garden, London WC2H 9HJ
01-379 3109

Promotes the importance of common animals, plants and local landscapes; forges practical and philosophical links between the arts and conservation of nature and landscapes; acts as a catalyst furthering ideas and bringing different groups of people together. No formal membership.

Conchological Society of Great Britain and Ireland
c/o Hon Secretary, 51 Wynchwood Avenue, Luton, Beds. LU2 7HT

Devoted to the serious study of molluscs, including the many species of marine molluscs, from razor shells to sea-slugs.

Conservation Association of Botanical Societies (CABS)
323 Norwood Road, London SE24 9AQ

Established as recently as 1986, this new association encourages and co-ordinates a variety of projects, including an assessment of the damage to wild plants that will result from the building of the Channel Tunnel.

Conservation Foundation
11A West Halkin Street, London SW1X 8JL 01-235 1743

With Dr David Bellamy as a Director, encourages industry and business people to support conservation by publicizing the efforts of practical conservation workers and providing financial help; projects include the Bisto Kids Wonderful World of Nature Rivers and Streams Project.

Conservation Society (ConSoc)
12A Guildford Street, Chertsey, Surrey KT16 9BQ 09328-60975

Works for a sustainable and equitable society and argues for policies that will reduce the depletion of resources and reverse the degradation of the environment; campaigns have included one against the dumping of poisonous wastes.

Council for Environmental Conservation (CoEnCo)
London Ecology Centre, 80 York Way, London N1 9AG 01-278 4736

Provides a forum for discussion on major environmental issues and co-ordinates the activities of the voluntary conservation movement at a national level in Britain. Involved in many campaigns, including the Council of Europe Water's Edge Campaign.

Council for Environmental Education (CEE)
School of Education, University of Reading, London Road, Reading, Berks. RG1 5AQ 0734-875234 ext. 218

Encourages and promotes environmental education by co-ordinating activities of over 60 national organizations and providing support and

information programmes, especially in the school and youth sectors. Involved in many projects, including campaigns against the drainage of wetlands and the impact of the Channel Tunnel.

Council for the Protection of Rural England (CPRE)
4 Hobart Place, London SW1W 0HY
01-235 9481

Promotes and encourages the improvement and protection of the countryside and of rural amenities; campaigns include those on energy policy and water strategy.

Countryside Commission
John Dower House, Cresent Place, Cheltenham, Glos. GL50 3RA 0242-521381

Advises central and local government on rural conservation and recreation in England and Wales; encourages conservation of landscape beauty. Involved in the creation of National Parks (many including beautiful coastlines, e.g. Pembrokeshire Coast), Country Parks, AONBs (including Isles of Scilly and Suffolk Coasts and Heaths) and Heritage Coasts. Also responsible for the creation and maintenance of various coastal footpaths. Has 8 regional offices in England and Wales.

Countryside Commission for Scotland (CCS)
Battleby, Redgorton, Perth PH1 3EW
0738-27921

Carries out, in Scotland, similar work to that of the Countryside Commission.

Crofters Commission
4–6 Castle Wynd, Inverness, Highlands IV2 3EQ 0463-237231

Promotes the interests of crofters in the seven crofting counties of Scotland.

Dolphin Survey Project
Dept. of Anatomy, University of Cambridge, Downing Street, Cambridge CB2 3DY 0223-333768

Co-ordinates sightings of dolphins and porpoises and observations of their behaviour; reports should be sent in as quickly as possible, including name, address and telephone number, or name of vessel, and exact location. Stranded dolphins and porpoises should also be reported to the RSPCA. (See also International Dolphin Watch.)

Fauna and Flora Preservation Society (FFPS)
8–12 Camden High Street, London NW1 0JH 01-387 9656

Works for the international conservation of wild animals and plants, especially those that are endangered. Current special projects include bat conservation and the conservation of reptiles and amphibians. Welcomes interest and support through membership.

Field Studies Council (FSC)
Preston Montford, Montford Bridge, Shrewsbury, Shropshire SY4 1HW
0743-850674

Aims to encourage and increase an understanding and appreciation of the natural environment and its wildlife through education. Runs courses in natural history, geology, archaeology and other subjects at its 10 field centres, which include several coastal ones, such as Skomer and Skokholm islands. Studies the

ecological effects of marine pollution, including oil pollution.

Friends of the Earth (FoE)
377 City Road, London EC1V 1NA
01-837 0731

Works to promote policies that will protect and improve the natural environment and to affect government policies on the environment by direct lobbying and public education. Campaigns include those against marine dumping of waste, TBT marine anti-fouling paint and the building of Sizewell B nuclear power station.

Institute of Estuarine and Coastal Studies
University of Hull, Cottingham Road, Hull, Humberside HU6 7RX
0482-46311 ext. 7511

Encourages research and teaching in estuarine and coastal studies within the university; provides links between the university and a wide range of outside bodies concerned with this area.

Institute for Marine Environmental Research (IMER)
Prospect Place, The Hoe, Plymouth, Devon PL1 3DH 0752-221371

A research institute of the Natural Environment Research Council which studies processes that determine the performance of marine and estuarine ecosystems, with the aim of detecting and predicting any effects of human activities.

Institute of Marine Studies
University College of Swansea, Singleton Park, Swansea, W. Glamorgan SA2 8PP
0792-205678

Investigates the marine environment, especially around south-west Wales, and associated problems, both in relation to human activities and natural processes.

International Dolphin Watch
Parklands, North Ferriby, Hull, Humberside HU14 3ET

Co-ordinates sightings of dolphins and porpoises and observations of their behaviour; reports should be sent to the above address, and to the Dolphin Survey Project.

International League for the Protection of Cetaceans (ILPC)
2 Meryon Court, Rye, E. Sussex TN31 7LY
0797-223649

Works towards the protection and conservation of whales, dolphins and porpoises; conducts and sponsors scientific research, informs the public and serves as an information network for relevant organizations.

International Society for the Prevention of Water Pollution
Little Orchard, Bentworth, Alton, Hants GU34 5RB 0420-62225/02514-24837

Aims to prevent water pollution worldwide; promotes research, disseminates information and raises funds.

IUCN Conservation Monitoring Centre
219C Huntingdon Road, Cambridge CB3 0DL 0223-277314

The IUCN promotes action directed towards the sustainable use and conservation of natural resources; the Monitoring Centre (with a botanical section at Kew) studies the distribution and numbers of animals and plants, especially endangered species.

Keep Britain Tidy Group (KBTG)

Bostel House, 37 West Street, Brighton,
E. Sussex BN1 2RE 0273-23585

Carries out annual surveys of rubbish, including
many toxic wastes, washed up on our seashores
as part of its Marine Litter Research Programme.
Results of surveys are used to put pressure on
the International Maritime Organization to
implement tougher controls on dumping waste
at sea.

Mammal Society Cetacean Group

c/o The Linnean Society, Burlington
House, Piccadilly, London W1V 0LQ
01-434 4479

Collects and disseminates information about
whales, dolphins and porpoises, bringing
together amateurs and professionals with an
interest in these mammals.

Marine Biological Association of the United Kingdom (MBA)

The Laboratory, Citadel Hill, Plymouth,
Devon PL1 2PB 0752-221761

Promotes all research that contributes towards
marine biological science, working to increase
understanding of life in the sea; runs the Marine
Pollution Information Centre which serves as a
national information and documentation centre

Marine Conservation Society (MCS)

4 Gloucester Road, Ross-on-Wye,
Herefordshire HR9 5BU 0989-66017

The only conservation organization that
concerns itself solely with coasts and offshore
waters, the MCS promotes the study and
conservation of the marine environment and
develops programmes of research, education and
publicity. A major recent achievement was in
persuading government to establish Lundy Island
as the first Statutory Marine Nature Reserve; the
MCS also runs a number of Voluntary Marine
Nature Reserves and is pressing for more
statutory ones; also runs many campaigns on
pollution, including pollution of beaches by
sewage and by TBT anti-fouling paint.

National Trust

36 Queen Anne's Gate, London SW1H 9AS
01-222 9251

Owns, maintains and protects over 450 miles of
Britain's most beautiful coastline (through the
Enterprise Neptune campaign) in England and
Wales, as well as more than 520,000 acres of
countryside and many historic houses,
prehistoric sites etc; owns 44 nature reserves
and various bird sanctuaries, some on the coast.
Has regional offices.

National Trust for Scotland

5 Charlotte Square, Edinburgh EH2 4DU
031-226 5922

Performs similar function, in Scotland, to that of
the National Trust. Has various local branches.

Nature Conservancy Council (NCC)

(including 'Seabirds at Sea' group)
Northminster House, Northminster Road,
Peterborough, Cambs. PE1 1UA
0733-40345

The government body that promotes nature
conservation in Britain. The NCC selects,
establishes and manages a series of National
Nature Reserves (NNRs), schedules and protects
Sites of Special Scientific Interest (SSSIs) and
Marine Nature Reserves. Has many regional
offices.

Royal Society for Nature Conservation (RSNC)

22 The Green, Nettleham, Lincoln
LN2 2NR 0522-752326

The umbrella group for the many local nature
conservation trusts, which manage over 1300
nature reserves, many on the coast. Current
campaigns include those on nitrate pollution of
rivers and estuaries, nuclear waste disposal and
marine conservation. See also Watch Trust.

Royal Society for the Prevention of Cruelty to Animals (RSPCA)

The Causeway, Horsham,
W. Sussex RH12 1HG 0403-64181

Runs an oiled seabird rescue centre at Little
Geech, Taunton, Somerset; report any oiled or
otherwise injured birds, also stranded whales,
dolphins and porpoises, to your local RSPCA
office in England and Wales.

Royal Society for the Protection of Birds (RSPB)

The Lodge, Sandy, Beds. SG19 2DL
0767-80551

Conserves and protects wild birds, promotes the
appreciation and enjoyment of birds; acquires
and manages nature reserves and conducts
research, surveys and campaigns, many
concerned with coastal birds. Regional offices.
Includes Young Ornithologists' Club (YOC).

Scottish Field Studies Association (SFSA)

Young Street Financial Services Ltd,
31 Rutland Square, Edinburgh EH1 2BW
031-229 7933

Performs similar function, in Scotland, to that
of the Field Studies Council.

Scottish Marine Biological Association (SMBA)

Dunstaffnage Marine Research Laboratory,
PO Box 3, Oban, Argyll,
Strathclyde PA34 4AD
0631-62244

Studies all aspects of marine research;
particularly concerned with waters off the west
coast of Scotland.

Scottish Society for the Prevention of Cruelty to Animals (SSPCA)

19 Melville Street, Edinburgh EH3 7PL
031-225 6418/6419

Performs similar function, in Scotland, to that of
the RSPCA. Contact your local office.

Seabird Group

c/o Royal Society for the Protection of
Birds, The Lodge, Sandy, Beds. SG19 2DL
0767-80551

Promotes co-operative research on seabirds and
circulates results of projects, including annual
surveys of breeding seabirds and collection of
seabird corpses for scientific examination.

Wader Study Group

44 The Pastures, Edlesborough, Dunstable,
Beds. LU6 2HL
Establishes contacts between amateurs and
professionals studying waders; organizes
co-operative studies.

Watch Trust for Environmental Education Ltd (WATCH)

22 The Green, Nettleham,
Lincoln LN2 2NR 0522-752326

Run by the Royal Society for Nature
Conservation to enable young people (up to 18
years) to increase their knowledge of wildlife and
take an active part in conservation.

Wildfowl Trust

Gatehouse, Slimbridge, Glos. GL2 7BT
045389-333 ext. 210

Promotes study and conservation of wildfowl and
wetland habitats, with 7 centres and reserves
around the country. Projects include Mute Swan
Survey and regular wildlife counts (since 1947).

World Wildlife Fund – UK (WWF – UK)

Panda House, 11–13 Ockford Road,
Godalming, Surrey GU7 1QU 04868-20551

Campaigns and raises money for the
conservation of endangered wildlife and wild
places and promotes the wise use of the earth's
resources. Current projects relevant to the
British coastline include the protection of
estuaries and other wetlands under the Ramsar
Convention and studies of coastal Otters in
Scotland.

GREENPEACE

In its capacity as an international non-
governmental organization, Greenpeace is expressly concerned with the
protection of the environment. It
currently represents the views of over
a million members in 17 nations and has
proved itself a vital source of independent scientific advice. For ten years it
has been involved in campaigning to
stem the tide of pollution that
threatens the North Sea and other
bodies of water around Britain's coastline. It has campaigned consistently for
the preservation of marine wildlife and
against all coastal and estuarine contaminants; it has had considerable successes in these fields. Its 1986 *Beluga*
survey was the first independent scientific survey ever undertaken of
Britain's coastal and estuarine waters
and it represented the start of the new
Greenpeace Coastal Campaign.

Greenpeace
30–31 Islington Green, London N1 8XE
01-354 5100/01-359 7396

INDEX

Page numbers in **bold** *type refer to illustrations.*
Page numbers preceded by an m refer to maps.
Abbreviations used: Br. = Bridge; i = installation(s)